Ciné Parkour

**A cinematic and theoretical contribution to the
understanding of the practice of parkour.**

Julie Angel

Films

submitted as part of this research, found on the Ciné Parkour DVD are:

ASID, profile of a freerunner (2005)

Le Singe est de Retour (2006)

MySpace (2006)

Jump Westminster (2007)

Visions (2007)

Rain (2008)

Feedback Loop (2008)

Sarcelles (2008)

Environmental visions (2005)

First step (2007)

Go Girls! (2008)

City Gents (2007)

The Outside in (2007)

Indoor Parkour class (2007)

Julie Angel

INTRODUCTION

This thesis represents my interest and adventures in collaborative documentary filmmaking, alongside a curiosity for how people find new ways to experience, play, confront fear and participate in their environments. My practice-led research will attempt to explore, understand, represent and document the practice of parkour beyond its dominant mediatised representation as a performance spectacle. My research consists of a practical and theoretical exploration of the relationship between self, body and the environment beyond societal norms and conventional, regulated opportunities for outdoor, creative spatial and physical practices, through parkour.

My aim in theorising parkour is to advance our understanding of what it means to explore and transcend the real and imagined boundaries of what is possible in terms of the relationship with the self and the environment.

I will endeavour to understand the nature and essence of what constitutes the everyday practice of parkour and what role it plays in the lives of certain practitioners. Whilst parkour is practiced in different ways in different places, my aim has been to understand the local reality and knowledge of how it is experienced and understood by those who were instrumental in its creation and development. The founders have since passed their understanding and knowledge regarding their methods, motivations and ethics of

5

the practice onto new generations, many of whom are my key informants.

I aim to provide a culturally and historically situated understanding of the cultural norms of the parkour world and to theorise the debates that parkour can ignite. This research project is the result of a journey into exploring the formation of values, ethics, motivations, social tensions and 'normal' behaviours in parkour culture relating to socialisation, appropriation, voluntary risk-taking, fear, notions of freedom, autonomy, architectural determinism and identity.

Parkour is a relatively new phenomena and this is the first piece of extensive, qualitative, participant observation research which has accessed the founders of the practice, as opposed to short-term observations of those who have learnt from representations of parkour primarily on the internet and television rather than from extensive first-hand instruction or guidance. My research focuses on the lived, subjective experience of parkour in terms of the inter-related relations of the physical, psychological, spatial, political and social inherent in the practise.

This research project consists of two parts, firstly the films produced as research and representation, and secondly this written dissertation. The filmmaking occurred before any theorisation of parkour as this was the method by which to gain first-hand knowledge and experience of the practice. By choosing to commence the research with qualitative, participant observation documentary filmmaking as my chosen methodology, I have been able to explore the lived experience as opposed to a theoretical conceptualisation based on existing predominantly 'performance-for-spectacle' representations of the practice. I recommend viewing the films before reading the thesis.

Documentary filmmaking as audio-visual research provides a creative means by which to translate and reveal knowledge in a way that descriptive writing does not allow. The camera can represent the spatial, social and temporal, providing an opportunity to play back the images to those you have filmed, demonstrating your points of relevance, priorities and interest. Film and video production can be applied as part of the academic process, providing both the means by which a dialogue is formed, as well as, being the final representation in the form of an edited piece of work. The dialogue between the film's producers and those who are being represented can provoke new encounters, questions, situations and, film productions.

My own filmmaking practice has developed towards participatory- observation and shared cinemas, relying on forming friendships and an open dialogue over an extended period of time with those whose lives and activities I attempt to access, understand and represent. This process relies on an accountable feedback loop of production, trust and friendship to reveal layers and segments of knowledge. I endeavored to become an insider in the parkour community, seeing the world through parkour eyes, enabling me to reflect on my own lived experiences as cultural knowledge, as well as having the empathy to listen and learn from the experienced members of the parkour community.

The starting point for the filmic encounters is one of minimal disruption and observation that subsequently leads to interactions over a period of time. The stylistic considerations for a film's production can only be established once knowledge is gained as to what is appropriate and suitable as an effective means to communicate certain aspects, knowledge and representations of a culture. The productions are no longer 'about' but led by the knowledge gained throughout the process of participant observation and a shared feedback loop of production.

I have attempted to theorise my filmmaking practice, as well as, parkour during the research. The films and written work both explore issues of authenticity and the differences between performances of the everyday and performance for spectacle. The main theoretical issues regarding my filmmaking are based around the challenges of participant observation and issues of representation.

In trying to examine the theoretical aspects associated with parkour no single theory or framework has been sufficient for finding explanations for such a multi-layered and contradictory practice as parkour. However, Henning Eichberg's theories on 'body cultures', Belinda Wheaton's research on 'lifestyle sports' subcultural theory and identity, Mihaly Csikszentmihalyi's work on optimal flow states, Maurice Merleau-Ponty's writing on existential phenomenology, Stephen Lyng's 'edgework' and Eric Brymers work on transcendence through 'extreme sports' have all provided useful theories for examining the physical and emotional phenomena of parkour. When exploring the social and political aspects of parkour, Foucauldian theorising of parkour as a practice of freedom, alongside the work of Michel deCerteau, Charles Taylor and Barry Wellmann has proved beneficial in focusing on the appropriation of public space; power relations; socialisation; networked individualism; modern identity; authenticity and autonomy.

In the written dissertation, Chapter 1 offers a history of the origins of parkour, based on interviews and interactions with the key personnel involved in developing the practice. Chapter 2 provides a chronology of the practice-led fieldwork along with a contextualisaion and analysis of the films produced. This chapter documents the adventures, challenges and experiences of participant observation, the documentary filmmaking and the search for authentic voices within the parkour community and my informants. Chapter 3 theorises parkour in terms of the emotional, spatial, physical, political and social experiences. Chapter 4 identifies and examines the paradoxes of parkour as it continues to adapt and change to new contexts of sportification and performance as new practitioners find their way.

During my fieldwork from 2004-2010 many things have changed in the way in which parkour is perceived and represented. Access to certain individuals, particularly the founders, changed overtime. I have attempted to keep track of the changing influences and debates that surround parkour. Although my fieldwork for this thesis has ended my involvement and participation in parkour has not.

Chapter 1

Le parcours, l'art du déplacement, parkour and freerunning, a historical overview

Parcours: *l'art du déplacement*: **parkour and freerunning,** an art, a discipline, a sport, a culture of movement? There are numerous definitions of what parkour maybe, as presented by different individuals depending on their experience, motivations and knowledge of the origins of the activity. *L'art du déplacement-*parkour-freerunning, is a physical training methodology and a particular approach and way of thinking about movement and creative spatial mapping. It is a physical and emotional activity that involves using only the body to overcome obstacles (physical and emotional) within a route. This may involve running; climbing; vaulting; jumping; traversing; balancing, or any other physical means to get from one point to another. Some simplify this stating it as finding a way of getting from 'point A' to 'point B'. It is a method that involves learning to overcome one's fears and limitations by mastering the body-mind-nexus and co-ordination of one's own movement in any terrain. (See Appendix 1 for a glossary of some of the fundamental methods and techniques of the movements.)

The discipline was originally referred to as *parcours*, French for 'a course' or 'route', it was subsequently known as, '*l'art du déplacement*' (that translates as 'the art of moving'), then parkour, and more recently, the term freerunning was introduced in 2003. Although the names have changed and are used by various individuals and groups for their own distinctive recognition, there are vast similarities among these practices, and the essence of these arts is the same. (See Appendix 2 for the terminology timeline and an explanation of the different terms created, when and by whom.) The various terms were created by a group of young men who are credited as the founders and pioneers of this relatively new activity and cultural phenomena that began to evolve circa 1986/7.

I will refer to *parcours*, *l'art du déplacement*, parkour and freerunning throughout this thesis depending on the timeline of events I am discussing and the context of the particular informants. Out of respect for my informants, it is important that I use the appropriate terms especially when discussing certain histories in this chapter. I believe it is important to distinguish between the respective disciplines and individuals as it is deeply tied into - and part of - the founders' identities, even if the practices appear to be the same from a mainstream or even traceur perspective. Elsewhere in this thesis I will more-generally refer to the disciplines as 'parkour', for the sake of simplicity, apart from when relating to a specific time or event.

Previously published research that includes a history of parkour (Marshall 2010, Atkinson 2009, Mould 2009, Geyh, to name but a few) have erroneously named a limited company, 'urban freeflow' as being another name for the discipline. Whilst this is proof of the company's success as a brand, it demonstrates a lack of understanding of the timeline of events and an overdependence on internet sources for research, choosing not to use interviews with the individuals concerned, as few researchers fail to acknowledge the term l'art du déplacement.

This research is the first detailed account of the various histories from the key individuals woven together. The individuals interviewed were willing to share this research space, after some of them have been apart for over a decade. Whilst there are the multiple histories that resulted in *l'art du déplacement*, parkour and freerunning, there is an overwhelming consensus and acknowledgement by the key individuals involved, that it was through a collaboration of different personalities, motivations and influences that resulted in what we know today generally as either *l'art du déplacement*, parkour or freerunning.

The origins of the influences that shaped the phenomena are hard to conclusively trace in that so much is reminiscent of other past-times. There are elements of child's play within the spatial awareness and actions; the approach to the training is similar to the discipline found in martial arts; the levels of risk involved has parallels with solo freeclimbing, the ability to adapt and seek out opportunities in the environment is reminiscent of 'the art of escape', and the passing over of obstacles connects back to the military obstacle course, *'le parcours du combattant'*. However, what sets *l'art du déplacement*, parkour and freerunning apart is that they encompass all of these elements.

The will to explore, challenge, create, play, climb and jump, are inherent in the lives of most people growing up but are abandoned for other more-practical and less-challenging pursuits as people mature. These more-practical activities normally occur in a certain terrain or regulated timeframe, not as an unregulated practice within public spaces. However, were it so easy to dismiss these practices as merely grown-up, risk-fuelled child's play then they would have established themselves within mainstream popular culture well before the time of my research and not be viewed as a new way of moving and perceiving the built and natural environments, as well as a training methodology of interest to sports scientists (Parkour Generations, [142]).

Historical Research Methodology

The creation of these arts did not come out of a single moment, nor were they 'invented' or conceived of by one person. It has not been possible to interview all of the participants from the founding generation of practitioners as there are many, but I have spoken to many of them as well as spending time filming with them, to try and gain a reasonable assessment of what took place, when, where, with whom and out of what kind of social and political context. This includes recent specific interviews relating to the early period in the discipline's development. It was only after five years of research, participation and documenting the culture, that I had the opportunity to interview David Belle and Sébastien Foucan who are two of the acknowledged 'founders' of 'parkour'. Sometimes it has been the people who arrived a little later on the scene, the second generation of practitioners such as the Vigroux brothers, Stephane and Johann, and Thomas Couetdic who have also provided valuable insights, as they are at times more objective than those at the heart of the matter. These second generation practitioners have the endorsement of their peers from the first generation and as such they are reliable informants to help shed light and insight to the discipline.

The record of events presented here is the result of audio and video interviews I have conducted, along with emailed questions and first hand conversations with the key individuals involved. They are: Châu Belle-Dinh; David Belle; Williams Belle; Yann Hnautra; Sebastien Foucan; Laurent Pietmontesi; Katty Belle and Stephane Vigroux. Not all of the my informants speak English and my French is at best 'conversational', therefore, translations have been made by my bi-lingual informants: Katty Belle; Stephane Vigroux; Johann Vigroux; Thomas Coutedic; Annty Marais and Gogoly Yao, all of whom are part of my research group. They were well-suited to being able to understand the activity, vocabulary of the discipline, vernacular slang, and to contextualise how the informants relate to each other. The relationship between the interviewer and source is key in this methodology (Perks & Thomson, ix) and for this reason it was important that my choice of interpreter was already familiar with the internal dynamics and politics of the group.

Perks and Thomson describe oral history as "the interviewing of eye witness participants in the events of the past for the purposes of historical reconstruction" (Perks & Thomson, ix). "Oral history . . . refers [to] what the source [i.e., the narrator] and the historian [i.e. the interviewer] do together at the moment of their encounter in the interview" (Portelli, 3). Perks and Thomson suggest that oral history can be empowering and has allowed for previously "hidden from history" voices to be given an outlet, allowing personal relations and the participants' personal interpretations of the lived experience to contribute. The challenges and debates surrounding oral histories are concerned with the "relationships between memory and history, past and present" (Perks & Thomson, x). This methodology allowed my informants to express, recount and make sense of their own everyday experiences and present their own interpretations of history, the interviewee being in effect the historian as well as the source.

Whilst there are a variety of ways of interpreting the past, my aim is to present a brief overview of the key influences that have resulted in the parkour culture that I have witnessed and researched. My role has been to find the connections between individual and group memories. As with the filmic research discussed in Chapter 2, I needed to consider issues of performance and authenticity within the presentation of my informants's individual histories and to consider what the recollections meant to them then and what they mean now. As Linda Shopes states, "an interview can be a history lecture, a confessional, a verbal sparring match, an exercise in nostalgia, or any other of the dozens of ways people talk about their experiences" (Shopes, 3).

Even though various forms or interpretations of the activity are practiced today by thousands of people all over the world (Sandbag [166]) and the disciplines have reached a global audience of millions through representations in various feature films (*Yamakasi: Les samouraïs des temps modernes, District 13, Casino Royale*), internet videos, television advertisements and documentaries (*Jump London, Jump Britain)* and even inspiring video games (*Mirror's Edge*), this has happened in a relatively short period of time.

According to David Belle, the very early formative days began with a maximum of 30 or 40 people who started practicing and developing a way of training, (Belle D. 2009a) with friends from Sarcelles, Lisses and Évry moving together. This then filtered down to a smaller number as the activity started to evolve into a more-focussed discipline and obsession, rather than merely a sporting, leisure past-time. Those who were committed to the discipline 'full-time' see it as an art, and these were the main pioneers. It is these few, the smaller group, who pursued and devoted their time to creating the disciplines we now know as *l'art du déplacement*, parkour and freerunning. It is their personal and private story of families and friendships that I have attempted to access. Bonds were made and broken, family members cut ties with one another, and other ties forged, never realising at the time that what they were doing would one day become an international phenomenon, even if it was their dream. They did all, however, believe that what they were doing had a positive value. The individual contexts, motivations and ambitions behind the practices shaped the varying narratives and reflections on what occurred two decades ago in two Parisian suburbs. (Appendix 3, the '*Parcours* Timeline' provides an overview of the key figures, moments and events that occurred from 1986 until the start of my research.)

Whilst some of the versions of events differ slightly (crediting different people for different things regarding the chronology of events), the question that I found to be more relevant and of more concern to the founding participants, was not, who did what and when, but **why**. The focus on the reasons of 'why' rather than 'who' and 'when' could partially account for the lack of an agreed history of events being constructed until now, and is also indicative of what the disciplines mean to those involved in their creation. The individual personal motivations sustained the passion for improvement and training that led to such extraordinary achievements, inspiring new approaches to movement as well as a new level of understanding of human, physical potential.

However, the history of this culture of self-development and movement has not been a simple narrative to follow, having been complicated by the various media and individual discourses and misrepresentations of the practice by lazy journalists over the past 13 years since its initial TV coverage. The effect of this has been to inflame feelings of injustice over the lack of recognition or omission of some people in the formation of the disciplines. The history, as presented to me, for this research is occurring at a more reflective time as the participants mature. Whilst there are individual interpretations of events, I have no reason to privilege one account over another, but to try and understand their context.

The origins of the movement

The modern history of the development of the disciplines began as a result of the combined cultural and environmental influences on the children (and later their multi-cultural friends) from two families situated in opposite Parisian suburbs; the French Vietnamese Belle family based in Sarcelles and the French New Caledonian Hnautra family in Évry. The young David Belle was the link and catalyst between the Belle and Hnautra families.

David (who lived with his mother and sister in Lisses, next to Évry) would visit his father, Raymond Belle, in Sarcelles. Raymond was living with the extended Belle family for a period; and David's cousins (Phung, Châu, and Williams Belle) would accompany their aunts on visits to Lisses to see David. David's cousins became acquainted with his friends, in particular, David Malgogne, Yann and Frederick Hnautra, then later with Sébastien Foucan, Charles Perrière, Laurent Piemontesi, Guilain N'Guba-Boyeke and Malik Diouf. The friends were all active and interested in physical sports such as athletics or martial arts, as well as enjoying normal teenage adventures and training together outside. After a time, David's friends from Lisses and Évry would accompany him on trips to Sarcelles, training in the forest of Ecouene, a relaxed atmosphere in contrast to the hard streets of Évry. The Belle's home in Sarcelles and the Hnautra's home in Évry both became an 'open house' to the group of friends, where everyone was always welcomed (Hnautra 2009).

Sarcelles is 16kms north of Paris, (where the extended first generation Vietnamese immigrant Belle family lived). Although the city consisted of many high-rise residential areas of moderated rents (or HLMs – "*habitation à loyer modéré*" as they are known in France) the Belles lived in a quieter, greener corner of Sarcelles, very close to the forrest of Ecouen. Katty Belle, the fourth youngest in a family of five, describes the general atmosphere of growing up in Sarcelles as one of an aggressive and hard environment, a contentious melting-pot, home to many nationalities and religious viewpoints (Belle K. 2009).

Like Sarcelles, Évry and also nearby Lisses were new multi-cultural suburbs largely populated by first-generation immigrant families, located 25km south of the centre of Paris. According to Marshall, the population of Évry has increased tenfold to 8000 in the 40 years since 1968 (Marshall, 165) and has one of the youngest populations in France. Valérie Orlando says that the urban neighbourhoods situated on the outskirts of France's larger cities have been coined '*banlieues*' by the French media to create negative stereotypes: "Where once banlieue was used to connote the pristine white middle to upper middle class neighbourhoods around Paris and other large, urban centres it is now, more often than not, a highly charged word used to describe a hyper-masculinized, violent space saturated with delinquency, social unrest, gangs, and random car burnings" (Orlando, 395).

How the practices evolved

Two of the key individuals involved in shaping parkour's development were David Belle and Yann Hnautra. Yann spent the first part of his life, until his early teenage years, growing up 'in nature' in New Caledonia. He was a self-confessed tough kid, "a bit wild, free" (Hnautra 2009). Yann already had a strong, disciplined physicality and knew various sporting techniques and types of training when he arrived in France, having been trained and pushed by his father, a career soldier. The Hnautra family were the first black family to move into their street in Évry and he was seen as one of the 'strong' people in his area (Hnautra 2009). Yann describes his neighbourhood as tough: stating "If you wanted to just walk in certain streets, you had to be a man, but a man with a big 'M', you had to be able to cope with anything that could happen to you," (Hnautra 2008). According to Stephane Vigroux there was a lot of street-fighting and the Hnautra brothers Yann and Frederick were regularly involved and successful in their fights (Vigroux S. 2009). It was normal for Yann to make new friends as a result of tense conflicts and situations; assessing someone's character by their response to his actions. If they challenged him in return, he respected their anger and confrontation, as was the case when he first met David Belle when they were both teenagers (Hnautra 2009). However Yann also placed great value on strong social bonds among friends and family, if he knew someone was part of a friend's social network, conflicts wouldn't arise.

Both David Belle and Yann Hnautra had strong patriarchal fathers who had served in the military. This was highly-influential in nurturing a combative spirit amongst the friends, as well as the subsequent levels of self-imposed danger, risk and suffering the young generation of Belles, Hnautras and their friends chose to inflict on themselves.

David was not raised by his father, Raymond Belle, but his father's reputation preceded him. David heard his grandfather's stories: "Your father is a 'force of nature', he did some incredible things" (Belle D. 2009a). Before meeting him, David admits he imagined his father as a giant of a man, two metres high. The concept of the hero-figure with super-human abilities was very present in David's imagination through his interests and information regarding his father, as well as his love of the Marvel comics such as "Strange" and characters like Spiderman.

Raymond Belle was born in 1939 in Indo-China, one of a family of nine siblings to a French father and Vietnamese mother. While on holiday visiting an uncle, he became separated from his parents due to the Vietnamese war. He continued to live with his uncle until the age of seven (Belle D. 2009c, 23-24). He was sexually-abused whilst living at his uncles (Belle D. 2009c, 26-27) and was subsequently sent to live in a French military school in Dalat as the family struggled to cope (Belle D. 2009c, 23-24). As a consequence and reaction to the abuse, Raymond Belle decided to build a "strong shell" as a coping-strategy, creating an impenetrable exterior so no-one would be able to touch him again (Belle D. 2009c, 27). He was trained and educated as a boy soldier in Dalat where it was "walk or die" (Belle D. 2009c, 24). David recalls his father telling him of the different types of training he would do alone at night, in addition to the required training. This was various courses or '*parcours*' such as ones that focussed on endurance, agility, resilience and silence or stealth, also making up courses of his own, inflicting pain on himself to strengthen his physical and mental resolve (Belle D. 2009c, 41-42).

Raymond Belle was also aware of George Herbert's '*Méthode Naturelle*' physical-training methodology that had originally been inspired by Herbert's observations of the functional strength of indigenous peoples in Africa and used as a way for sailors to train whilst on boats (Marshall, 167). Herbert's system evolved into the obstacle course training route, the *'parcours du combattant'* used by the French military as well as some educational systems and other international physical training services including the French fire brigade.

After the fall of Dien Bien Phu in 1954, Raymond Belle was sent back to France and stayed within the French military education system until 1958 (Belle D. 2009c, 25). He then began work as a military fire-fighter using his then, already-celebrated, athletic and gymnastic skills, winning many awards (Belle J.F., [28]). He chose to apply all of his training to rescuing and saving lives rather than to fight and kill. Raymond located some of his family who had also escaped to France and were living in Sarcelles.

Although not part of the core group, Katty Belle grew up with parkour and to date still participates in the activity as a leisure practice. Katty Belle recalled how parkour started for her when she was seven or eight years old, when "Tonton Raymond", her Grandmother's brother (Raymond Belle), came to live with their family in Sarcelles for a period of time (Belle K. 2007).

While staying with his relatives in Sarcelles, Raymond Belle would collect Katty and her brothers Phung, Châu and Williams after school and take them to the nearby forest of Ecouen and encourage them to climb, run, and explore, asking 'Can you do this? Can you do this?' teaching them how to move and adapt to their surroundings. They would run along the top of the wall surrounding the forest to get to the children's play area. This was how they spent their time together, after school and during their holidays. They were not children who were told to stay away from the edge, but - on the contrary - to explore it, to know it, to be careful of it but not fear it. Moving and exploring movement was the family's way of spending time together outside: the male and female members of the family all took part, aunts and sisters, as well as, uncles and brothers (Belle K. 2009).

Châu Belle-Dinh leads members of Majestic Force and Parkour Generations training in the forest of Ecouene, Sarcelles, 2008.

David's account of first discovering parkour as a concept is when he asked his father to explain how as a fire-fighter he had achieved a certain jump that resulted in helping a woman who was about to commit suicide. David questioned his father's celebrated bravery and physicality, keen to understand the 'recipe' that had created this man who was so capable, strong and fearless. His father's explanation was, "When I was young I was doing *parcours*" David asked "*Parcours*? What is *parcours*?" David recalls his father replied "*Parcours*, it's like in life, you have obstacles and you train to overcome them, you search for the best technique, you try all techniques, you keep the best, you repeat it and then you get better" (Belle D. 2009a). David states that his father had practised parcours since he was seven years old. However, as those were periods of great suffering and harshness, his father was reluctant to recall these memories.

The context and motivation Raymond Belle communicated to his son was one of a training that prepared you to always be ready, in a state of alert and to train yourself to be of assistance to others. You maybe able to do a jump when you have warmed up or are comfortable he told his son, but will you be able to perform the same jump with no preparations under duress? This was the mental and physical preparation, "be strong to be useful" (Belle D. 2009c, 141).

David says that his father encouraged him to be more active and to train, instilling an 'ethic of parcours' in him. David describes it as having "lit the fire within me to illuminate my own path" (Belle D., [28]). While David's relationship and will to know his father was key to his personal motivation, according to Châu Belle-Dinh, it was not only Raymond Belle who encouraged these ideas, but Châu's parents, their other uncles and also friends of the family, all of whom had escaped Vietnam. The philosophy behind the training, movements, games and challenges they did were rooted in the Belle family's belief in strength and resourcefulness, harnessed by a will to be strong as a product from their experiences and time in Vietnam. Williams Belle explained that being a "Belle" meant you had to be strong as part of the Belle family's identity.

As well as the physical training that Raymond showed Phung, Châu, Williams, Katty and David, he encouraged a creative vision and mapping of the terrain, inviting them to question what things were made of and how they could be used. Both Katty and David Belle attribute Raymond Belle with introducing them to looking at things in a different way, seeing what the possibilities were from their environment in Sarcelles. David recalled how his father would encourage him to question what surfaces were made of and how they could be used, (not being aware of the architecture that was available to David in Lisses and Évry) (Belle D. 2009a).

David took the *parcours* concept from his father in Sarcelles back to his local architecture in Lisses and Évry where he shared this vision with his friends. Yann remembers that David clearly wanted to know and understand his family, searching to create his own identity and change his destiny using sport. He wanted to

20

impress on his father that he too could be capable of the type of things his father had endured and achieved (Hnautra 09).

Games and training

David's friends and cousins were already active and interested in various sports: Châu practiced martial arts while Laurent and Sébastien did athletics (Belle D. 2009a). They wanted to change their lives quickly and were looking for efficient ways to do it, finding a social haven and freedom through sports as an alternative to the rising culture of gangs that surrounded them. All of the participants interviewed state that they were 'searching for something' at the start of their *parcours* experience. Yann states, "there was the problem of ethnic diversity so where could we open up to everything? At the church? At the mosque? Even there they don't accept each other; so where? At school?" (Hnautra 2009).

The group was only interested in its training. Each of the group had their own role models and inspirations; for Yann it was aspiring to be worthy of his clan's name in New Caledonia, for David it was connected to his father. What started off as games, regular levels of sport, physical challenges and adventures, soon no longer satisfied the hunger for self-knowledge and change felt by some members of the group. Yann states "at the beginning it was games, but I started to do that as training. Some of us wanted to get stronger and improve, and games didn't necessarily give you all these opportunities" (Hnautra 2009). The games had names like 'route of faith' or 'legend' (Hnautra 2009). There was an exchange of ideas and skills, fuelled by everyone's motivations. Sébastien Foucan recalled that it was Yann, the eldest of the friends, who led the training in the early days and helped train and encourage David. People were training different aspects of their skills. For example, David, aided by Frederick Hnautra, was practicing handstands at height in a bid to understand what some of the 'firemen of Paris' could do. Yann had already climbed the Dame du Lac (an enormous climbing wall in Lisses) when he first met David and taught him how to do it. David recalls that Yann taught him fighting and self-defense skills. When Châu and his older brother Phung first trained at the Dame du Lac (never having seen anyone train there before) they created new routes, ones that Yann and David had previously thought impossible as they had believed they had exhausted all the possibilities on the site (Hnautra 2009). Consequently Yann and David then trained the new routes, with everyone's abilities and ideas contributing to a growing ideology, that of surpassing individual goals and reaching new levels, making the impossible possible. The group were all drawn to each others strengths and abilities, Yann states, "to be strong you have to get closer to strong people, it's logical" (Hnautra 2009).

The types of training that the group did became increasingly more challenging as they worked primarily on their physical and mental strength as opposed to actual techniques. They would run to Paris and back, just to know they could. They did extensive long-distance *quadrupédle* work (see Appendix 1). (David stated he would do '*quadrupédie*' on his fists in the snow.) They incorporated large numbers of repetitions into the drills, for example, to do 1000 pistol squats, 500 drop jumps or 100 catleaps (see Appendix 1). They would only jump on one leg from dawn until dusk. And the jumps and drops became bigger; the rocks they lifted heavier. They would play a version of volleyball, throwing and catching heavy boulders over a wooden plank. The edges and ledges from which they hung became smaller and higher, and they would hang there for ever-increasing amounts of time.

In an interview with the press, David Belle described people who wanted to do parkour as "warriors", explaining that parkour was "A training method for warriors." He made the point that, "So many people try to train easy 'come do Parkour! It's really cool!' But if tomorrow I made you do real training, you would end up crying. That's what you need to know: you are going to cry, you are going to bleed and you are going to sweat like never before." [23]

David stated in my interview with him that it makes him suffer to think about his training sessions now as he endured so much pain. Some have compared parkour to military training but as David said, after having experienced the physical training during his national service "compared to my Parkour training, the army felt like an amusement park." (Belle D. 2009a: 116). The group all took risks together, they cried and bled together, they gave of themselves to create new experiences, a 'new sport', their art, and their identities.

It was a unique context within this group of friends. To experience pain and fear was normalised in their training as they worked within the freedom of their own structures.

Over a period of years a training ethos developed whereby they only took on difficult challenges: "We started to build ourselves like that, to only do the hard things, and believe in unbelievable actions, to try and understand them, in order to change things" (Hnautra 2009). They were all obsessed with their training, linked by a will to transcend their own limitations, so much so that they avoided alcohol and/or drugs unlike other youths around them.

The approach to training for this group was to create challenges or situations for themselves where the individual and collective achievements were made with great physical or emotional effort. The group belived that some element of suffering and/or fear would lead to innovative solutions based on mental and physical strength. Their challenges forced one to find mental and physical techniques to find a way through, a route. The group believed that if faced with two options, one should take the hardest route as nothing will be learnt from taking the easy route. Williams explained that, at times, this could mean training and might involve choosing to go without food or water or sleeping without a blanket to endure the cold.

Yann Hnautra reflected on this period of time by stating, "our trainings were really hard because we were living with hard people, and we were living in very complicated times, so we had to be respected, and we cultivated that state of mind" (Hnautra 2008). The friends moved and challenged each other in the same way in both the built and natural environment (Angel, *Parkour Generations: Rendezvous 4 Q&A part1* 2009).

The forest of Ecouen in Sarcelles. Running precision by Thomas Couetdic, 2008.

Évry, Running precision by Forrest in Lisses, 2006.

At the beginning there were single jumps and big drops as well as incorporating acrobatic movements. It was only later that this evolved into combinations of movements and certain techniques such as the "diving kong", "double kong" or "palm spin" (see Appendix 1). Yann Hnautra, David and Williams Belle all compare this stage of learning to that of a child first learning to speak, then progressing to sentences, stories and finally the creative application of these skills to formulate poetry. This art was not only a method of exploring the self, it was also a tool for self-expression.

At this time there were no names for moves, just basic jumps, drops, climbing, traversing, and strength challenges. The techniques were created as individuals adapted and found ways to move over obstacles.

A tictac at *La Dame du Lac*, Lisses, by Stephane Vigroux, 2006.

Yann Hnautra credits Williams Belle with creating many new techniques. Williams, the youngest of the group and not always welcomed by the others, spent a lot of time training on his own. Williams felt the 'violence' of many of the drops and impact on the body. He wanted to train in a way that was challenging yet not as 'hardcore' as the training that was being practiced by the others. As part of this, he developed a style of 'moving-like-water', flowing over rails that involved a considerable strength and co-ordination but was not so violent on the body (Belle W. 2010). Yann reflected that they wasted a lot of time in their training and could have been 'softer' in what they were doing. The level of sporting prowess and abilities of Raymond Belle were a guiding influence on the 'ways of being' of his son, nephews and their friends. The hard nature of their training was as much a demonstration of strength as a method of training. Their priority at this time was to extend and work on their mental resolve rather than rationalising how best to improve and be efficient in their methods (this was something that would come later as they communicated the discipline to others).

The able sporting body was a driving cultural signifier within the creation of *l'art du déplacement*, parkour and freerunning. The everyday importance was in the acts of commitment to a confrontation of fear, a disciplined working of the body, the values of self-belief, adaptability and creativity, responding to ideas, reactions and actions. They associated discipline with pleasure in the physical acts of what they did. Everything was a process of self-reflection, of revealing weaknesses or flaws. Yann describes the goal of the practice as a journey and a way to "dress wounds", to know, heal and re-enforce oneself, to instigate change and as a way of breaking patterns of behaviour (Hnautra 2009).

The theme of 'suffering' (and an empathy for their relatives who had suffered) was a continuing theme for the young men's motivations. David Belle states his reasons for doing parkour as, "for me, it's just that I wanted to show that if I could be brave and surpass myself, if I could become someone, I was making my father immortal, because by being recognised, I was making him known, and he won't have done all he did for nothing" (Belle D. 2009b). Whilst David's relationship with his father was core to his motivation, the other members of the group also maintained a strong motivation and desire to change and improve themselves for the purpose of helping others. They were all prepared to suffer to improve.

Some were inspired by fantastical characters of the superheroes of comic books and the urban myths and realities of Raymond Belle's achievements. Sébastien said of Raymond Belle, "he didn't do sport, he WAS sport" (Foucan 2009). During this period

Sébastien states there were times when they would go out to train and they would not know if they would come back. Stephane Vigroux also recalls that in this very early period the levels of risk they undertook were akin to madness; claiming they could have died at least ten times a day. Williams Belle also stated that the suffering they willingly undertook was a sort of madness, driven by their individual motivations. However, for all the potentially fatal risks they took, they were never seriously injured beyond cuts, bruises and strains. Sébastien attributes this to their training. They had focused on being precise and controlled as well as building up sufficient physical strength to withstand the potentially violent impact of the drops and landings that their actions involved (Foucan 2010). The aim was for their landings to be soft, quiet and controlled, it was not enough to be able to do it, it was to "do it, do it well, do it well and fast" (Belle D. 2009c: 76-77).

Within the group there was a commonality for the desire to achieve a functional strength, focussing on the utilitarian nature of how they were moving. David Belle in particular pushed the level of achievement at this time, exceeding anyone's expectations of what was possible (Belle W. 2010, Foucan 2009). Yann acknowledges David's transformation, describing him in the early days as "a bag of bones", a "skinny kid without any muscles" (Hnautra 2009). David admits, "When I started Parkour, I found a way to exist. I wasn't feeling well in my mind, and I wanted to get back to my true self and listen to my desires and not what others expected of me" (Belle D., 2009c: 52).

Sporting effort, pain as pleasure

The levels of risk these young men inflicted upon themselves brought them a mixture of emotions such as fear, disappointment, anger, excitement and pleasure. There seems to have been a mix of joy and sporting pain in the practice. Going out to train was equivalent to going on an adventure of embodied risks and tensions, confrontational thrills and the excitement of intense games that demanded great skill; a mixture of pleasure and pain, confidence and fear, wellbeing and injury. Elias and Dunning (1986) claim that sport can allow people to engage in thrills and excitement that is otherwise missing from the routines and controls that form everyday-life in civilised societies (Elias & Dunning in Pringle, 211-212).

There were multiple pleasures inherent in the training, such as, friendship, teamwork and physical contact with each other (including carrying one another), as well as experiencing the environment, and the development and displays of skill, fitness, adaptability and creativity. Richard Pringle contends that one of the outcomes of the human search for pleasure is "the contemporary political, economic, and social significance of sport" (Pringle, 213). How pleasure is experienced, used, managed and understood can vary, for example, pleasure can be playing sport in pain or doing painful exercises (Pringle, 214). The participants were unconsciously tied to constructing local identities of 'a strong man', a hero, being fast, agile, and brave.

The social processes that resulted in the construction of pleasure in the group's training were based around the participants' 'field of knowledge', their context, the rules they set and adhered to and the social relations. They deemed their behaviour to be 'normal' as for them young men should be athletic, strong, participating in outdoor-sports and having a disciplined approach to their bodies, driven by a willful mental resolve. Williams commented that it took him a while to realise that what they were doing and the levels of risk they were taking was not 'normal'. Yet what was initially a process of normalisation was taken to new levels of extremes as the games became life-threatening. This perhaps explains why their training was only shared by so few once the full extent of their emotional and physical approach was apparent. Their training was exclusive as each individual had to have a certain ability and be able to keep up.

Edgework

Stephen Lyng suggests that the level at which a person chooses to voluntarily engage with risk-taking experiences is the result of an attraction to "exploring the limits of human cognition and capacity in search of new possibilities of being" (Lyng 2005: 4). Lyng conceptualises this as 'edgework', borrowing the term from the "gonzo journalist" Hunter S. Thompson who wrote about the behaviour of "outlaw bikers" and predicted a rise in risk-taking leisure pursuits of the baby-boom generation as they matured (Lyng 2005: 19).

Lyng sees edgework as a way of negotiating the boundaries or 'edges' between, for example, sanity and insanity; consciousness and unconsciousness; life and death. He concludes that the reason why people are drawn to edgework activities "is the intensely seductive character of the experience itself" (Lyng 2005: 4-5). Edgework can be seen as a response to alienation and 'over-socialisation', providing participants with feelings of self-determination and control (Lyng 2005: 5).

"When the 'me' is obliterated by fear or the demands of immediate survival, action is no longer constrained by social forces, and the individual is left with a sense of self-determination. [...] Behaviour in edgework appears to the individual as an innate response arising from sources deep within the individual, untouched by socialising influences" (Lyng 1990: 879).

The edgework that this group of young *parcours* men participated in was not a temporary escape from institutions or working conditions, they were not 'weekend warriors'. They chose to immerse themselves full-time in their active risk-taking. Lyng believes "Those who venture close to the edge are attracted by embodied pleasures of such high intensity that they often have addictive consequences" (Lyng 2005: 18). Yann adds: "If there wasn't the art of movement, there wouldn't be anything free to give us the opportunity to mix sport, art of life, with the research, or our personal identity, living in an idea. It's rare. Otherwise we would have had to enter ancient sports, very ancient. New sports are so different that they don't necessarily meet people's everyday needs" (Hnautra 2009). Yann concluded that the aim of their actions, no matter how intense or dangerous, was for them simply to accept themselves (Hnautra 2009).

Fantasy, imagination and real world actions

Whilst the levels of hardship in the training were a direct influence from their peers (as well as the contentious urban environments around them), the group was also largely inspired and gained motivation from the superheroes they followed in the Japanese anime and manga series at the time, such as, *Dragon Ball* and *Dragon Ball Z*, as well as the comic and graphic novel characters the *X-Men*, *Spiderman* and *Iron Man*. The energy of the characters, as well as the actions and the classic tales of bravery and endeavour of great achievements, fed into their conscious. Sébastien recalled that in *Dragon Ball* "there was a tournament, and there was training for the tournament to achieve a physical and spiritual level. I loved it, for me it was a perfect moment, it gave me strength to go outside and practice." He describes himself then as being a dreamer, being inspired by and a fan of all of the superheroes, dreaming and believing he could fly (Foucan 2010). The friends' culture of self-improvement traversed the realms of fantasy and realism, incorporating an active imagination to create new situations and encounters.

According to the humanistic geographer Yi-Fu Tuan, "to understand human reality better, it helps to see people and their works as compounded of realism and fantasy." He continues to say that fantasy "plays a key role in the enlivenment and transformation of culture" (Tuan 1990: 435). The fantasy, followed by the imagination to create or try a particular move, turned into a realistic act for the founders of *l'art du déplacement*, parkour and freerunning, only to be seen as fantastical acts by those who witnessed such spectacles. Whilst the creation of their culture was highly influenced by the fantastical, their reality could not have had a more heightened sense of realism and been more practical; the risks were too great for them not to be. Their precise landings and 'body armour' had prepared and enabled such flights of fantasy to be successfully achieved. Today the health of these men, now in their mid to late 30's, reflects the success of their efforts; despite the repetition of severe levels of impact there are no knee or joint injuries among them. They are all active and are still training in varying degrees.

Tuan argues that realism tends to be seen as good, whereas fantasy can be perceived more negatively. One of the characteristics of fantasy is that it can be isolating: a fantasist lives in their own world, not sharing the view of their community (Tuan 1990: 442). In the case of this group of friends they created their own sense of community as they shared collective fantastical ideas of superheroes and the local stories and myths such as those surrounding Raymond Belle's achievements. Tuan states that fantasy can "set us free from established culture" and that it can be "an occasional reminder that human reality is not wholly bounded by the tragicomedies of socioeconomic life." "One of the proper and moral uses of fantasy is to envisage the good - a possible world that does justice not only to human yearnings but to human potential" (Tuan 1990: 443).

Richard Knowles states that fantasy is often seen as separate from the subject's life context (Knowles, 87). For my informants from this period, their actions chose to merge their preoccupation with fantasy characters into their daily actions. Ernest Becker suggests that fantasy emerges out of fear (Knowles, 88) and that a fantasy "self and situation" is developed as a way of creating something less- alarming and reducing something down to a more-manageable level than the one being dealt with. The fantasy becomes the ego or character and is a response to fear.

Whilst the 'fantasy self' is opposed to change, the ego can be maintained potentially for a lifetime, into and throughout adulthood, never realising an authentic self. The person can try to live out the fantasy as if it were true but when they themselves know this is not the case then there is an ambivalence towards it. Knowles suggests there is then the possibility for a change in the fantasy self. Fantasy can be challenged by a crisis and from commitment (Knowles, 91) and may then invoke change. This involves a letting go and confrontation of fear; admitting to a vulnerability within risk-taking.

For my informants the letting go of fear (the crisis), involved an active imagination and the commitment to action, for example, to vault, traverse, balance or climb. This was key to them finding and realising a more authentic sense of self, applying a disciplined commitment to the control over their emotions and bodies in their movments whilst in the air as well as when in contact with the environment.

Motivated by the fantasy of heroic acts and abilities, imagination for my informants was expressed in how they saw the environment; what actions they chose to commit to followed by the authentic experience of being which they experienced as a result. Knowles states that imagination is a movement toward action, even if that action is intellectual or meditative, rather than physical. Imagination may then be regarded as active as opposed to fantasy being passive. There is an opening up of one's perception and a crossover that could have derived from fantasy. The imaginative mode also involves a willingness and commitment towards engagement moving towards it. As Knowles explains, "Imagination is a way of moving in harmony with the rhythm of the world and others" (Knowles, 94).

"Unless we can imagine ourselves doing something, we cannot do it. What usually interferes with our authentic imagining is fear and its rigidity, fantasy and its passivity, a wilful or wishy-washy attitude. In the rare moments when we are able to imagine, there is a letting go of the more habitual ways, a willingness to encounter things and people as they are and a move into risk and uncertainty. The fears, fantasies and resolutions and wishes take on a particular form, are seen in a creative Gestalt and offer to the person a sense of purpose, a way of moving in the world which is more real" (Knowles, 95).

During the imaginative encounter these young men entered an experimental field of new cultural experiences, a transitional space where there was an active negotiation of fantasy, imagination and reality, one of 'self and non-self' that opened up opportunities for communication, confrontation and expression that contribute to creating personal identity and a sense of being (Midol & Broyer, 206). Midol and Broyer state that, "it is within a transitional space that sports pioneers have had to invent new motor forms, new means of communication, and a new kind of community" (Midol & Broyer, 207). The culture the group created is a new form of activity and like other 'new sports' is free from restrictions on safety (Midol & Broyer, 207) as it practices transgressive behaviours that create new values, living in the moment in their intense relationship and experience as they transcend their own lives. By doing this they embrace something that has been more-traditionally defined as feminine, that is, to value that which comes out of a state of being while keeping a capacity for action (Midol & Broyer, 208).

The group's quest for belonging, an acceptance of themselves, and authenticity through processes of self-knowledge, gave it a sense of freedom. As individuals they were liberated from fixed, socially- constructed positions and notions of self.

Alison Weir argues that "the question of *authenticity* is not just about knowing the truth of the self; it is about being true *to* oneself" and involves an ethics and quest for a meaningful life. Charles Taylor suggests that the question of 'what gives my life meaning' is central to the question of modern identity and committing to a relationship of integrity with oneself. (Taylor 1991, Weir 537, 543) This ethic of authenticity is specific to modern culture (Taylor 1991: 25). Taylor suggests that finding meaning to one's life involves experiences of being 'connected' in some way, to find a 'personal resonance' (Taylor 1989: 510), a social self that gives value based on ideas of communities, through relationships with others and with the world, and that the relationship to oneself can only be achieved through being embedded in communities and "background horizons of meanings" (Weir, 538). Weir suggests that "The need to discover and define one's own meaning, and the belief that one can do so, are specific to modern western culture" (Weir, 537).

The types of training the individuals focussed on were based around self-awareness and identity-construction; giving value to their relationships and authenticity; their connections to shared values, actions and experiences. Their desire for connections without constraint; a form of social autonomy, their training was a form of 'personal resonance'. The participants revealed themselves to each other during their training sessions, through, for example the blood and tears, they each so openly and often remember.

A philosophical approach

As the training activities continued throughout the 1980s, the practitioners started to understand what the physical and creative aspects were bringing to their lives in terms of their psychological outlook. The utilitarian influences of the older generation of Belles and Hnautras emphasised the need that to be strong meant that it should also be of use to others: the motivation should not be entirely selfish. The training was not a performative practice.

Out of all the friends who were moving and practising *parcours* at this time, there was a core of nine, who, for various reasons, continued to train in a more-dedicated way. Some of the young men had to fulfil their obligation to national service, others were getting jobs while some were keen to use parcours in their spare time as an activity for the weekends and holidays. People were making choices.

David Belle was the driving force behind the will to create something out of *parcours*. Yann states that while they realised that their way of life was consumed by their training, they wanted to be part of society. Furthermore, there was the realisation that they were old enough to have to work so they decided to try and make something from parcours and make a go of it. The all male core group of nine, dedicated to their own trainings were:

Châu Belle-Dinh, Williams Belle, David Belle, Guylain N'Guba-Boyeke, Malik Diouf Sébastien Foucan, Yann Hnautra, Charles Perrière, Laurent Piemontesi

The approach to transcending physical and emotional limits, their philosophy and training ethics along with the discipline, the movements and techniques was by now firmly fixed in each of the group's minds. At this stage, they were not concerned with aesthetics, grace or agility. Furthermore, they were all very protective of how their culture was represented having invested so much of themselves. The group became more closed – elitist even – and it was much harder for anyone to gain admission and to learn the discipline from them (Belle K. 2009). For those that did, it was necessary to demonstrate their commitment and respect for the process: thus, gaining access to these key individuals and their tutorage became harder, not least, because they were occupied with developing their own practice.

Dissemination of an art, conclusion to first phase of evolution

The discipline evolved locally in Sarcelles, Évry and Lisses over a period of approximately 10 years. It began in the mid-1980s, gaining local and then national publicity, initially from a magazine article published in Lisses (Hnautra 2009). Techniques continued to be developed after this period but the psychological and physical training methodology and approach had been firmly established by this stage. In 1997, David Belle's brother Jean Francois Belle who like his father, (Raymond Belle,) was a firefighter, asked his brother and their friends to arrange a performance for the public fire-service show in Paris   ([27]). Jean Francois was instrumental in and determined to show off his brother and his friends skills to an audience beyond Sarcelles, Évry and Lisses so he shot some video footage of the group and sent it to the French TV channel Stad2.

For the fire-fighters show the group decided to give themselves the name 'Yamakasi' meaning 'strong-man, strong-spirit' in Lingala, a Bantu language spoken mainly in Congo-Kinshasa and Congo-Brazzaville, from where one of the individual's family - Guylain N'Guba-Boyeke -originated (Hnautra 2009). The group members' ages ranged from 15 (Williams Belle) to 25 (Yann Hnautra). They were self-managed, with no experience of how to organise themselves and unaware of the challenges that performances and/or publicity might pose. At this time, Sébastien Foucan, who had an interest in the visual arts, came up with the name *l'art du déplacement* (Foucan 2009).

The group was made up of strong-willed characters, a product of their own extreme training and individual self-belief that encouraged autonomy. Both Sébastien Foucan and David Belle recall they had doubts as to the plausibility of a group ever being able to work together, as at this point in their lives people were starting to have different obligations and responsibilities (Belle D. 2009, Foucan 2010).

After viewing Jean Francois Belle's footage of the group of young men, the national French television Stad 2 broadcast a report on the group of young men from the Parisian suburbs, celebrating their athletic accomplishments, innovative approach and style of movement. This was the first and only positive portrayal in the French media regarding their training and the discipline itself for a long time. Subsequent reports were negative: this *'parcours'* *l'art du déplacement* was socially devalued through negative stereotyping of the multicultural group and the neighbourhoods from which they came (Foucan, 2010). It would be almost 20 years before the discipline was accepted in Évry, not viewed as trespassing or an activity based around some form of ill-intent. And yet, reactions to the performance aspect were positive and continued to celebrate the spectacle of what these young men could do.

After the first semi-public performance at the fire-fighters event, the negative or positive attention that followed signalled the breakup of the short-lived original line-up of the Yamakasi. The Yamakasi were asked to perform in *Notre-Dame de Paris*, a French-Canadian musical. Not everyone wanted to take part and there were concerns as to how this activity - their *l'art du déplacement* - was being perceived as an acrobatic show, as a performance that didn't demonstrate the other aspects of the discipline, such as, their warrior training; the strength of character; mental resolve; their ethics and values. David Belle and Sébastien Foucan independently decided to leave the group. They remained friends for a while and were both in the group 'Tracers' (see Appendix 2) but, eventually, after some time, each was to chose to concentrate on his own projects and responsibilities. David believes the split of the first line-up of the 'Yamakasi' would have happened regardless of the show as people had different obligations at this time (Belle D. 2009a).

Katty Belle explained that at the time of the invitation to perform at the *Notre-Dame de Paris*, there were already fractures; David left wanting to be an actor and Sébastien wanted to teach rather than perform. The remaining seven 'Yamakasi' performed in the show, bringing their skills and abilities to the awareness of Luc Besson, the celebrated French writer and filmmaker. Both David Belle and the remaining seven members of the Yamakasi group would go on to work on film projects by Besson in the future.

David's friend Hubert Kunde suggested to him that he change the name and make the practice his own, he could replace the 'c' in "*parcour*" with a 'k'. David did this and the word would then be written with a 'k', although the spoken word was the same. David's training became known as "parkour".

After the split, the remaining Yamaksi group continued to refer to the discipline as "*l'art du déplacement*", avoiding the term "parkour", not wanting to associate so closely with David for personal reasons, not because of any difference in the essence of the practice. Châu Belle-Dinh concurs with his statement at the question and answer session of the international training event Rendezvous 2, stating that David Belle uses the name "parkour", whilst for him and the other remaining Yamakasi members use the term "*l'art du déplacement*", stressing that the importance is the mentality or approach you have when you are moving. "You do parkour, *l'art du déplacement*, motion art, freerunning, it's the same thing, your heart, your 'way' is very important" (Angel, *Yamakasi Q&A Rendezvous II pt.1* 2007).

When the Yamakasi group separated Sébastien Foucan went on to have various jobs as a fire security guard; David Belle also worked as a security guard then choosing to travel for a while. They both still trained although not so intensively during this time. David wanted to be an actor and made a promotional showreel of his abilities, the video *Speed Air Man* in an attempt to be involved in the 2002 film *Spiderman*.

The issue of how the discipline is used or displayed in a performative context continues to be contentious and cause factions within the international parkour community as discussed in chapter 4. The incorporation, or not, of acrobatic movements, as to when something is or is not parkour, still resonates to-date between different groups of practitioners. The source of the initial conflict seems to stem from acrobatics being seen as a fun and an optional act that does not align itself with the functionality and utilitarian ideal of being 'strong to be useful'. The physical skills attained by the core group through their training meant acrobatics were easily achieved and some saw this as the thing they did once training had finished. The representation of parkour as it was presented in David's early video *SpeedAirMan* was key to the classifying in the minds of many new practitioners what was or was not parkour. There was no explanation of what was behind the movement, no presentation of the training methodology, ethics, values or suffering that had been endured, just a spectacular display. It is still little known today, amongst the parkour community, that the video was itself a performance created as an audition tape for the film *Spiderman*. The visual representation of parkour is discussed in Chapter 2.

Variations on a theme

The lack of recognition by some of the group towards others of their level and of their contribution to helping create the disciplines within the end of the first formative decade, led to the future appropriation of the practice by all of the core group at some point. Whilst there were these differences, they do however all agree, that it is all rooted in the same practice: *parcours*.

For Yann Hnautra, Châu Belle-Dinh, Laurent Pietmonetsi and Williams Belle, they chose to continue to use the term *l'art du déplacement* and developed a more participatory, compassionate and inclusive approach to the discipline, creating trainings that were not all 'hardcore'. They continued to perform and also began teaching small groups and individuals from 2001 onwards, adapting the teaching to suit individuals' abilities, ages and gender. Williams Belle views *l'art du déplacement* as an umbrella-term that includes parkour and freerunning, equivalent to how the term 'martial arts' can describe a multitude of fighting-arts such as karate or taekwondo. He acknowledges, however, that if you were to train parkour with David or those who had followed David's path, their approach would be slightly different than if you were training freerunning or *l'art du déplacement*.

For David Belle, parkour is a complete training method that he believes his father had communicated only to him, clearly distinguishing it from George Hebert's *Method Naturelle*. He does, however, also recognise the input and influences from the group of friends who were all participating in the activity at the time. "The act of getting together and sharing all these sporting experiences with people who came from athletics or martial arts and all these things, it contributed to this phenomenon of parkour, it creates loads of new motivations" (Belle D. 2009a).

While there are several different names for the practices that came out of *parcours*, in an interview at the New Yorker festival, David made it clear that, for him, "There are not different kinds of parkour: someone who can fight - a real fighter - can fight on the ground, small, big, anywhere, parkour is the same; you must adapt, you adapt to everything that's around us here. There are not derivatives, then acrobatics are different, you can do it here but you can't do it for one hour, but you can do parkour and discover your surroundings for a long time. (Belle D. [24]).

For David, parkour is about becoming a disciplined athlete. However, at times his views are contradictory. He sometimes comments that he wants people to enjoy themselves and have fun; at other times they have to be warriors who endure brutal training that can be done outside. But what is clear is that he does not want to, in any way, discredit his father's abilities, his father, who is, the source of David's motivation and teachings. However as Stephane Vigroux stated, David's way of training was very very particular and only a few people stayed with him and followed his level and methods of training (Angel, *Le Singe est de Retour* 2006).

Sébastien Foucan, used the term parkour for several years then chose to create freerunning after appropriating the term that had been used as a direct translation for parkour in the documentary *Jump London*. He has developed this as a more inclusive and participatory practice than David's parkour, encouraging creativity and expression. At times, however, Sébastien uses both terms – parkour and freerunning – interchangeably (foucan.com).

The personal investment in terms of time, suffering, passion, effort and belief in the potential of the practice, coupled with a group of young men inexperienced in managing their sudden media attention, led to divisions that would take decades to heal. Over the next twenty years all of the 9 core Yamakasi group would use the skills they had gained for performative roles in features films, commercials and other projects. Some of the group (Chau, Yann and Laurent) focused on the teaching aspect, working towards creating a coaching certificate that would ensure the continuation of their training methods and standards. Others put their energy into media roles, but all of them still trained and shared the common bond of their early experiences. This is an unfinished history and, even whilst this research is being written, there are talks and a will for the nine men to meet together and work together to create an agreed definition of their practice, confirm the collective essence of what to them is an art, and find a way to help the discipline, as a training methodology, be given the recognition they feel it warrants.

To an outsider there are few if any visible differences between the disciplines *l'art du déplacement*, parkour and freerunning. However, subtle differences in the approaches, along with the strong-willed personalities and different motivations within the founding group exist. Even though this may be only miniscule, amongst the group itself, these differences are important as they represent who each individual is. For many practitioners, however, it is irrelevant to their own training, and only makes a difference in who they choose to align themselves with and follow as role-models or 'heroes'.

Conclusion

The disciplines born out of '*parcours*' stem from a search for an authentic identity, inclusion, (suffering), freedom, expression and innovation. As the anthropologist James Clifford states, "It is easier to register the loss of traditional orders of difference than to perceive the emergence of new ones" (Clifford, 15). "Twentieth-century identities no longer presuppose continuous cultures or traditions. Everywhere individuals and groups improvise local performances from (re)collected pasts". The disciplines - these 'arts of movement'- are the product of what Clifford calls "historical transplanting" (Clifford, 14-15). There are local narratives of cultural-continuity from the Belles and Hnautras as well as other cultural backgrounds from the various friends, but there is no single master-narrative to the events that occurred.

Michel de Certeau wrote that the acculturation phenomena, the experience of being culturally in-between results in producing a degree of "plurality and creativity" in peoples "ways of operating" (deCerteau, 30), strategies to become autonomous, as was the case for my informants. They transcended their histories and localities to become something of a myth, incorporating elements of the wild into the 'civilised'. Their journeys, *parcours* and explorations may have been fuelled by individual motivations, but as a group of friends they shared, and were linked by, their collective experiences. When the friends began to unconsciously create their own social culture of movement, those involved were adolescents - between child and adult - open to new ideas but not yet fully-developed in terms of identity and socialisation.

Midol and Broyer suggest, "A culture is held together through the exchange of representations, the sharing of prohibitions and taboos, the acknowledgement of recognized rules of behaviour, and the acceptance of sanctions for misbehaviour. The culture reflects a certain type of collective suppression on the basis of which are elaborated the unconscious personality structures of individuals." This forms a "collective unconsciousness" (Midol & Broyer, 205).

The culture of movements - *l'art du déplacement*, parkour and freerunning - are all imaginative open-ended projects. As Knowles believes, "A project is imaginative rather than fantastic when: its spirit is one of openness and relaxation rather than one of rigidity and fear; it is characterized by receptivity rather than passivity; it admits and organises the chaos and uncertainty of life rather than attempting to eliminate them or becoming lost in them; the project is articulated in such a way that it invites rather than coerces, leaving people free; it is available for inter-objective validation rather than calling for blind faith; it opens up a future which inspires to action rather than relying upon nostalgia or guilt; and the thinking involved and the practice acknowledge the unfinished and open-ended nature of the project" (Knowles, 96-97).

The culture of *l'art du déplacement*, parkour and freerunning, is an expression of adaptability and the product of personalities that were in a constant state of transformation. The experiences of the group of friends in the developmental period were born from a state-of- mind specific to that time and context and as such cannot - and should not - be taught in the same way as that of the founders when they created it, through their constant 'hardcore' experiences. It would be irresponsible as well as dangerous. However, the early

41

experiences created the values, ethics, spirit and essence of the disciplines as they are taught and practiced today.

Although the individuals have not trained together since 1997, they all continue to share a positive message about their discipline based on their own experiences and belief that their approach to training and the environment can – and should - play a major role in many educational aspects. They, also, all warn of the dangerous potential in the practice and the pitfalls of wanting to strive too quickly for recognition, to be careful of one's own 'ego' when practicing. As David states, "Parkour is truly a long distance discipline" (Belle D., 2009c: 56). Williams Belle stresses the importance that the discipline is a dangerous sport and, as such, it has to bring you something; it has to be beneficial to you, in your life, and, because of this, it is not for everyone (Angel *Parkour Generations: Rendezvous 4, Day1 of 2* 2009).

To conclude, the essence of parcours that became known as, *l'art du déplacement*, parkour and freerunning, comprises of the ability to transcend one's own limitations emotionally and physically. The result of this is to explore one's own identity and develop a more autonomous and authentic sense of self, free from what Weir suggests are more traditional "hierarchical social positions defined by categories like race, class, gender and sexuality" (Weir, 541). As David Belle said at the *NewYorker* festival, parkour makes you self-reliant, always confronting your own abilities, limitations and motivations, measuring risks and challenges (Belle D. [24]). The result of these explorations can be feelings of empowerment and emancipation.

Yann Hnautra monkey walks on wall in the forest of Ecouen, Sarcelles, 2008.

While there may not have been a combined written history of events by the group themselves, I conclude that although there are small differences among the memories of some of these individuals about the who, when and where, there are no great contradictions in the main premise of how the activity came about. It is the result of the initial patriarchal, military influences and inspirations from the Belle and Hnautra families, coupled with the energy, will and imagination from a group of young men who were prepared to challenge, support and suffer to achieve great physical feats that forced them to confront their own fears and limitations, and ultimately explore their own identities. As a result, they found their own identity against a background of contentious, local environments.

The *parcours* timeline (see Appendix 3) illustrates the key moments in the period from 2001 to 2004, at which point I first became aware of parkour after watching the BBC TV ident *Rush Hour* featuring David Belle, and then the subsequent Channel 4 documentary, *'Jump London'* featuring Sébastien Foucan, Johann Vigroux, Jerome Ben-Aoues and Stephane Vigroux, broadcast in 2003.

Chapter 2

Documenting Movement: a shared participatory ciné parkour

This chapter aims to discuss and describe the methodologies used in my practice based qualitative research analysing several film productions on the development of a ciné parkour. I will be documenting the processes and challenges of participant observation, collaborative filmmaking, creating a shared cinema and development of a ciné parkour. I will also be documenting how the presence of the camera and filmmaker can stimulate, modify, and accelerate actions and act as a catalyst, allowing - and inviting people - to share their knowledge. As Feld commented on the work of ethnographic filmmaker and "prolific" photographer, (Henley, xii) Jean Rouch, who used a similar approach, "people respond by revealing themselves, and meanings emerge in that revelation" (Feld in Rouch,16).

I wanted to research, document and represent parkour in a way that neither the parkour community nor mainstream media was doing. I wanted to concentrate on the 'everyday' as opposed to the existing dominant spectacle and performance-orientated representations of the practice.

I wanted to document how the practitioners experienced parkour, to understand the nature of the activity and the role it plays in their lives. I was interested in detecting their motivations and insights. What is it that parkour has that sets it apart from other activities? And what makes it so appealing?

Were traceurs (see Appendix 1) moving around cities simply because they had no other place to go? In London - a site of growing popularity for parkour - the press reported regular closures of school playing-fields and sites for play and exercise (Curtis, [53]). Acts of physically-creative expressions, whilst sanctioned for performances, were not to be encouraged as unregulated past-times. Was parkour simply a product of, and reaction to, an increased sense of regulation and ownership by the state and private corporations? The sedentary, risk-averse culture of the 'no ball games, no skateboarding and no cycling', signs, discouraged movement, yet traceurs were moving freely, whenever and wherever they saw fit, conquering their fears while, at the same time, embracing the risks of their activity. Was there a link between diminished options for play and expression and the increase in people who were willing to confront their fears and limitations by moving unconventionally around the built environment?

Parkour is a cultural movement and, as sports ethnographer Robert Sands explains, "In the case of sport ethnography, it is possible to conceive of an athletic team or group, even athletes of a sport, as a culture" (Sands, 17). Culturally, traceurs' movements, spatial tactics and how they read and experience their environment is a variation on the normative practices of how people choose to navigate and view their surroundings.

Methodologies and motivations

My methodology was rooted in what Steven Feld states as " the most basic ethnographic field methods, participation and feedback" (Rouch, 12). My intention was for the research to be long-term. Although not trained as an anthropologist, my reliance on participant observation, collaborative filmmaking and feedback, situated it as an ethnographic practice, but, what constitutes an ethnographic film is a point-of-debate among various theorists (Ruby, 29). My work could be categorised as an example of what Jay Ruby describes as "anthropologically intended films" (Ruby, 6). Historian and cultural theorist James Clifford writes, "Modern ethnography appears in several forms, traditional and innovative. As an academic practice it cannot be separated from anthropology. Seen more generally, it is simply diverse ways of thinking and writing about culture from a standpoint of participant observation" (Clifford, 9).

Clifford states "Participant observation obliges its practitioners to experience, at a bodily as well as an intellectual level, the vicissitudes of translation." Fieldwork should produce knowledge as a result of an "intense, intersubjective engagement" (Clifford, 24) usually over a long period of time.

My methods of production fell between the expository, ethnographic, artistic, and experimental, at times incorporating empathetic provocations (questioning, making requests and presenting ideas) beyond the experiential and observational passivity that I used as a starting point for the research. I also used staging, re-enactment and performance, techniques Nichols states are more normally associated with fiction. (Nichols 2001: xi). This was to create what the French filmmaker Jean Rouch describes as "cinema 'reality' ", which is what he claims Robert Flaherty and Dziga Vertov did, although they each employed different approaches; Flaherty, the geographer-explorer, chose to stage reality, while Vertov, the futurist poet, chose to seize "improvising life" (Rouch, 31-33).

Nichols suggests there are four "dominant organisational" modes of representation in documentary around which most "texts" are structured; expository, observational, interactive and reflexive. Each contains its own limitations, constraints and viewer expectations, forcing a search for, and creation of, new hybrid forms combining multiple elements of the four forms, out of which "New modes convey a fresh, new perspective on reality" (Nichols 1991: 32-34). He later added two further modes, the poetic and performative (Nichols 2001: 99).

I incorporated a hybrid of documentary forms, choosing elements of direct cinema; cinema verité; ethnography; ethno-docudrama and the avant-garde which combined, allowed me to remain adaptive and responsive to experiences and knowledge gained throughout my research. The end result is a diverse body of work in form and duration, reflecting a range and variety of themes and knowledge present within parkour culture.

It was important to my research that it was done in a spirit of collaboration. I invited and received feedback from my respondents during both the filming and editing stages. There were discussions on, for example, what was the best angle for filming and framing a shot and this, at times, led to several different versions being filmed. There were also occasions when I 'passed the camera', inviting my research participants to take the camera and take some of the footage. By showing and sharing the footage and edits, it enhanced the participation of the informants, which created a production feedback loop. It established a shared ciné parkour, giving the participants some control and influence over the individual and collective representations of parkour and themselves.

My knowledge of parkour has come from observational and first-hand experience. My style of filming and editing evolved with my experiences and understanding of parkour. My initial approach was to prioritise the experiential and familiarise myself with parkour before applying an analytical frame that would identify the authoritative voices, and selecting appropriate and effective stylistic strategies to communicate and represent parkour.

I believe, like the filmmaker David MacDougall, that the analytical and experiential perspectives are, "complementary and of comparable importance" (MacDougall, 93). By concentrating on certain elements and attributes of parkour within individual productions, I endeavoured to build a picture of a larger social whole. A tradition which Clifford tells us fieldworkers have always done (Clifford, 63).

My approach was informal and without any strict theoretical framework. What mattered was the quality of contact, something Rouch states is more important than producing a technically-professional film (Rouch, 37). I wanted to become an accepted participant and find a role within the parkour culture. To access and understand parkour I began by filming observationally; relying on the experiential to form the basis for interpretation, introspection and analysis. This culminated in showing both the raw unedited footage and edits of existing footage to the participants. Their feedback then helped to inform decisions that contributed to the style and content necessary to communicate themes and actions. Filming observationally also meant having to be present in the situation, as Brian Winston states, "Mindless observational filming is not documentary, it is surveillance" (Winston in ten Brink, 305). By being mindful of that which I chose to focus on, frame and observe, shaped on the participants' feedback, I was taught how to observe parkour from an informed traceurs' perspective.

This approach evolved into a collaborative process, working within a framework of a shared cinema, a feedback loop in production and post-production. Editing was not a strict linear process that began as soon as all filming had finished; in general there were as many potential edits as there were possible shoots. What was important was that there was adequate time for a collaborative analysis of how the representations should be portrayed. The films became sites of a common-ground of perception, expressing the parkour I had observed and experienced, aligned with the lived experience of the participating traceurs. The films contain multiple voices; those being filmed and the filmmaker. The films do not follow a narrative logic, but one which is more fragmented or mosaic, a logic that has been created over time and shared publicly.

Nichols believes "The documentary tradition relies heavily on being able to convey to us the impression of authenticity" (Nichols 2001: xiii) and that the authenticity of an image itself is a matter of trust (Nichols 2003: xvi). The viewer or audience has to believe that the filmmaker has portrayed an accurate representation of his subject. And I had to trust in the authority and feedback of my informants relying as much on their judgements of authenticity as my own. Long-term access and participation were necessary to ensure 'trust' could be built and maintained among all parties to enable such films to be made.

I needed to develop a predictive and anticipatory style of camera work which would allow me to follow and continually frame and reframe movements. I needed to learn to adapt and respond to moments that were of relevance and concern to the participants, based on their actions of where and how they moved. An example of this is where certain foot or hand placements are going to be and where they would move to next. I needed to share their parkour vision, following the body in motion as well as within a fixed frame of space. This was achievable as a result of being exposed to parkour over a long period of time and my own experiences of doing parkour. This led to my ability to operate the camera in a more dynamic way whilst also paying close attention to the sounds created. There was a need to remove, and look beyond the spectacle to reveal the empathy, difficulty, fear, effort, playful creativity, discipline, accuracy and repetition present in parkour. I wanted the films to allow an audience to see and experience the world through parkour eyes, following in the tradition of Jean Rouch, Sol Worth and John Adair (Ruby, 13).

My methodology involved relying on the experiences of the observer (myself) and observed sharing power and influence inherent in the filmmaking-process by trusting in the collaborative feedback loop and my ability to contextualise the social relations at play. This approach was successful in developing filming and editing strategies and determining which participants I wished to continue working with to develop a ciné parkour. This, ultimately, led to a change in the individuals with whom I collaborated for my research project.

The heavy reliance on constant feedback throughout various stages in the production cycle meant my methodology provided an ethically-accountable mode of production. It was only by having the active participation of the informants that made it possible to pursue this approach over an extended period. As Ruby explains, "The need to justify is more commonly experienced by ethnographers than documentary filmmakers because ethnographers tend to stay in the field for prolonged periods and often wish to return for a restudy. They become temporary members of a community and, as such, assume certain obligations" (Ruby, 33).

This lengthy, collaborative and accountable approach resulted in creating accurate representations of parkour culture that reflect the experiential qualities and authority of the informants and filmmaker/researcher. Working collaboratively meant I had to discuss and explain my creative choices in the representation of the participants and parkour. This included explanations on what I had included of their thoughts and actions, how I framed them, the use of shots, and the style of editing. Why, for example, a shot was left out or one 'take' was chosen over another was the most frequent point of discussion. The second most-debated topic was the composition of the shot, determining what were the important aspects on which to focus. My hope was that by combining my audio-visual communication skills with the participants' expertise and knowledge, it would be possible to create films - fragments of knowledge - that would help an audience to understand what the traceurs did and why they felt compelled to do it. An insight that went beyond the spectacle of existing parkour representations.

The research was adaptive throughout and resulted in various improvisations and experimentations. As Sarah Pink discusses when looking for the kind of approach sometimes necessary when doing visual ethnography it is "not unusual to make up methods as you go along" (Pink, 5). I relied on the building of friendships and mutual respect for my process of enquiry and pursuit of parkour.

I was initially motivated by that which I understood parkour to be. My first impressions of the art came from watching *Rush Hour*, and *Jump London*. I interpreted parkour as a reaction to, as well as a tool to enjoy an otherwise banal urban environment, finding new ways and places to play. When I began my research parkour had been presented purely as an urban past-time, with a tendency to explore routes above the city. When I interviewed Mike Christie, the director of both Channel 4 documentaries *Jump London* and *Jump Britain*, he expressed his belief that parkour was a product of boredom and modernity (Christie: 2005a). This I later established is contrary to the original motivations of the founders. Christie's films, hybrids of performance and documentary, made little reference to the fact that Sébastien Foucan (who was central to the Jump films) and his friends in Sarcelles, Lisses and Évry were all very active, involved in sport, and many of them came from families with strong athletic and military backgrounds. Sébastien states in an interview (on the extras) on the *Jump London* dvd that parkour was the product of both the natural and urban environments and can be practiced in both. This was omitted from the main content of the film and urban representations of parkour continue to dominate mainstream media and any discussions on parkour. By omitting the rural potential and context of parkour it alludes to the practice as being more of a response to the urban than I was to discover it was.

I was drawn to the implicit politics of parkour, the re-appropriation of public space that seemed to represent a reversal of power in the dominant culture. I recognised certain parallels with skateboarding from my research and film on pool and pipe-skating in Southern California, as these activities shared the concept of a multiplicity and a creative vision of urban spaces (Spasic, *Chlorine* 2003).

Practice led research

I deemed moving images to be the appropriate medium and mode of research especially for moving participants. It also provided me with an accessible way to share and collaborate with the informants during the research process. Barbash and Taylor make the point that, "Film also has the possibility of reaching a far vaster audience than most academic writers could ever imagine. The subjects of your film are better able to judge your representation of them than if you write a book about them in another language. Your films can be seen and evaluated by all sorts of communities to which you'd otherwise have no access" (Barbash & Taylor, 2). Rouch commented on his own practice that, "by studying this film on a small moviescope viewer with my informants, I was able to gather more information in two weeks than I could get in three months of direct observation and interview" (Rouch, 44). It is this gathering of information and exchange that is possible during practice-led research when working collaboratively. As Ruby states in his research into the possibilities of an anthropology of the visible, "Culture is manifested through visible symbols embedded in gestures, ceremonies, rituals, and artefacts situated in constructed and natural environments" (Ruby, ix). The spatial relations of the traceur to the built environment and their symbolic use of space lends itself to visual documentation that the written would struggle to explore as effectively. I believe, as Paul Henley suggests Rouch did, to share "a commitment to the medium of film as a unique and unprecedented way of promoting humanity's understanding of itself" (Henley, 254). The process of sharing the footage with my informants helped me to understand how they read the built environment and helped to make me aware of moments of relevance. This also allowed them to see what I did and did not know, the scope of my understanding through my representations of them. They embraced the feedback loop and actively participated in the filmmaking process. As film theorist Bill Nichols explains, "the idea of representation itself is central to documentary" (Nichols 2001: 5).

By attempting to represent the 'everyday' of parkour culture, the films were largely for the parkour community and participants, however, they were also for me, the filmmaker, as evidence of the knowledge and experience gained, and ultimately, also for the largest audience possible, the public; to expand the understanding of parkour. The films offer the potential for a discourse on ideas of public space, encounters, expression, identity, fear, risk, play, and effort in sport, as well as, demonstrating what parkour really is.

Representations of parkour

At the start of my research, the existing commercially-motivated representations of parkour had to impress, entertain and satisfy audiences for those people financing the films. Mike Christie, the writer and director of *Jump London*, exemplified this commercial approach when he discussed some of the constraints and realities of his documentary. He stated that, with regards to what was shown and the locations and structures where traceurs did parkour for the benefit of the documentary, if the traceurs had **their own way**, "they wouldn't have been doing parkour on them" (Christi [44]). This performance of parkour, away from its preferred style of environments, resulted in a piece of televised performance-art. In contrast to this, my research would focus on what and where the traceurs chose, that is, **their own 'way'**. They would have autonomy over, not just the locations but also the form, as well as the content for the research documentaries. I wanted to find a way to film parkour that conveyed the experience of it for the traceurs. In contrast, Christie states "at no point was anyone going 'do you know how to film Parkour?' People were more worried about it being edited in a sexy way and the buildings being filmed in an interesting way" (Christie [44]). As Neil Archer comments on the research by Fuggle and Saville, "mainstream representations of the parkour spectacle occlude the exploratory, bodily experience of individual practice" (Archer 95).

Whilst *Jump London* was an example of the mainstream media's perspective of parkour, representations of parkour from within its own culture were equally spectacle - and performance led - even if less cinematic, playing out as showreels or records of achievements. They were not intended to provide any explanation or discussion of the culture but simply highlighted the more visually spectacular aspects of it. Having a visual record of how you achieve something is also a learning-tool to observe your technique. Video analysis is a common training method for sports professionals and coaches.

Ruby claims that: "The agendas of people representing a culture in which they are native have to be different from those who are not. Once it is acknowledged that no one can speak for or represent a culture, but only his or her relationship to it, then a multiplicity of viewpoints is possible and welcome – some from within and others from without and all the marvellously grey areas in between" (Ruby, 31).

The most widely-seen video from within the parkour community at the time (created in 1998) was the short film *SpeedAirMan* featuring David Belle. David had put the film together as an audition showreel for the first Spiderman feature film, the title itself a play on the French pronunciation. He had not initially intended the film to be broadcast on the web, or for it to be interpreted as a guide to what was or was not parkour (as some traceurs would later do). A friend of David's had uploaded it onto the web and it quickly became a sensation. The video did not fail to impress: the images of David traversing the Dam du Lac 'climbing-wall' structure with astonishing ease and speed as though he were moving on flat ground, seemed like digital effects. The distance and height of the jumps and speed of the 180 catleaps does not fail to astonish even today when there is arguably so much more spectacular parkour footage available. The agility and accuracy of the movements on the outdoor staircase seem more akin to the movements of a wild animal than a man. The physical capabilities of this man and what he was doing had rarely been seen beyond the closed community of parkour's French founders.

Whilst the performative and visually-spectacular image potential of parkour had been widely-viewed, the under-represented 'everyday' aspect of the practice had, in my view, not been presented and any potential insights that might materialise had not yet been revealed.

Finding my way

During my six years of research filming and documenting parkour (complimented by an 'inside' understanding of it which was gained from my own training and participation) I have worked with various traceurs and groups starting my research with participants who had little experience or understanding of parkour and its essence. While there were many reasons for, and benefits of this, ultimately, I hoped to gain access to the founders of parkour. Eventually, my efforts and patience were rewarded and I was introduced to – and able to interview – the key individuals involved. It is my belief that this was made possible due to a continuation of collaboration, trust and endorsement personally, socially, and professionally.

London, 2004. I decided to base my research in London where I live, to allow for continuity and an extended period of access to the participants. I contacted Urban Freeflow, a London-based parkour organisation that had been featured in an article in the Guardian guide, a supplement to The Guardian newspaper.

After several months of emails, telephone calls and showing examples of my work, the manager and then co-owner Paul 'Ez' Corkery, invited me to meet the team in central London. Ez was the gatekeeper for access to the Urban Freeflow traceurs. I was invited to meet the group socially, that is, not to film. Rouch advocates the benefits of not filming immediately but of building a relationship for a period of a year (Rouch, 36). I did not want to wait this long. In hindsight, I believe that it can take, at least, this long to understand the social relations at play. Although my relationship with the individuals of Urban Freeflow were in their infancy, I did gain valuable experience, during that first year, of learning how best to film and edit parkour.

First impressions were of a chaotic but fun-loving male group of friends, with an average age of twenty. The group had an older, and determined, commercially-minded manager who was then also doing parkour. My request for access could compliment Ez's ambitions for UrbanFreeflow.

Sands comments that the early periods of new experiences in the field are often perceived as chaotic "culture scenes" where actions and knowledge is shared between participants, defining how and where cultural knowledge is generated. A 'cultural scene' is "ultimately the specific knowledge used in cultural situations" (Sands, 28). In parkour the culture scenes were often at sites such as entrance areas to housing estates, walkways, and others areas that offered opportunities for parkour. The knowledge was the language of parkour, the moves such as 'the kong', 'tic tac', and 'cat leap', as well as where to see the opportunities for movement.

Although I was familiar with some of the locations, I had never seen them utilised in such a manner. Rouch described culture scenes as a "readymade *mise-en-scene"*, one where the director has to create their own reality, improvising the framing, camera movements, and lengths of shots; all of these are subjective choices from the filmmakers inspiration (Henley, 256).

Seeing parkour first-hand was disappointing. After all, I had only witnessed the stylised television spectacle of the skills demonstrated by the first and second generation French traceurs in *Jump London* and *Rush Hour*. To my outsiders' eyes, viewing them without the dramatic camera angles and edit-style of mainstream entertainment television, this group's movements in comparison, seemed heavy and awkward. After an hour observing and socialising with the group, team member Paul Joseph, known as 'Blue' arrived. He moved with control, a light touch and apparent ease over the low-level concrete structures. Blue's background in inline-skating and basketball had helped to physically prepare him for parkour.

Two of the team, Yusuf Yirtici, known as Asid, and his brother Hasan, lived relatively close to me and expressed an interest in working on a documentary together. Asid was eager and enthusiastic to discuss parkour. Based on his experience in sports ethnographies of sprinting, basketball and football, Sands says "Athletes love to talk, mostly about themselves, but also about their skills and their sport" (Sands, 114). Asid was no exception and was keen to participate. Over the following months Asid brought me videos of David Belle to watch. He wanted to educate me in parkour. Hasan was involved but Asid was the focus of the film.

I wanted to build a rapport with my informants, to understand their parkour world, relying on the experiential and personal relations to form the basis for interpretation and representation. Clifford describes this kind of ethnographic experience as "the building up of a common, meaningful world, drawing on intuitive styles of feeling, perception, and guesswork. This activity makes use of clues, traces, gestures, and scraps of sense prior to the development of stable interpretations" (Clifford, 36).

I was aware I had the challenge of understanding the activity and its terminology, as well as, working to gain the trust and participation of the traceurs. I was not familiar with their terminology or culture. I did not know what 'a precision' was or a 'tictac to cat'. My priority was to get to know the people, and through them, the knowledge of the parkour would come. I viewed the experience as an ongoing process-of-inquiry into the subject and participants; clearly expressing to them, that they were the 'experts' in their field, and never highlighting any of their contradictions or flaws.

The challenges of participant observation

My approach and methodology of firstly getting to know and experience the parkour world was very similar to Rouch's methodology, as discussed by Paul Stoller, "Friendship is a key component of Rouch's notion of participatory anthropology" (Stoller,

24). "While his fieldwork is based on scientific principles and intellectual problems, it is also founded on the principle of long-term friendship and mutual respect" (Stoller, 47). I agree with Rouch's distinction that 'doing' ethnography and ethnographic film – which are interpenetrating rather than separate domains for him – is a profoundly human endeavour" (Stoller, 47). Steven Feld comments that, "Rouch's films enunciate a dedication to participation, involvement, long-term ethnographic commitment, and interpersonal engagement" (Feld in Rouch, 20).

Using the experiential as a basis for knowledge, as I did, is not without its challenges. Filmmaker David MacDougall reasons that for an anthropologist there is the problem and paradox of "reconciling the analytical with the experiential", stating that, "If I am to understand this socio-cultural system properly, I must not adopt the indigenous view; but if I do not adopt the indigenous view I cannot understand it properly" (MacDougall, 93). This neatly outlines the central challenge of producing research films with an ethnographic tendency.

My methodology followed the indigenous/non-indigenous model, creating a duality of roles from filmmaker/researcher to filmmaker/participant and back again; being aware of the shifts in these roles and acquiring the necessary skills of empathy, humility, the ability to communicate my intent and to share my knowledge and influence of the filmmaking process.

At the start of my research I was an outsider and, therefore, relied on qualitative research and experience, and an empathic enquiry and investigation into the social phenomena of parkour. I was aware of how my context and my age when I began (34), gender (female), ethnicity (white British) and class (middle) situated me within the ethnographic context. Sarah Pink states that ethnographers need to be aware of how they represent themselves to their informants and "how their identities are constructed and understood by the people with whom they work" (Pink, 24) as this can have implications for the knowledge that is produced. Key to this - and what helped in gaining and sustaining my initial access - was my previous work as a 'professional' independent filmmaker, rather than as a researcher, academic or student. I was welcomed particularly by Ez as someone capable of high production values and a willingness to involve the participants, rather than just an academic researcher.

To become a participant observer is not to say that I have trained in parkour in the same way that my informants have: it describes a relationship between myself and the informants that allowed me to find a role within their culture, one that involved filmmaking, friendship and shared experiences, and enabled me to be accepted as part of their social landscape and most importantly to me, the observer and documentarian of their actions. According to Clifford, "Participant observation serves as a shorthand for a continuous tacking between the "inside" and "outside" of events" (Clifford, 34). The insider being the participant, interpreting and representing culture as a result of the experiential. Clifford also, however, warns of the temptation to "translate all meaningful experience into interpretation", which might also be a veiled attempt as a validation for ethnographic authority (Clifford, 35). This process of validating what was or was not meaningful meant I had to trust in my informants' understanding and presentation of parkour.

Collaborative visual ethnography

My filming sessions with Asid and Hasan began in February 2005. I began filming observationally, not knowing what would be an appropriate or effective film style to utilise for subjects and themes that were, as yet, unknown to me. I attempted to be as unintrusive as possible and to prevent disrupting their actions. However, as Rouch states, "Every time a film is made there is a cultural disruption" (Rouch, 37). It is my belief that my perceived context as a 'professional', rather than 'research', filmmaker perhaps influenced and disrupted the participants' behaviour (particularly in the early days of my research) creating an eagerness to perform for the camera. Thus, my presence created something that was not representative of the 'everyday'. Over time this ceased to be the case.

My initial approach to observe (rather than intervene or choreograph sequences), allowed the moving images to reproduce the movements and their personalities. Combining elements of cinéma vérité and cinéma direct, I used a lightweight handheld digital video camera (Sony PD-150, Sony Z1, Sony Z5), worked only with available light, operated alone and never put myself in front of the camera. As Winston states, putting the filmmaker on screen is no guarantee of truthfulness nor will it prevent you from being as unreliable on screen as off-screen (Winston in ten Brink, 300). I was the director, the producer, the cameraperson and the editor.

My two years spent studying sound engineering and recording techniques definitely helped in being able to record interviews without having to wear headphones. The less-visible the recording technology, the more relaxed my informants were. MacDougall advocates that by de-emphasising the filmmaking process, as well as spending long amounts of time with your subjects, they will lose interest in the camera, "They must finally go on with their lives, and they tend to do so in their accustomed ways. This may seem improbable to those who have not witnessed it, yet to filmmakers it is a familiar phenomenon" (MacDougall, 128). Similarly, Fredrick Wiseman suggests that his method of filmmaking involves de-mystifying the process of filmmaking. If anyone asks how the camera works, he shows them, as he believes it is important for the filmmaker to act 'normally', although for him, this also meant not asking questions and not appearing arrogant in assuming any knowledge about, or around, the topic being filmed (Wiseman, 2010).

Over time, in addition to filming observationally, I began to intervene, to direct the content of conversations and to ask specific questions, assisting in the construction of the film. Answers would lead to new questions and help enlighten me through more cultural knowledge.

Filming Asid, Liverpool street, London, 2005.
Image courtesy of Paul Holmes

To work collaboratively, I used a process Paul Stoller refers to as 'participatory cinema', a term he used when describing Rouch's work. My work, like Rouch's, involved spending a lot of time listening but then also screening and 'sharing' the films with the participants during the filmmaking process. I played back what had been shot for the participants and made copies of the rushes and partial edits, viewing works in-progress and working on the final edits together. The first film production was the most intensive period of learning for ideas of framing and filming parkour as I was a complete outsider. The subjects of a film can have high standards and judge themselves accordingly as they are more informed and qualified to give feedback on their actions. Thus, I found Asid and Hasan's feedback extremely useful.

Asid and Hasan frequently filmed themselves, more often with Hasan filming as Asid performed, creating new showreels for Asid to present to casting companies in his attempts to get work. Having experience both in front of, and behind the camera, meant that Asid had great concern for his own representation and we discussed what considerations were important for him regarding his personality and parkour. This concern, at times bordered on vanity which could impede my task, but this simply served to help me clarify my own purpose.

Asid and Hasan checking through their own footage, Victoria Park, London 2005. *Image courtesy of Paul Holmes*

Asid's own parkour films demonstrated to me his personal visual style and influences. They were very heavily choreographed towards a visual spectacle; edited to impress; highlighting the complexity and manner in which he moved; reflecting his interest in martial arts films and used a fish eye lens to exaggerate the perspective of the shots (Yirtici, *Psychoactive* 2003). My role as a documentary researcher provided a very different agenda to that of Asid's own filmmaking.

Asid's films, like those of other traceurs, offered no explanation for his actions, nor the impact parkour had on his life. Finding the meanings and motivations behind the movements were fundamental to my criteria, not his. Like Asid's films, my work with him contained many performances. At times when filming observationally, the camera's presence provoked performance rather than a continuation of the everyday. Asid always knew where I was and when I was filming. His enthusiasm to perform began to impact on the research as the bravado notably increased when the camera was on and out of its bag. At times he chose to perform directly to the camera rather than to interact with me.

Although I wanted to find a role and be a participant observer, it does not and cannot really exist until friendship and trust have been established and tested, as both sides will have their own agenda. My presence was tolerated; there was a working relationship and beneficial exchange of reciprocity. I had access to people who did parkour, and in exchange Asid and his manager received publicity and exposure, all the while influencing its content.

Learning to film and understand parkour was a humbling experience. I was inexperienced in framing bodies beyond the conventional acts of walking and running. I underestimated the height jumped, the distances landed and the speed at which it occurred, missing many, if not all, of the relevant moments. I needed to learn the options for movement that different obstacles presented: would it be a precision jump where I should pay attention to the accuracy and softness of the landing or a tictac. How fast would that happen and where would they land? I had to share the parkour vision of my informants. The camera needed to become an empathetic extension of the movements of a traceur. Like Rouch's ideal ethnographic filmmaker, I needed my shooting to be "simply reduced to reflexes" in terms of sound and vision, camera movement, framing and shot length, creating a "participating camera" (Rouch, 39-40).

Whilst my filmmaking was 'mobile' in terms of documenting more- conventional forms of movement, my mobility and intuition in a parkour context was inadequate. As Rouch tells us in an interview with Enrico Fulchignoni, "Making a film, for me, means writing it with your eyes, with your ears, with your body. It means entering into it - being invisible and present at the same time - which never happens in traditional cinema. It's being able to be with friends, with light equipment, being able to talk to them, have them answer, and not with a clap stick slate, floodlights, staged framing, and so forth" (Rouch, 147).

Creating a ciné parkour

To 'enter in' to the filmmaking I needed to find the parkour equivalent to Rouch's ciné-trance, a ciné-parkour. In Rouch's experiences of filming possession ceremonies of the Gonghay-Zarma, he describes that the filmmaker/observer was also unconsciously modified by the possession ceremony (what was being filmed) and by the impact of the filming process itself and this, he says, needs to be given critical attention (Rouch, 87-88). He describes the observer's role as both active and involuntary in this context. Paul Henley summarises the key principles of Rouch's shooting praxis stating for Rouch there needed to be a collective unison in the inspiration and "performance on *both* sides of the lens, by the subjects as well as by the filmmaker" (Henley, 257). Henley also suggests that Rouch describes his ciné-trance as having been possessed "by what he would later describe as a sort of "enthusiasm", which "cannot be defined but which is essential to poetic creativity" (Henley, 274). This is something Henley says many filmmakers can relate to; that under certain circumstances there is a sense that "complicity is established between filmmakers and subjects, giving rise to a conviction that both parties are conspiring to produce a sequence of the highest quality" (Henley, 276).

As I spent more time around parkour, I started to have my own 'inspired' 'enthusiastic' experiences of it, getting into what I refer to as 'the parkour zone', which included developing parkour vision - following with the camera and predicting the moves and routes of the traceurs - and experiencing what psychologist Mihaly Csikszentmihalyi describes as a "flow" state when filming. In addition, and because of this, my environmental perspectives changed as a result of my involvement with and filming parkour.

Parkour, as well as my filming of it, is an activity that fits into Csikszentmihalyi's research theory on optimal experience that he calls "flow". He describes flow as a "phenomenology of enjoyment" (Csikszentmihalyi, 49) that is made up of eight component parts. Flow occurs when there are some, if not all, of the elements listed below, Parkour includes all eight elements:

1. A task is confronted that there is a chance of successfully completing, (a challenge).

2. There must be a level of concentration exerted.

3. The task or challenge has clear goals.

4. Immediate feedback is possible.

5. Awareness of the 'everyday' is removed due to being deeply involved in the act.

6. There is a level of control over the actions by the participant.

7. Concern for the self disappears but is re-affirmed immediately after.

8. The sense of time is changed through involvement with the activity.

For me there was a joy to the filming of parkour and, as with parkour, the action of filming and capturing parkour included all of the above elements. My own experiences and that of the parkour culture were full of unpredictable responses that allow the individual to break free from society's real and imagined controls of predictability. As a parkour filmmaker I needed to be able to learn to predict as well as follow, aiming for a harmony of improvisations on my part with the improvised movements of the traceur.

However, I was unsure of the impact my presence was having and how I was affecting the traceurs and their parkour. What was my role in documenting the traceurs dialogue with the environment? Was I, or could I, be neutral? Would my presence of looking and recording them, their awareness of being seen, alter their parkour? I was not watching Asid and Hasan, I was looking through my lens at Asid and Hasan, my observations were subjective not objective. Rouch describes the kinds of bodily improvisations of the director-cameraman being rooted in Vertov's idea: "The ciné-eye is: I *edit* when I choose my subject (from among millions of possible subjects). I *edit* when I observe (i.e., film) my subject (making a choice among millions of possible observations)" (Vertov in Rouch, 39).

When I was filming, (*Julie the filmmaker/researcher*), I was not seen as the same person by Asid, as when my eye was not fixed to the viewfinder. However, Rouch claims that it is because of this duality of roles, the change due to the filming behaviour and equipment, that allows the filmmaker to enter into the same experience as those being filmed (Rouch, 99). For Rouch it was the trance possession- ceremony that allowed him to enter his own "ciné-transe" (Rouch, 99). I had to get into the parkour zone, re-conceptualising space and place, allowing the camera to participate, react and capture, like Rouch freeing myself of "filmic and ethnographic theories necessary to rediscover the " '*barbarie de l'invention*' " (Rouch, 100). Ciné-parkour was only possible by the experience of doing it. By 'doing' I mean a combination of observing, filming, interpreting and also physically experiencing parkour so I could empathetically relate to what the traceurs were doing.

This early period of observing and filming parkour was less-complex than the task of interpreting what I had seen and filmed, freeing myself of ideas of form to create reflective parkour-led films as opposed to films about parkour. Interpretation was a far more-delicate process than the observations. The only way to create a ciné-parkour was to spend time with parkour and the people doing it, gaining knowledge and experience through collaboration and participation. Filtering and selecting what constituted performance for the camera, or a performance of the everyday, the moments when the camera captured actions inherent in my informants' daily lives.

Doing parkour

In April 2005, half way through the first film production I went to my first parkour class. Francois 'Forrest' Mahop had set up and was running the first structured indoor parkour classes, to my knowledge, in the UK. I started attending these classes (Mahop [117]).

Had I not been an 'insider' of the parkour community, as an older, middle-class female, prior to the formal creation of classes, I would not have felt comfortable in attempting to access and learn from a group of young males moving somewhat unpredictably around the environment. I would not have known when and where to find them, if I would have been welcomed, and if they would be willing to share their knowledge with me. I would not have known how to start. There would have also been concerns over whether they would be sufficiently informed to take care of me when communicating such a risk-fuelled practice. I had not seen examples of female parkour videos but because I had been witness to the ground-level training, it seemed feasible that the female body was equally capable of parkour as the male body.

A major shift in my awareness of parkour occurred as a result of experiencing parkour myself. This was the extent to which fear plays an active role and how the sense of time is warped as a result; the anticipation and freezing that can occur before you are ready to let go and try. Traceurs refer to this dialogue with fear as 'breaking the jump'.

Doing parkour revealed unconscious fears I had in my day-to-day life when conforming to normative behaviour, moving through pre-defined routes. In parkour, like other risk-associated activities, whilst someone might physically be capable of a movement, without the confrontation and subsequent release from fear, they will not achieve it. I experienced different levels of fear when doing and sometimes filming parkour because of the height and position of where I was and having to operate the camera.

Sands comments that when undertaking a participant observer role in a sports ethnography there is the possibility of physical and emotional injury, however, the exposure to such risks, "makes the experience of participation more real to the ethnographer. The experience becomes a part of the cultural reality that is being formed through fieldwork" (Sands, 97). During my participation in parkour over the past six years I have suffered one injury; a sprained ankle that was caused from slipping on a mat in an indoor training session.

Filming Sébastien Goudot in District 13, Paris.

The conscious fears I experienced in doing and filming parkour were often my own realisation of the inherent risk and potential injury: the consequences of failing; the inability to successfully achieve the desired move; losing balance; falling; over-estimating the landing; catching your foot; losing your grip.

As a result of my experiences, I was profoundly aware that physical enquiry, play, risk taking, fear and self-improvement are at the forefront of traceurs' lives. A traceur's movements are the resemblance of their "object of perception", (Merleau–Ponty 2004: 71) bringing a visibility to the potential and possibilities that they themselves experience.

Fear and risk are ever-present within the parkour context, embraced openly and positively. At times when a camera angle involved a precarious balancing or positioning that I was uncomfortable with I would pass the camera to one of the traceurs, explaining the desired framing or intention of the shot. At times they would help to find solutions or support me so that I could overcome my fear to continue the filming myself, for example by holding my legs or standing below me in case I fell. I expanded the range of possibilities of how and/or where I would film from and became more comfortable with my own previously unacknowledged fears, incorporating more mobility and fluidity into my filming as my experience and confidence with parkour grew. The filming had to become as playful as the parkour, the camera becoming the extended parkour body, moving through railings as though doing an underbar, running, balancing, following.

Explaining the shot and framing to traceur Alli Shelton, who shot some parkour action from a position I was not comfortable with in the film *City Gents*.

There was a physical practicality and mobility to my following and documenting parkour. At times I had to climb over walls or fences to be with my informants. I worked with the minimum equipment necessary to facilitate my mobility, (a small camera-rucksack). My own competence in moving was observed by the informants, and was sometimes commented on in a positive way. In New York 2008, during the open training session held in Central

Park, I climbed over numerous fences during the day and when filming *Sarcelles* I had to get on top of the wall that the traceurs ran and performed quadrepedal on. The traceurs always helped me in such situations: when filming *Sarcelles*, they sent out a search party when I got left behind after filming them running off into the distance.

As a result of doing (at a constantly low level) and observing parkour, I acquired parkour vision (see chapter 3) and experienced an increase in personal confidence as well as changes in my perception and relationship to my environment. I had never before felt enthusiasm for railings, the placement of small walls in alignment with other walls, whether the height of a wall was sufficient for me to attempt and work towards completing a wall run. Areas I previously avoided, associating them with crime and anti-social behaviour, were now havens of activity, possibility, challenges, effort, engagement, concentration and joy, replacing fear and passivity with positive emotions and activity. The negative associations of fear have the potential to isolate and alienate you from geographical as well as social spaces.

Feedback loops of production

After experiencing parkour myself, a change started to evolve in my approach to capturing, representing and understanding parkour. This had a positive effect on the relationship with my informants as they could see my understanding of their practice develop. My understanding at this time dictated that the camera needed to be more dynamic and listen more closely. The films needed to communicate empathy, fear, focus, playful creativity, accuracy and repetition. I incorporated this awareness into the remaining filming sessions with Asid, moving the camera more closely to follow his movements and holding the hesitation witnessed in a shot before deciding to take off and jump. An example of this uncertainty revealed itself at the square blocks in Victoria Park when he initially fails several attempts at a precision jump (Angel, *Asid, profile of a freerunner* 2005).

I had a more informed appreciation for my informants' capabilities, sensitivities, the risks they took and how they had to overcome fear. When people are very good at something, they can make it look relatively easy. I had underestimated the strength and mental focus needed for nearly all of the moves: the dynamic power needed to execute the vaults; the upper body strength to be able to pull the body up from a catleap position or traverse a wall; the intense impact of the landings on the body; the strength needed to land softly and move fluidly and the focus and accuracy needed for safe landings.

The concern for the moments of relevance became clearer the more I experienced parkour. The sound of the movements and landings in particular were important indicators of the skill and competence of the traceur.

To represent parkour it was necessary for the filming and editing to be a closer reflection to the way that parkour was experienced by the participants. I could empathise with this far more after my own experiences of parkour. My camera had been too static, un-engaged, distant and unaware of the points of relevance. I wanted to reflect the dynamic nature and experience of the traceur. I needed to respond to and reflect the phenomenology of the body that the traceurs reconnect with. As the human geographer Yi-fu Tuan explains, "Space is perceived through the senses: the eyes can discern objects and the mind postulates space as their matrix and frame. At a deeper level the notion of space is derived from the experience, beginning with infanthood, that we are free to move the body and parts of the body" (Tuan 1971xv: 3). I needed my camera to reflect the traceur's perception of space.

Ruby writes that researchers in the field can "grapple with questions about which aspects of culture are visible and how they might convey that knowledge and other fundamental questions about doing ethnography with a camera. How can you translate experience into images? Do images merely illustrate ideas, or are there "pictorial" ideas? Can you actually explore and discover with a camera, or must you wait until you know in order to film? When you are dealing with people whose sense of space, place, body movement, and event are different from your own, how do you know what you are looking at and when to turn the camera on or off?" (Ruby, 37).

By trying to develop a ciné parkour I hoped to be able to answer some of Ruby's questions. The collaborative nature of the feedback loop informed me how best to translate the experiences of the traceurs into images. My experience of exploration with the camera as a tool that revealed my knowledge and understanding that led to an awareness of what questions to ask, and what to select in terms of framing and editing. It was only by filming and sharing that I could then 'know'.

By visually and audibly exploring with the camera, it was important to achieve a balance of representations of emotions, dynamic movements, and being able to contextualise the parkour spatially within the environment. This documented the emotional, physical and spatial aspects of parkour. It was important to depict the risk involved in a move and therefore empathise with the fear experienced by the traceur as well as reflect on the subtleties of mood, interactions, ambience and emotion within the final edit. Skill, speed, focus, fear and accuracy had to be present within the films as well as a representation of where and by whom.

Over time I developed three distinct styles or approaches to the camera work for ciné parkour:

1. Following in Motion (the parkour camera): the physical

2. The Body in Space: the spatial

3. Optimal Flow: the emotional/psychological

'Following in Motion' is the product of longer exposure to parkour, doing parkour, and time spent with the more experienced traceurs. The idea of uninhibited motion and a sense of the energy and fluidity that they experience and desire, reflects the dynamic nature and texture of their movements. The use of synchronised sound is also an important feature in helping to convey this and the quality of the movements. This is demonstrated in the films *MySpace, Visions* and *Sarcelles.*

I worked mainly with a handheld camera, this allowed for playful movement and the necessary mobility to adapt and reframe predicted movements. This also minimised the impact of the technology present, therefore focusing on social interactions and observations. As Rouch says of a handheld camera "You can film anything anywhere" (Rouch, 8).

The 'Body in Space' allows for the architectural references and contextualisation of a movement and is not reliant on sync sound. The camera is generally still or has very little movement. We see the body pass through a space, allowing us to gauge the height, width and dimensions of the space moved within. The scale and often the amount of fear associated with a movement is communicated this way. The surfaces taken off from, as well as landed onto, are visible to the viewer. An informed traceur will be able to appreciate the angle of the take-off as well as the difficulties of the landing. This approach is more widely used by filmmakers with less experience and understanding of the activity whose interest is to demonstrate the body in space, rather than a more subjective perspective.

Filming Sebastien Goudot in District 13, Paris.

'Optimal Flow' is similar to both of the previous techniques but always relies on handheld camerawork and is based on a harmony of improvisations and inspired performances linking the traceur to the environment and the filmmaker within that. Optimal flow involves filmmaking that has the minimal cultural disruption by the camera and filmmaker and is constantly adaptive and responsive, relying on intuitive framings, spontaneity and chance. This approach requires knowing when, where and how to film within the existing mis-en-scene.

I continued filming and receiving feedback from Asid and Hasan, gaining a greater insight into the activity, retaining a level of humility when receiving the detailed feedback. They indicated what edit points and changes from their perspectives would more accurately represent their movements and experience. They were active participants in the filmmaking as well as appearing within the film. They advised me that the slow motion sections should represent the 'hang-time', that is, when the body is in mid-air, particularly when jumping down or across, as time feels extended by the participant. They communicated what frames should be taken out or added to the edit, in particular to show the full extent of the landings, as this demonstrates the successful completion of a movement or not, and was something that I found to be of great concern to all of the practitioners I worked with. There were discussions about which 'takes' might be better examples of moves relative to their movements and which camera angles contextualised the parkour to make the viewer aware of the difficulty.

Previous parkour commercials and documentaries had largely neglected to show the landings and completion of moves as these tend to extend the shot length, dramatically altering the pace of an edit. The concern in many commercial contexts was to focus on the position of the body in space, scale of the jump or drop, rather than the clean, safe complete execution of a movement. Did the traceur make it ok? Were they injured? Would they be able to repeat the action again? The landings demonstrate the strength, control and experience of the traceur. Whilst the production companies did have a concern for the traceurs safety, they were also sometimes restricted from showing this due to Health and Safety regulations that stipulated that they use crash mats. Because these productions were setting up parkour action and paying the traceur to perform it, rather than filming what was happening anyway, they had to comply to set health and safety standards and duties of care. Commercial productions that featured parkour resulted in different representations compared to ones that were parkour-led or not-for-commercial purposes.

In my experience of being involved with commercial parkour productions, I saw many accidents occur due to the use of crash mats, not directly because of the risk of parkour. The soft landings and slippery surface of the mats make it easy for people to twist their ankles or slip on landing. Rarely did the traceurs ask for a crash mat on commercial productions, if they did, it was because they were tired and having to perform the move as part of their job. Traceurs do not take unnecessary risks, it is not in their interest to want to injure themselves.

I did not provide crash mats or any safety measures on my shoots, I was not paying them to perform, the traceurs were, to my mind, their own best safety regulators. At the start I filmed whatever it was they were doing but over time as friendship and trust built up and I became more familiar and accustomed to different traceur's abilities and styles, together we discussed what would be interesting to film to reveal different aspects of parkour. There was a combination of observational filming as well as collaborative choreographing.

Just one more: the ethics of filming

Whilst the complexity of maintaining and developing social relations demands more time, tolerance and patience than the act of filming or editing, there was always an ethical obligation on my part to consider the repercussions of my informants' actions on them. The will and enthusiasm to perform for the camera, capturing the most spectacular (or not) representation of parkour, could result in a traceur putting themselves unnecessarily at risk.

To maintain good relations it was important to develop an approach to the filming as well as the edit collaborations. There needed to be informed consent from the informants. They needed to be aware of the research project and the potential ramifications of the study after its completion. Their participation was voluntary and could be withdrawn at any time. I developed the following guidelines for filming parkour due to parkour's inherent risk and out of respect for my informants:

- do not ask someone to do parkour, let them determine what they will do

- do not ask someone to do anything a repeated a number of times

- do play the footage back to them

- do ask their advice on how to film it

- do not have expectations of what they can and cannot do

- do ask them how long they are happy to be moving, it is their energy levels and schedule that is the priority, not the filmmakers.

As a filmmaker/researcher I had to respect my informants' context and realisation of the physical demands that parkour exerts on the body. Different styles of filmmaking dictated different approaches. Observational filming did not involve so many of the guidelines, but still my presence could influence what I was able to observe or not. When collaborating in choreographed sequences, re-enactments of previous achievements and performances, the process of an active dialogue dictating the scale of the action, number of repetitions and the time spent filming necessitated an honest and open dialogue between myself and the participants. If I wanted to record more takes it was important to let them know, I had to lose the habit of the commercial director who says "Great! Just one more!" instead saying, "How many more do you think you can do? I need x number of angles" for this, and explain my reasons.

Asid, Hasan and others in the Urban Freeflow team informed and influenced my parkour filming and editing to achieve a more accurate representation of their actions, experiences and understanding of parkour during the first film production. Even though our encounter began with me as 'the filmmaker' they were teaching me this role in the context of documenting parkour. Being a 'parkour filmmaker' involved different sensitivities to that of a 'documentary filmmaker' or even a 'general sports filmmaker' (Edwardes & Mahop, 2008).

During the first six months of research I edited sections immediately after they were shot, and some of the most rewarding edits came as a result of capturing and editing immediately after filming. The energy and memory of the moments from the shoot informed and shaped the edit. The immediate processing of shots into a sequence incorporated the pace and rhythm of the parkour experienced during the shoot. The subtleties of mood, levels of risk, fear and number of attempts all translated into the edit and as a result a style of editing evolved based on a combination of the experiential and observational. What the traceurs did or said during a shoot inspired and influenced the film produced. At times I would film observationally, at others it would be a more interactive engagement; they were all actions and reactions based on the social encounters. Each edit would further influence and feed into the next filming session.

The more I shared evolving edits, the more support I was given in return. Technical self-sufficiency in terms of shooting and editing equipment was essential for this methodology and I continued to work in this manner whenever possible on all of the parkour research productions.

ASID profile of a freerunner

In the spirit of collaboration, Asid and Hasan wanted to contribute their own footage to the project and volunteered to film sections showing Asid visiting his local mosque and the team's visit to New York, investing their own creativity and vision into the project. Overall, the filming for *ASID profile of a freerunner* took place from January to July 2005. I shot 23 tapes (dvCam) of 40 minutes each in total, amassing over 15 hours of material. 75% of that time was spent filming Asid and his fellow teammates' existing parkour commitments, the remaining 25% was designated filming sessions between Asid, myself and Hasan.

Whilst this initial period was very collaborative, there were also competing voices within Asid's film. Ez wanted to maintain his position as gatekeeper and influence the team, not allowing autonomous projects to take place between '**his**' athletes, without **his** control, without **his** influence. Ez was focused on the commercial exploitation of the team and brand Urban Freeflow.

In maintaining access there was always an understanding of agreeing with Asid and Ez what to show in the films produced. I was not creating an investigative piece of journalism, but a reflection of how Asid saw his world and more importantly, perhaps, how Asid would like others to see him and parkour. Although my initial aim was to present the everyday actions of a traceur, this is not ultimately what I achieved. Asid was a performer only sometimes letting his guard down. Some sections of the film demonstrate this but it is very much in the background, in contrast with his main 'performance' style during the film.

The film *ASID profile of a freerunner*, is a product of my first impressions and introduction to parkour. The opening montage of Asid reflects the conflicting elements of performance, observation and re-enactment present within the film. It was only in the latter part of the production that I was trying to develop a ciné parkour that allowed me to break free from established rules and forms of documentary. Many elements of the film conformed to existing representations of parkour as my master interview with Asid was conducted on the rooftop terrace where I lived, positioning Asid above the city, as the BBC had done in *Rush Hour* and Christie had done in *Jump London*, perpetuating the notion of parkour as a rooftop activity. Whilst I wanted to document parkour beyond the spectacle, I again conformed to performance spectacles through the night-time action montage and the framing of Asid's martial arts moves in the park.

Asid and Hasan during the rooftop interview.

Asid is positioned as the social actor presenting his "pseudomonolgue". Nichols states that the pseudomonologue "appears to deliver the thoughts, impressions, feelings, and memories of the individual witness directly to the viewer. The filmmaker achieves a suturing effect, placing the viewer in direct relation to the interviewee, by absenting him - or herself" (Nichols 1991: 54).

The film incorporates elements of observational cinema, performance re-enactments, expository and reflexive documentary. Whilst the knowledge and understanding communicated was Asid's personal presentation of parkour, the visual representations developed throughout the making of the film contributed towards the development of a ciné parkour although the film itself is not a product of a ciné parkour.

Through the process of making the film I became more informed on how to be a parkour filmmaker and the narrative development in the film reflects my acquisition and growing knowledge of parkour. Making the documentary introduced me to parkour as an expressive and creative form of movement, providing me with themes that required further research. These were, parkour vision; spatial creativity; fear; play and the sensitivities to points of relevance when filming.

A multiplicity of voices and networks of informants

My role of parkour filmmaker at this stage was based on audiovisual reciprocity not trust or friendship. However, working collaboratively, laid the foundations for future parkour films and access. I was asked by Ez to be involved with a new project shooting a parkour tutorial with Urban Freeflow. I travelled to Japan, America, Greece and France with various Urban Freeflow team members as part of the tutorial project during the summer of 2005. As ten Brink writes of Rouch, "One of the main purposes in making films is to create the possibility for further films to be made" (ten Brink, 5).

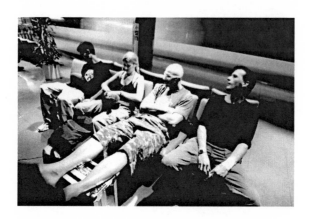

Travelling to and filming in Tokyo, June 2005.
Images courtesy of Andy Day

I had become useful to Urban Freeflow, filming events and putting edits together for their publicity, such as, a women's only workshop and a performance in Trafalgar Square (Urbanfreeflow [187]). The traceurs continued to make their own parkour films and I advised them on how they could better represent themselves, offering feedback on their edits, advising Ez on many aspects of marketing and representation. While they understood what a camera could record in terms of sound and visuals, they were unaware of how some of the messages they portrayed in their own films could be read by a wider audience. On a trip to the United States sponsored by Boost mobile, Ez filmed and worked on an edit with Ben 'Bam' Milner. A large part of one edit was based around waiting for a lapdancer to arrive in the hotel room and the actions that followed. I advised against making this public as whilst it had been entertaining for them at the time they could not see the negative potential of putting such footage out or how it could contrast with representations of them as 'responsible athletes'. They didn't realise this contrasted with the positive responsible sports image and 'discipline' they professed to be involved in.

Within Urban Freeflow I formed important friendships with Francois 'Forrest' Mahop, my parkour teacher; Andy Day (known as Kiell) the stills photographer and a practitioner working with Urban Freeflow and Dan Edwardes, a traceur and writer who was present at many events and accompanied Urban Freeflow on the trip to

Japan. They were older, highly-educated and also interested in reflecting on, documenting and understanding their experiences of parkour, thus more closely reflecting my own position.

Forrest first experienced parkour as a result of attending the same athletics club as one of the founders, Sébastien Foucan (Mahop [118]). He then went on to take care of, and rehabilitate, Stephane Vigroux after a knee injury. Andy Day had become involved with Urban Freeflow due to his own research into urban representation in film as part of his Masters in American Literature and Film at Birmingham University. He began photographing parkour as a means to document it then began practising it himself (Day, www.kiell.com). Dan Edwardes had first seen parkour when studying in Japan and on his return to London met Ez and became more involved with Urban Freeflow. I also had a good relationship with Johnny 'Sticky' Budden and Paul 'Blue' Joseph who were both involved in their own creative practices alongside their parkour. Sticky is a graphic designer and Blue a musician. My creative commonality as a filmmaker meant a dialogue was possible beyond parkour that allowed a friendship to grow rather than relations built purely on audio-visual reciprocity.

Forrest and Asid at the Southbank Centre, London, June 2006.
Images courtesy of Paul Holmes

In addition to my contact with Urban Freeflow, I followed parkour within the mainstream media and on the internet. Other parkour groups had a negative view of Urban Freeflow as they dominated much of the UK scene's media and commercial parkour work, presenting themselves as 'experts' and 'professionals'. The filtering of experiences to produce an 'authoritative' account was the main challenge for my research at this stage. It took at least one year, if not more, for me to comprehend the internal dynamics of the parkour culture. I had to trust my informants to be accurate in how they presented information to me as an outsider. I found myself negotiating a route between the experiential and the multiple voices of parkour. MacDougall states that the experience of individual social actors could be suggestive but an unreliable indicator of a collective experience (MacDougall, 94). This discourse, navigating multiple positions of authority, led to a change over time in my choice of informants and participants as I accumulated greater knowledge and understanding of parkour, learning what had gone before and comparing it to what I had experienced with Urban Freeflow. I had wanted to understand parkour as it was for those who had created it.

The social relations formed through the process of participant observation presented opportunities to connect with other more experienced traceurs than those with whom I had been working. During the process of building up a relationship with my informants, friendship and mutual respect were challenged at times as a result of the growing commercialisation and subsequent factions and divisions among individuals in the UK and international parkour communities with whom I had begun to work. The people with whom I have maintained contact and friendship are those who feature most heavily in the films and with whom I continue to collaborate. As Sands explains, "Many cultural members become lifelong friends, some become lifelong enemies, but that is life" (Sands, 118).

Rites of passage, recording a ghost

In December 2005 I had the opportunity to interview Stephane Vigroux. He had been trained by David Belle for five years at the tail end of the art's developmental phase. He then spent two years with Sébastien Foucan and other founding members of the discipline. Stephane is widely credited with bringing several key elements such as fluidity and softness to the art as well as techniques such as the 'kong vault' movement. Stephane was living in Thailand at this time but was going to be in Paris for two weeks visiting his family. I had Forrest's endorsement; this was crucial to gaining access and a willingness on Stephane's part to be filmed. At the start of the filming I had no set goal or fixed outcome to the filming and any potential edit. My understanding of parkour, and therefore how I represented it, changed after meeting Stephane.

Stephane presented a case for parkour as a disciplined, particular way and approach to training and conditioning the body and mind, alongside the creative vision and imaginative reading of the landscape. I had not been exposed or made aware of this key element of parkour from my time spent with Urban Freeflow. It was a 'eureka' moment. Parkour was a specific training methodology that if followed could produce incredible results physically and psychologically whilst, at the same time, keeping the participant safe in the process. Stephane's everyday parkour was very different to that which I had witnessed with Asid. This was big news to me and I think to many others at the time. After two days spent listening and filming with Stephane - and the generous donation of some of Stephane and his brother Johann's early parkour footage - I had all the elements for the documentary *Le Singe est de Retour* (*The Monkey is Back*). In Stephane I had found an authority on parkour, an artist and humble practitioner who was happy to share his journey, experiences and understanding of parkour.

Stephane is discreet, generally very shy and was apprehensive when we first met. My approach was to observe and listen. As Rouch did, at times I also took the approach of "intervening to provoke a certain reality" (Rouch, 141). Open-ended questions and conversations when filming were also important as otherwise it would have been an observation of Stephane and Forrest training. It was, however, also important to retain a sensitivity to know when and what to ask. I did not think that passive observation would give the greatest insights within the limited time-frame; I saw the venture as a conversation. At the start of the filming I spoke to Stephane away from the others who were present (Ez, Andy Day, Forrest and Dan Edwardes) to let Stephane know what my approach was. If he did not want to talk about something or if he did not want something filmed then he should just say. He would have the final editorial clearance of anything that was put together and nothing would be made public unless he agreed.

Lisses, December 2005 Stephane and I at the start of the day's filming discussing the approach to the shoot away from the others.
Image courtesy of Andy Day.

It was clear Stephane had a particular message to communicate. He was renowned within the international parkour community for his great skills and dedication but had, to my knowledge, never been interviewed and little was known about his views on parkour other than the fact that he had been very close to David Belle. His discretion led to his nickname, 'the ghost'.

My outsider status and inexperience of parkour, especially in Stephane's eyes, made it easier to ask many questions that a known traceur would have looked naïve in asking but may nonetheless have wanted to know. I shot eight tapes of 40 minutes over the two day period. Day 1 was spent following Stephane and Forrest on a guided tour of Lisses and Évry as Stephane recalled his early days of training with David Belle, interspersed with some training. Day 2 involved a formal interview in the warmth of Forrest's parents' house where we were staying.

There had been a great increase in the number of videos posted on the internet of people showing their biggest most impressive jumps. Stephane and many of the experienced French traceurs saw this as reckless and dangerous. Their motivations for doing parkour and their vision for it had not stemmed from a desire to impress or share with the world on the internet their most recent achievements. They had gradually built up their skills over a long period of time. According to them the art had a particular disciplined training methodology that they valued highly, calling it the 'spirit' of parkour. This had not been represented in the mainstream media or by the parkour community. Parkour was being transformed into a reckless past-time more akin to the American MTV series *Jackass* than to the specific mindset, training methods and approach the founders, and those close to them, valued so highly.

Stephane believed there was no need to rush in trying to achieve big jumps early on in people's progression. He believed many people did not have the physical condition to be able to do such movements without injuring themselves and people were ignorant of the risks. They lacked 'body armour'. In an interview with a Thai website, Stephane commented, "You must always do every move, no matter how small, perfectly. You have to know what your body is doing the whole time, even in the air. You have to do it over and over maybe hundreds of times until it is perfect! That's what David taught me"_(Vigroux [192]).

There were many motivations for people to do parkour yet the internet and mainstream media representations encouraged spectacle rather than any other aspects of the art. However, while there were many promoting the spectacle, there was also many wanting to learn about parkour but access to the small group of traceurs who held this knowledge (which according to David Belle was a group of approximately 40 people in the early period of parkour), was difficult to come by, especially for those who did not speak French. Stephane's understanding of parkour was what I had been searching for; a link to the origins of the art and an explanation of what it was.

Stephane was humble about his continued parkour training and his move to Thailand had been a rejection of the early commercialisation of parkour and the competing parkour factions in France. Stephane communicated a well-thought understanding of the practice based on what David Belle had taught him, and of his his experiences with Sébastien Foucan. He was also heavily influenced by Williams Belle who had shown him a more compassionate and inclusive approach to training and teaching the discipline, promoting the idea of a 'non violent' way, compared to David Belle's.

Back in London I began to piece the edit together. Unlike with Asid's project, Stephane could not provide regular feedback. I did not share any footage with Stephane during the shoot as this would have disrupted the social interactions and flow of the days' events, but if asked, I would have willingly shown him. Forrest viewed the edit in progress and talked through various elements with me. He believed I had captured the essence of his friend. A dvd of the edit was sent to Stephane in Thailand and he emailed his feedback and requests for changes and additional elements, such as, an image of his brother Johann with whom he had shared so much of his parkour experience. Stephane's endorsement of the documentary and appreciation that he had final editorial control, opened the door for me to work with other first and second generation traceurs.

Meeting Stephane was a major turning point. The final edit of the documentary with Stephane was initially released on Urban Freeflow's own video stream hosted on their website www.urbanfreeflow.com under the title *U$FTV volume 3, Le Singe est de Retour.*

Le Singe est de Retour demonstrates my understanding of parkour as it was revealed to me. The edit follows the sequence of events on the first day of filming, reinforced by the static interview. The camera remained at a distance during Day one but the interview presented an opportunity for a closer and more-intimate framing as Stephane presented his understanding and experiences of parkour. The film is the result of the social encounter between myself, Stephane and the others who were present.

The film utilised observational filming and interactive modes, remaining aware of when to disrupt and provoke answers and when to allow events to unfold such as when Stephane challenges Forrest to balance along the rail. The film contains the products of interactions and conversations with others present on the day.

After the release of the film, Stephane took up Ez's invitation to join Urban Freeflow. Stephane hoped to influence Ez and the wider parkour community and communicate the understanding of parkour that he shared with the pioneers and founders of the art and which he felt was missing.

The understanding of parkour that Stephane provided informed my future representations of the art and the development of a ciné parkour. The parkour films needed to incorporate difficulty, effort and discipline in addition to what I was already aware of. Existing representations including mine had failed to communicate an everyday parkour as lived by experienced traceurs such as Stephane.

Discovering my space

Le Singe est de Retour was very well-received and welcomed by the growing international parkour community. It had an impact on the understanding of how to train and the spirit of the practice, not just for me and the development of a ciné parkour, but for those who were training. They too were learning of an approach. Meanwhile, the Urban Freeflow tutorial project was at a standstill but I began to spend more time with Forrest who was training Dan Edwardes at the time.

After Stephane's insights, the focus of my research films shifted towards the practice and lived experience of parkour; parkour as a training methodology and ethos rather than participant-focussed films or a longer format master narrative. I wanted to communicate the spirit of the original practice. I started to experiment with different forms and conventions. As Jean Rouch highlights in his essay *The Camera and Man*, there remains the essential question of, "Must one 'stage' reality (the staging of 'real life') as did Flaherty, or should one, like Vertov, film 'without awareness' ('seizing improvised life')" (Rouch, 33)?

Forrest and Dan had been training in a south London housing estate and asked if I would film them so they could review their progress for their own video analysis. The area they were moving in was small and dense. What they were doing encapsulated the concept of how parkour can utilise space in a creative way. We discussed how their training could be made into a short film focussing on that space. I also wanted to focus on the sounds of parkour, something other representations failed to do. The short film format offered a more effective platform to present fragments of information expressed in a way that would expand on the parkour themes being explored.

Having observed Forrest and Dan's ritual training and movements of parkour, we started to explore and discuss different ways of filming and framing the action. I regularly played back the rushes to them and they viewed sections of edited content and work-in-progress. As the training progressed and they created new routes and movements within the space, we shot more, updating the potentiality of the space in the edit to reflect their experiences. The film incorporated the feedback loop of production.

The collaborative filmmaking was more present in the process than evident onscreen. The film's location, an unassuming set of stairs, rails and a walkway, contrasted greatly to the splendour and significance of the locations featured in the '*Jump*' documentaries. It was neither cinematic nor iconic. The documentary was parkour-led, using locations that were chosen for parkour not vice versa as was the case with *Jump London* and *Jump Britain,* even though in those documentaries the traceurs still dictated everything that they did. Mike Christie explained such productions as his, "It's a bit strange because sometimes it was the status of the location rather than suitability to Parkour but you know, it's a balancing act when you're making a piece of television like that. You've got to satisfy a big audience and an international desire to see landmarks with a space that delivers great moves" (Christie [44]). The research films created only needed to satisfy the participants and myself.

We agreed that the focus of the film was the interaction between parkour and architecture so elected not to record any talking heads, using the audio from the interview content as a basis for the narration. Forrest and Dan understood the purpose of showing training and the parkour vision. We were all confident that the film portrayed a different representation of parkour than had been previously seen. It avoided the obvious spectacle normally shown, instead displaying complex and difficult sequences of movements set within a singular confined space rather than an open one or set on multiple unconnected sites. The film demonstrated creativity and fluidity, juxtaposed by the slow movements of one of the residents entering the building and the local children's observations, claiming they too wanted to be "monkey men" (Angel, *MySpace* 2006). Forrest and Dan had befriended many of the local residents who even joked with them that sometimes they arrived later on some days than on others.

The end result was the film *MySpace*, a creative collaboration that explored modes of representation of parkour around themes of parkour vision, architecture and training. The film was shot as a mixture of observational and choreographed sequences, incorporating the ciné parkour styles of following in motion, the body in space, and optimal flow. I used static tripod shots for the solid fixed architecture in contrast to the soft dynamic predictive style that follows the traceurs. The body is seen in space, as well as, a more experiential view, balancing a concern for the relevance of contextualising the movement within the limited spaces of the architecture and also incorporating elements of reflexivity as the filmmaking process itself is revealed, such as, at the start when you hear my comment, "Ok, the wind's dropped" (Angel, *MySpace* 2006).

MySpace explored the creative potential of space and the traceur's (in this instance Forrest and Dan) ability to see the potential for lines of movement, routes and opportunities for parkour training within a small confined area. The video demonstrated the kinds of repetitive conditioning movements they practiced in their training, as well as some of the failed attempts. It revealed a process of imagination initially suggested through the film's opening audio signifiers, then a montage of engagement, activity and a lack of predicted actions in both the traceurs' movements and breaks in continuity editing, as moves are incomplete and suggested at times. Fear and failure is present in the repetition of hypnotic and seemingly-balletic choreographed moves. Whilst the degree of difficulty in the parkour was higher than a lot of larger jumps or drops, the footage rejected the idea of spectacle and was a communication of the active dialogue of the potential between the traceur and the built environment.

MySpace was the first example of a film made that incorporated a ciné parkour based on a more extensive understanding on the nature of the practice. The collaborative nature of the methodology and friendship allowed for time to experiment with audio-visual representation as Dan and Forrest spent a lot of time working with me on the edit as well as the viewing and feedback that occurred during filming.

In a reflective interview with Dan and Forrest, I enquired as to what they felt set our film collaborations apart from other parkour films. Dan commented that; "You have a much better idea of what parkour really is and therefore you can portray it better, which is more pleasing for us." Forrest agreed that it was through an extended amount of time and exposure to the activity that I had an appreciation for the details and skills of the athletes that informed me how best to then visually-represent parkour's different elements. Forrest made the point that "You've had to learn all these things, you came from another background but after the experiences in parkour you realise how ok, maybe if I do a tracking (shot) it will be more interesting for the movement, maybe if I do this angle with this close up I will give more sensitivity for the audience about the dynamic, about the speed about the strength, about all these things. The difference is that you pay attention about all these details because you know the athletes quite well but most of the filmmakers even if they are good filmmakers, they don't really know for themselves exactly what kind of angle will give them the best dynamic, the best expression of the movement." Whilst the spoken content presented one form of knowledge, there was equal concern for the visual portrayal of their movements (Edwardes & Mahop 2008).

Forrest and Dan during the reflective interview.

Shared cinema

To work within the idea of a 'shared cinema', I wanted to find ways to share the footage with my informants, beyond the few who participated and collaborated in the films. At the start of my research in 2004 there were very few video file-sharing websites so rushes were exchanged on dv tape, dvd or as compressed quicktime files. After completing *MySpace,* we (Forrest, Dan and I) wanted to share the film with a wider audience, primarily other traceurs, to communicate a specific representation of parkour. I initially hosted the film on my personal website *www.julieangel.com* but the launch of the video file-sharing site *YouTube.com* in November 2005 presented the opportunity to share the film with no additional costs or effort to a potentially wider audience. I uploaded *MySpace*, giving it the title, *'Parkour Documentary'* with the following description: "This film is a study of architectural potential and the body within a limited space. Parkour, conditioning, combinations, foot and hand placement, they've got flow. I've been shooting parkour action for nearly 2 years and this is the piece of work I am the most proud of. Enjoy!" (Angel [11]).

Whilst YouTube was not a scholarly context to present the films, if films are conceptualised as Ruby states as, "a medium of communication" (Ruby, 22) or as John Grierson positions them, "Cinema is neither an art nor an entertainment, it is a form of publication, and may publish in a hundred different ways for a hundred different audiences" (Grierson in Hardy 1979: 185, in Ruby, 22), then YouTube was an appropriate outlet for a culture and community proficient in using the web while, simultaneously, opening up the viewing potential of this ciné-parkour to a wider audience. Many traceurs had initially found, and been inspired to take up parkour, from content viewed online.

My motivation was the same as Rouch's, in an interview with Lucien Taylor he expressed a desire in his work to share and "to produce in a medium that allows dialogue and dissent across societal lines" (Rouch, 137). I believe free-to-view video sharing websites that allow comments, such as YouTube, provide this cross-cultural and societal dialogue, allowing viewers to comment and reply; creating and contributing to a dialogue, if the channel user allows the comments. For example a comment left for the film *Visions* in answer to another comment, "Parkour isn't about doing massive jumps between buildings, even if you get that vision from the media. I can't understand why you offend them; they're great athletes and have a VERY high physical standard which you will understand if you TRAIN with them. Plus. who said parkour is about entertainment? This video gives inspiration if you're practitioner. If it was all about entertaining people there would have been massive jumps, flips and such. But it's not. It's just a playfull day" (Angel [12]).

The majority of parkour-related content on YouTube at this time continued to focus on performance and spectacle. The parkour community had created its own niche 'subcultural media'. Videos were characterised by a montage of images showcasing a range of parkour movements in unrelated and unconnected urban sites, focusing on the traceurs achievements. Unsuccessful attempts, sync sound or spoken content were rarely incorporated. None of the process and methodology of the practice was revealed. Edits were set to music, chosen to reflect the traceur's or filmmaker's current tastes. Forrest and Dan were both highly-skilled traceurs in comparison to many of the newcomers posting videos. Another distinction reflecting my, and the participant's understanding, was that *MySpace* demonstrated combinations of moves that created routes, rather than single movements and actions that, in effect, went nowhere.

Video file-sharing websites such as YouTube allow for multiple 'readings' and viewings of the films, as the parkour community, general public, as well as those involved in its production, commented and created a dialogue. The traceurs' readings decoded the images differently which can be seen by the comments left by them compared to other interpretations of the film that are typified by comparing the traceurs to ninjas and how parkour should be used for escaping from the police.

I have continued to upload collaborative parkour videos (more than 50) onto YouTube. To date, the media that I have put in the public domain as part of this research process has amassed more than 16 million views (Angel, www.youtube.com/slamcamspam). This is not due to a lack of parkour content on YouTube. Andrew Bangs, a sports editor and participation manager at YouTube, informed me that a video tagged with the word "parkour" is currently uploaded every 20-30 minutes (Bangs 2009). Michael Wesch comments in his film, *An Anthropological Introduction to YouTube*, that in anthropology if your work reaches more than 200 people it is significant (Wesch [198]).

Video file-sharing on the web as a means for distribution and sharing films, provides the opportunity for a shared cinema unimaginable in Rouch's day. The roles of digital networks and video file-sharing websites have played a huge role in the dissemination and representation of parkour, leading to a massive increase in the number of practitioners evident since I have been conducting my research. This is discussed in more detail in chapters 3 and 4.

Creating performance spectacles for consumption

Over time, my awareness and considerations for the impact the filming had on the traceurs, coupled with understanding their sensitivities and concerns for their representation, meant I became my informants' filmmaker of choice. I was put forward as the director and videographer for several parkour-related advertising campaigns. I had considerations for their well-being beyond capturing images for the commercial shoot due to the friendships formed. For example, if a traceur was carrying an injury but had still chosen to perform, I suggested movements that would avoid or minimise using the injured area, yet presenting the traceur as fit and able to the client. In these contexts I was an insider, part of the parkour culture, hired along with them for the job.

Participating in commercial parkour productions was a continuation but also a shift in the multiplicity of my roles. I was the researcher and endorsed filmmaker, a participant observer in parkour culture; while the research films were exploring parkour beyond the spectacle, I was also contributing to spectacle-based representations of parkour by working on these productions and was aware of this paradox. On commercial productions, the traceurs and I made suggestions to clients that assisted in the more realistic and credible representation of parkour and satisfied their commercial needs, for example, incorporating combinations of movements as opposed to single movements and rejecting ideas that were visually uninteresting and not credible to parkour. The contradiction of producing parkour-led research films and commercial performance spectacles, echoed the contradictions that I witnessed in my informants. While there was a will to explain and present parkour as a credible 'sporting' practice, there was always great enthusiasm for the potential for communicating, sharing and creating spectacular parkour images. The budgets and locations that were made available on some of the commercial productions provided opportunities for capturing a celebration of my informants' everyday training. The advertising jobs were, generally speaking, well-paid and provided more time for training than holding down any regular job for the traceurs. The experiences I gained on such productions provided valuable insights into the traceurs lives as well as how parkour was being commodified for commercial purposes. This is discussed further in chapter 4.

In June 2006 I travelled to Singapore with Ez, Forrest, Asid, Sticky and Tracey Tiltman for a shoot that also involved Williams Belle, the youngest member of the original Yamakasi group. This was my first encounter with one of the first generation of traceurs and founders. I was struck by Williams' motivations in contrast to the English traceurs. Williams' conduct on set confused and angered Ez as he attempted moves with an extremely high risk factor. These moves were done for his own pleasure rather than for the benefit of the camera. Like Stephane, there was a different approach to parkour and he expressed his concern for others' motivations and participation in parkour. After a long day on set, Williams would then do his own disciplined training, again in contrast to the others (apart from Forrest). Williams spent time talking to Sticky about this and had a profound effect that stayed with him over the years, citing Williams' strength, motivation and discipline as one of his inspirations (Budden [39]). Meeting Williams re-enforced my priorities and concern for the representations and communication of parkour as Stephane had expressed.

Continued collaborations

I continued to document events and projects for Ez with Urban Freeflow but the reciprocity began to feel unbalanced in Ez's favour. In Asid's documentary, Ez commented that it was his job to keep the guys in the team grounded, but his actions and attitude led me to question who in turn was keeping Ez grounded, as the group was exposed to more commercial opportunities.

The nature of the group that I had started to document had changed; it had lost its friendly trusting nature that was evident at the start of my research. The fun-loving group of friends had become reliant on parkour for their income. The friendships and common interest of parkour that had originally brought Urban Freeflow together were tested as tensions rose over a lack of transparency in the portrayal of the rates of commission, pay and the commercial opportunities Urban Freeflow was being offered.

Whilst it might be the intention of a researcher to maintain contact with all their informants, this is not always possible, particularly if you want to base your research on respect and friendship. In November of 2006 I cut all ties with Asid and Ez due to their personal and professional behaviour and in my view Ez's blatant and conscious exploitation of team members in promotion of the "brand" Urban Freeflow. I was no longer dependant upon Ez as the gatekeeper, as I had formed my own relations with various traceurs.

I continued to work collaboratively with Dan Edwardes, Forrest, Andy Day, Stephane Vigroux and Tracey Tiltman (who had subsequently become part of the team). I also remained friends with Sticky and Blue. During this period I was filming a pilot programme run by Eugene Minogue of Westminster City Council's Positive Futures programme, following Forrest and Dan (for one year) teach parkour to young people aged between eight and fifteen who were deemed to be at risk from crime and anti-social behaviour by living in some of the most deprived wards in Westminster. The project was the first of its kind in the country and Forrest and Dan were keen to demonstrate how parkour could be a positive force for change in the lives of these young people, countering parkour's media identity as an activity of dramatic roof-jumping and wreckless stunts.

Meanwhile Stephane had become frustrated at the continuing lack of understanding and communication of the training methodology and original spirit of parkour. Despite many attempts, he had had little if any influence over Ez's presentation of parkour. With much encouragement from Châu Belle-Dinh, one of the Yamakasi founders and the support of Forrest, Stephane relocated to London and briefly appeared in the Westminster documentary. The project resulted in the film *Jump Westminster*, following in the tradition of the 'Jump' brand with permission from Mike Christie, optimistically hoping the film would have an impact and influence on the same scale of the previous 'Jump' documentaries.

Jump Westminster

Jump Westminster is a classic expository essay making a persuasive case for the positive potential of parkour as a tool for engaging young people and making them physically active. The film addresses the issue of mimicking the kind of parkour seen in feature film stunts. It portrays parkour as an accessible, positive and scaleable activity for people of all ages and abilities; it was a way of physically training and a way of being creative with the environment.

The collaborative filmic feedback loop was employed in various ways during the production including the joint writing of the narration by Eugene Minogue of Westminster City Council to present the council's position, Dan Edwardes to present the parkour knowledge and myself to help guide these into a form that would create the general coherence of the documentary. Both Minogue and Edwardes appear and are interviewed in the film. The combined effort and voices of authority within the film collectively shared the same message from their own perspective and agenda.

While *Jump Westminster* is not a pure example of ciné parkour it has contributed to a growing continuity in the work produced to re-address the presentation and perception of parkour, by sharing and providing an outlet for the participants' perspective. The film involved observational filming and direct encounters, provoking responses from the young people and following their actions. My familiarity with framing parkour allowed me to film in a way that minimised the disruptions caused by filming in contrast to a press photographer who had to 'set up' shots with the young people and took away valuable teaching time.

Towards the end of the production, Stephane, Forrest, Dan, Andy Day and Tracey left Urban Freeflow. Stephane, Forrest and Dan formed a new company together, firstly called Parkour Coaching, later renaming it Parkour Generations. Their aim was and is to promote the original spirit and discipline of parkour, concentrating on teaching others. I gave them my full support in their venture and continue to be their resident parkour filmmaker (Angel, http://www.parkourgenerations.com/biography.php?p=julie). As David Belle says in his book *Parkour*, "Some came and trained with me for years and did get the spirit of Parkour. Then they moved on and created their own structure and went some way with it, like Stephane Vigroux who created *Parkour Generations* in England." (Belle D., 2009c: 83)

Nichols states that one of the functions of the documentary film is that it has the potential to effect change, of attending to social issues where there is already an awareness of. This was the case with parkour. That documentary "mimics the canons of expository argument, the making of a case, and the call to public rather than private response." (Nichols 1991: 4) *Jump Westminster* stated the case for a re-think of parkour as a way of not "training cat burglars of the future", or that parkour was "just about people jumping from roof to roof," (Angel, *Jump Westminster* 2007) but a way to engage young people and encourage them to be physically active whilst respecting themselves and re-evaluating their environment. The result of the impact that parkour had on the young people was that it improved their confidence, allowing them to overcome their fears, physically engaging some groups of people such as the Muslim girls, who had been previously hard-to-reach. Even though the majority of the classes were indoors, the concept of parkour presented a way for them to re-evaluate and have a new perception and connection to their environment, as well as, how they see themselves. When parkour was presented in a particular way it had an extremely positive effect on the participants. There was a significant drop in crime and anti-social behaviour within the workshop areas.

The *Jump Westminster* project was nominated for the 2007 Children and Young People's Services Award and was screened at the Home Office. It has the highest viewing figures of any film on the Community Channel on freeview TV. It has been used in numerous presentations and within Universities to teach community sports development as well as to discuss parkour. After watching the documentary, Sport England invited Westminster City Council to submit a bid for funds to help develop parkour as a sport. As a result of this, substantial funds have been secured for a permanent parkour park to be built in Westminster in 2011 and the creation of a National Governing Body, ParkourUK; Eugene Minogue, Stephane, Dan and Forrest are all involved.

Jump Westminster was the first visual evidence of the potential of parkour, beyond the hearsay of its pioneers and their followers. Some members of the original Yamakasi group were invited to London for the premiere screening of the documentary. They were aware of the project from Stephane but had not seen it. After the screening they gathered as many dvd copies of the film as possible to present to the authorities in France which had previously rejected their presentation of parkour as a force for positive social change and inclusion. Subsequently, *Jump Westminster* provided the impetus the Yamakasi founders needed. In May 2008, the Mayor of Evry signed a partnership with Majestic Force allocating funds for their own building and for them to set up their own international academy. (Chau Belle Dinh, Yann Hnautra, Laurent Pietmontesi and Williams Belle were now in a group called Majestic Force.)

Jump Westminster has been the springboard for a national 'parkour for schools' programme (Parkour Generations, http://www.parkourgenerations.com/classes.php?p=schools) as well as several international post graduate research projects into the influence of parkour as a method for social change.

Mike Christie, Eugene Minogue and I at the Jump Westminster premiere at the Institute for Contemporary Arts, London, 2007.

Generations and a parkour rendezvous

The newly-formed Parkour Generations was supported by various first and second generation traceurs (Yann Hnautra, Châu Belle-Dinh, Williams Belle, Laurent Pietmontesi, Thomas Couetdic, Kazuma and Sebastien Goudot) who all joined the collective. Key to their involvement was the trust and respect for Stephane, knowing that he understood the 'true' original spirit of parkour. They did not want their understanding of parkour to disappear once they themselves stopped training. Together they have since concentrated on teaching and working towards creating a certification system to qualify new coaches, spreading their understanding and approach to the art, as well as, promoting it through their own videos and our collaborations. They have also all continued their own training.

I have continued to be Parkour Generations resident filmmaker on commercial parkour productions and we have completed work for clients such as Canon, the BBC, Yota and Native Instruments.

On set of the BBC childrens drama series MI High, Annty Marais was the parkour stunt double, Stephane Vigroux the parkour choreographer and I was the director. London 2009.

To celebrate the newly formed Parkour Generations, a parkour 'Rendezvous' was organised. I videoed and made an edit of the Rendezvous event (Angel, *Rendezvous 1, 2007*). After the event, Stephane, Dan and Forrest wanted to show their friends one of their training areas nearby. I accompanied them, my insider, trusted, participatory role giving me access to this 'after hours' event. I filmed observationally not wanting to disrupt or take away from the joy of the successfully attended '*Rendezvous*' event between friends. The improvised unplanned video footage from the after hours session resulted in the film *Visions*.

Filming indoors at the Rendezvous event then with Thomas Couetdic and Yann Hnautra walking to the next location.

Visions is a product of the 'optimal flow' approach of filmmaking with 'inspired performances' of the everyday of the traceurs in unison with my improvised participatory camera. The film was not planned but instead a serendipitous and spontaneous event. I had been invited to the location and the participants all knew why I was there and what I was doing. I was an insider who did not disrupt yet whose presence at times provoked playful interactions. The result is a film that reveals the social aspects and encounters as well as the physicality and imagination inherent in parkour. It shows friends at play who share the understanding of what they do and why, in a parkour context, and of their creative explorations and challenges when doing parkour. In contrast to other parkour videos, the film revealed the extent of failed attempts and the process of achievement. Nichols states that the sense of observation is not just about the filmmakers ability to "record particularly revealing moments but also from the ability to include moments representative of lived time itself" (Nichols 1991: 40).

My understanding of relevance came from my experience of parkour and, in contrast to the previous films created at this time, I felt that *Visions* captured elements of the everyday of the traceurs, stylistically complying with the observational realism Nichols characterises as, "the representation of typicality". "Observational cinema affords the viewer an opportunity to look in on and overhear something of the lived experience of others, to gain some sense of the distinct rhythms of everyday life, to see the colours, shapes, and spatial relationships among people and their possessions, to hear the intonation, inflection, and accents that give a spoken language its "grain" and that distinguish one native speaker from another" (Nichols 1991: 42). Lucien Taylor concurs with this stating "observational cinema typically cares far more for people getting on with their lives than telling you about them, and for performances that are an integral part of the fabric of social life and not enacted especially for the camera" (MacDougall, 5).

This was the case with the representations in the film *Visions*. One sees a challenge - nobody is sure if it is achievable - but they all attempt it and contribute to finding solutions for it. Slowly each attempt enforces the reality that the challenge is achievable, guiding and helping one another until eventually it is accomplished. The film presents the emotional and perceptual understandings of the participants, their desires, creativity, and intentions within their parkour social space. Whilst the majority of the film remains in the observational form, there are also visible encounters between myself and the traceurs, for example when Yann Hnautra approaches the camera and says "ooooh c'est moi!" looking into the lens and when Forrest tells me "It's coming"; referring to Sebastien Goudot's indecision on whether to attempt a catleap from the wall to the tree. MacDougall claims that, by including people reacting to the camera and acknowledging the encounter between the filmmaker and the subjects, it breaks away from a filmic anonymity (MacDougall, 86). I was there, the participants were aware of this, but the 'performance' is one of the everyday. They were getting on with their actions. My familiarity informed my choices of where to be so as not to interfere with their routes and parkour: I knew how to film, where to film from and when to film. Stephane commented after seeing the first edit of the film that he had not realised I was there for most of the time. The traceurs were in their flow state and so was I.

The film was compiled solely with handheld camerawork and the framing of the shots reflect the moments of relevance, for example, the close-up slow-motion shots of the traceurs, moments before entering their 'flow' state, when the body is released from fear before attempting the precision down to the wall or the one armed catleap. The joy of the individual as well as collective achievements is represented. The comments and interactions beyond the parkour remain included in the edit, placing the social as an important aspect and contribution to, as well as product of, parkour. The rhythm of the edit reflects my memory and experience of the afternoon, one of gentle actions rather than dramatic or narrative peaks and troughs of intense training. This was parkour as a creative exploratory form of play but one that also included great risk-taking, for example, when Kazuma precision jumps down onto a small edge with a 30 foot drop on one side. This moment demonstrates the experience and focus of the traceurs with such an exceptional focus and skill but also how it was an informed risk as we see Sébastien Goudot check the landing surface beforehand and communicate to Kazuma that its 'ok' and what he should be aware of.

There is a musical accompaniment to the images reflecting the musicality, dance and play-like quality of the traceurs in their environment, concluding in the minimal lyrics; "life is beautiful", reflecting the traceurs phenomena of enjoyment from their actions and sharing the experience with one another.

Social encounters

I was in regular contact with Stephane, Dan and Forrest regarding creating new materials for Parkour Generations, such as the *Parkour Indoor Academy*, and I accompanied them and documented many of their international training seminars including trips to New York, Ohio, Rome and Paris (Angel, *Parkour Generations: training with Kazuma, Ohio, 2008*). I continued to do parkour as a hobby. My informants appreciated my interest and continued participation in their art, realising it could only benefit and further my understanding of it.

The social encounters and experiences shared between my informants and myself, in addition to collaborative filmmaking, formed the foundations of the relationship and dialogue. The open-ended conversations before, during or after shoots enabled me to access other layers of cultural knowledge. The times shared, especially when travelling, when everyone is outside of their normal routine and environment, created a bonding experience. The roles of researcher/filmmaker and informant/performer are temporarily suspended allowing for communication to be more open. The initial roles of the performer and the filmmaker are impossible to maintain over long periods of time and mixed experiences. For this reason, it is necessary to have extended access to allow for the layers of performance to be peeled away and reveal a more nuanced and less guarded experience.

Dan Edwardes, Kazuma, Johann Vigroux and Francois 'Forrest' Mahop, Cincinatti Airport, USA 2008.

Julie Angel

Members of Parkour Horizons, Parkour Generations, Chau Belle Dinh
and Yann Hnautra, Columbus Ohio, 2010.

Stephane Vigroux, Johnny 'Sticky' Budden and I, after surfing in
Nicaragua, 2010.

Adapting styles for themes

After spending more time with Stephane Vigroux, his brother Johann, Kazuma and Thomas Couetdic, new themes and methods of documenting parkour became apparent, born from a continuing process of observation, provocations and social encounters. Like Rouch, I believed new films and expressions of knowledge, required new experiments and options. There was no singular style of representation but an adaptive approach to find different forms relating to different concepts. As Nichols explains, what films say cannot be separated from how they say it; "Film signifiers come with images attached. They *are* images and sounds, and they are always concrete, material, and specific. What films have to say about the enduring human condition or about the pressing issues of the day can never be separated from *how* they say it, how this saying moves and affects us, how we engage with a work, not with a theory of it" (Nichols 1991: Xiii). There was an intention to explore and find appropriate representations of the people and issues surrounding parkour, so that viewers could engage with parkour as my informants and I had, something Nichols suggests is the "overriding ethical/political/ideological question to documentary filmmaking", that is, how to find such appropriate representations (Nichols 1991: 34).

Through my extended exposure to the experienced traceurs I became increasingly aware of the elements of suffering and work that existed in their practice. It was always, when outside of their comfort zone, that they felt their training began. At times parkour was joyful and reflected the camaraderie; the exploration and shared experiences of training together. At others it was truly laborious. Although Stephane had discussed this in *Le Singe est de Retour*, it had not been visually represented. I had filmed several of Kazuma's outdoor training sessions and on one occasion when I had arranged to film there was torrential rain which made both filming and the training itself more challenging. The footage from this one night was used to create the short film *Rain*.

The film *Rain* portrays the choice of the traceur to endure mental and physical hardships, exemplified by training in all weather conditions, preparing and adapting his or her training to different mental and physical challenges. The wet conditions necessitated a heightened focus and consideration for accuracy, the body responding to the surface textures whilst the mental obstacles of uncertainty and risk are magnified. The film contains hesitation, fear, failure and the collective experiences of the group. The motivation to train in such conditions links back to the original intentions for parkour; to be able to respond and adapt to unpredictable circumstances rather than the execution or the performance of movements in ideal scenarios, for example, when the surfaces are dry or when the traceur is warmed-up and prepared.

Rain was shot in a purely handheld observational mode using only available light. I followed the traceurs motion as well as framing their bodies in space to contextualise their movements. The camera framed the moments of concern, for example, the hand that steadies the traceurs balance when stood on top of a narrow wet rail about to take off for a downward precision jump, and the close ups of the feet's precise landing when jumping down from the rail to the small ledge. Every shot and linking audio is slowed down by 50% to mirror the extent of the internal dialogue of fear and risk that becomes extended and time is warped, due to the level of focus required, when doing parkour in such conditions.

The narration was recorded immediately after the class and informs the viewer on the traceurs' motivations and explanation of this inner dialogue, knowing the environmental conditions are contributing to that fear. There is a willingness to suffer by going through that process. This demonstrates a commitment to parkour beyond any motivation of entertainment or performance.

The film was shot in one evening and the edit was completed over the following two days. The music represents the ominous adventure they all undertake as Kazuma leads them from one spot to the next (his normal training was not compromised by the wet conditions). Throughout the session, the traceurs maintained their focus and little was said to one another or to me. At the end of the session they empathised and expressed their awareness that it must have been worse for me filming as I was static for a lot of the time and, therefore, very cold while they were training and were warm, even if wet.

Each film production reinforced new levels of trust with my informants and I formed new relationships that assisted in the research, particularly with Thomas Couetdic with whom I worked closely on the next film, *Feedback Loop.*

The traceurs perspective

Although the participants and I· had tried to communicate and represent their understanding and experiences of parkour through a ciné parkour, we had yet to present the traceur's active perspective; the world through their eyes whilst engaged in the act of parkour. The only way to do this was to film with them or have a camera on them recording POV (point of view) footage. I had started experimenting from 2007 onwards with various head and action cameras, trying to find the best approach, but the available technology involved attaching a camera to an external recording device. Although this was possible, the impact of the landings and the vibrations on the equipment resulted in very poor results, if anything was recorded at all. By improvising and adapting a camera that recorded directly to a card, and attaching an underwater wide-angle lens, it became possible to gain more effective results.

Stephane Vigroux with his brother Johann and then with Dan Edwardes on a day of camera-testing and experimenting at the Southbank centre in London.

My informants were very enthusiastic to explore this method; to visually share their experiences and create a film constructed entirely from their perspectives. Many of the Parkour Generations traceurs were involved in developing the project and the edited film incorporates footage by Stephane Vigroux as well as Thomas Couetdic whilst those who helped research different methods are in the credit sequence of the film, such as Lauren Stokes, Johann Vigroux, Dan Edwardes, James Gore, Yao Gogoly and Brian Opiah Obeng.

We experimented with how, and at what angle, to attach the camera, and what movements were possible beyond a blur of action. I brought my laptop to the shoots to review each take. We then planned, discussed and adapted the camera and traceurs' movements to improve the next take. This technique required precise choreography of foot and hand placement as well as where the traceur should look. Stephane Vigroux and Thomas Couetdic shot the footage for the main body of the film as the accuracy and choreography became extremely complex, on top of the normal inherent risks present in parkour.

Fixing the camera and interacting with whoever was wearing the camera for *Feedback Loop.*

Of all the films submitted as part of this research, *Feedback Loop,* is the clearest example of a collaborative process and product of a ciné parkour. I did not shoot any of the footage and was reliant on the tracers to capture the content.

Feedback Loop takes us on a tactile, hyper-mobile exploration of textures and objects in the built environment. Thomas Couetdic's narration guides us on his experiences beyond, and outside, of the everyday. His description of being in the moment reflects Csikszentmihalyi's flow state. The viewer experiences the positioning, height and speed of actions via a "ciné-eye" (Rouch on Vertov, Henley, 247). One viewer commented on the vertigo they experienced while watching it but Thomas moves with calm and ease in such positions. The camera perspective follows the moments of relevance, such as, the kicking off point of the tictac or the hands as they grab a wall and land a catleap.

Visually the film guides us through an example of the traceurs' processes of training and doing parkour; from the warm-up; the social inclusion of other traceurs present and identifying routes to take. Through editing, unrelated sites are bound together to create a sense of motion and variety in parkour movements, as well as, environments, from catbalancing, traversing and vaulting. The low resolution grain mixed with the surfaces and textures of walls and lampposts create an aesthetic for the altered half-conscious reality Thomas discusses. The approximation of the real is not achieved through the 'ciné-eye' resulting in an abstracted version of events disproportionate to the realism of the recorded events. The 'camera eye' struggles to reflect the visual focus and speed of every moment and frame of the traceur's movements. The images blur rapidly from one surface to another. At times the viewer is suspended in space needing a reference of the traceur's body to help situate the gaze and intention of the action.

Much of the film's content was devised from Thomas wearing the camera during 'everday' training sessions. After reviewing the footage, we identified moments where the tracuer's perspective communicated something of his engagement with the world and his process. At times this was then re-enacted to gain a better more-refined representation and recording, at other times, the original experiment was included in the final edit.

In 2009 a new action camera was released, recording in HD and with a very wide fixed angle lens that has allowed for this kind of recording to be far more easily and effectively achieved by traceurs as demonstrated in the YouTube film *Traceur.Ru – actioncam in Voronej.* and in the film *One* by Duncan Germaine (http://www.youtube.com/watch?v=AESeOE7A2uo).

Quality of contact

During the research, the quality of contact, collaboration and the quality of content produced has been fundamental to maintaining my relationship with my informants. For each production there has been a period of reflection by myself and the participants on the reasons for sharing the content, discussing the merits of what the video communicates and how it contributes to the knowledge and understanding of parkour. Nothing has been released without the consent of the key individuals within the films.

The films I have made since the creation of Parkour Generations in March 2007, (*Visions, Rain, Feedback Loop,* and *Sarcelles*) reflect and present an understanding of the realities and concerns of parkour from the experiences of a select group of traceurs that mirror the original intentions and actions of the founders of the art.

While working with Parkour Generations and the Paris-based Majestic Force team, I was asked to help create some promotional materials for the A.D.A.P.T. (Art du déplacement and parkour training) qualification they were working on. The two collectives spent several days training together in France which I filmed. The first day was in the Forrest of Ecouen in Sarcelles. I filmed observationally as they trained. As well as creating the promotional *A.D.A.P.T.* edit, the film *Sarcelles* was also created.

The film *Sarcelles* demonstrates the intensity of the parkour training my informants do when they are together, in contrast to previous films that show them playing, exploring or teaching parkour to others. The film features Yann Hnautra and Châu Belle-Dinh, two of the key founders of *l'art du déplacement*, who lead the training with many of my key informants; Stephane and Johann Vigroux, Thomas Couetdic, Forrest and Dan Edwardes.

The film focuses more on the method (the training approach) rather than the movements of parkour as other filmmakers and commentators tended to do. Also in contrast to existing representations of parkour, the film is set entirely in a rural environment as this location originally played a key role in the development of the parkour culture (as explained in Chapter 1.)

The film was shot as an observational encounter, relying on my relationship with the informants as well as my experience of ciné parkour (to predict, contextualise and follow movements.) The participants challenge and encourage each other simultaneously. As with the film *Visions*, there are visual records within the edit of encounters between myself and the traceurs.

By following many of the repetitions of the same exercise, the film communicates the effort and work involved in their level of training. Yann and Chau have been training for more than twenty years and their current physical state confirms how effective their methodology is. Their attention to the quality of the movements, enabled by their 'body armour', i.e. their level of physical condition, has kept them safe over the years whilst their creative vision allows them to see opportunities for training and movement in any environment.

The film communicates a level of concern and care the participants have for pushing and extending their own limits (as well as, a sense of care for those around them), creating their own community through the shared practice and a willingness to try, regardless of whether a movement is successful or not. Emotional engagement is welcomed in the training as everyone's effort is relative to their own abilities. *Sarcelles* demonstrates the self-competitive nature of the practice and focuses on the experience and encounter rather any direct goal or achievement. The training, effort, pain, creativity, friendship and joy communicated, present the participants as a community.

Parkour activism

After six years of collaboration and producing films, friendships have been made. I was no longer a "morally neutral observer," I had become a social activist. "Thus, because the ethnographer is committed to action that would benefit the members of the culture where fieldwork occurs, friendly, cooperative relations define such enquiry and the ethnographer becomes part of and serves the community studied" (Denzin in Sands, 110). During my research I witnessed the positive influence of parkour on many traceurs as well as in my own life and was willing to highlight the potential of parkour beyond a spectacle.

With many members of Parkour Generations and members of Majestic Force in France, 2008.

The third birthday party of Parkour Generations, March 2010.

Parkour Generations after the Rendezvous 5 event in London, 2010.

Filming the Rendezvous 4 event in London, 2009

Conclusions

The films that I have shared online as part of a participatory cinema of parkour, are, in my mind, products of, and a celebration of, the experiences and encounters of a relationship with the participants as well as the filming experience. The films, like those of Rouch's, combine "the familiarity that accrues from observation with the sense of contact and spontaneity that comes from rapport and participation" (Feld in Rouch, 12).

The films produced are subjective. The chronology of the films' productions demonstrate my levels of knowledge and understanding at different moments in time. By sharing edits and works in progress, my informants could gauge how I saw them and what they do; what I did and did not know. This provoked new dialogues and discussions that contributed to my continuing knowledge and understanding. Through a continual dialogue, both on and off camera, my informants and I explored various stylistic techniques that assisted in the communication and representation of their art.

The filmic feedback loop nurtured a sophisticated level of observing. I could have been present for five years yet, had I not formed the relationships and contacts I did, I would not have known specifically what to observe and/or how it was being read by my informants. The feedback loop informed me how to be a parkour filmmaker. It formed the basis for Ciné Parkour. The presence of the camera and myself in the role of filmmaker, had both a negative and positive impact at times. Negative encounters revealed themselves as moments of inauthentic performance. At times, the camera when used to directly provoke - to ask questions - was met with well-rehearsed lines, that is a performance. This also occurred at times when shooting observationally. It was only by prolonged exposure and extended knowledge that it was possible to select what was of value for the research.

The positive impact of filmmaking was to provoke and draw out the knowledge the informants had, revealing the essence of what parkour was and their relationship to it. Sharing the rushes and edits allowed me to engage and create a relationship where each party was willing to share and trust.

Although I have not produced nor intended to produce a single master narrative, I have produced fragmentary films of knowledge that have contributed accurate reflections and representations of parkour. My methodology required being familiar with a range of filmmaking conventions and techniques, letting the content or subject knowledge dictate the appropriate choice of film forms as a response.

The first 18 months to two years of my research was spent searching for authoritative voices on parkour. Collaborative filmmaking was the tool for this enquiry, the process of making the films was the research, relying on the social as well as the filmic to inform. Whilst I intended for the films to be parkour led, this was not achieved until I had a more complete understanding of the discipline. This occurred as a direct result of meeting Stephane Vigroux and then enforced by contact with other first and second generation traceurs such as Johann Vigroux, Thomas Couetdic, Kazuma, Williams Belle and other members of the Yamakasi founders. The subjective films constructed after the completion of *Le Singe est de Retour* reflect my growing awareness, knowledge and understanding of the art and are the products of a ciné parkour.

All of my key informants during my filmmaking research have been male. This has been due to my location and focus on gaining access to those who train and to understand parkour as it was originally practised. I have only observed men's experience of parkour although there have been some females present including myself during the past six years. As discussed in Chapter 1, there were female participants such as Katty Belle who were present in the early stages of the art's development. Although I had access to Katty for an interview, it has not been possible to do a dedicated film project with her as she was based in Thailand for the majority of my project. When she relocated to the UK (although we had planned to do a project together) she became pregnant and was not training. The interviews I conducted with her did, however, contribute to the insights I gained and my overall understanding of parkour. My research project has not focussed on the gender politics of parkour as this is a subject that requires its own dedicated research in the future.

My research was anchored in defining a clear role within the culture where I could demonstrate my commitment to the process of understanding parkour and of being an active participant and social activist over a period of years.

The aim of the films was not purely to achieve an effective method in the expression of movement and the sensitivities of the traceurs' experience of parkour, but for an exchange of ideas and knowledge, working with their authority to create an informed result achieved through multiple subjectivities and encounters. David MacDougall states that ethnographies "may contain an analysis that does not finally result in a set of formal assertions or conclusions. Indeed, it may be conceived of as neither a message nor a representation, but as a record of engagement with a different culture" (MacDougall, 75). I believe that the films produce both a representation of parkour as well as a record of engagement. The films have given a voice and visibility to previously under-represented aspects of the culture. They have tried to address the balance of representation and reverse engineer some of the commercially-motivated singular performative presentations of parkour.

My informants have always been open to learn more about the filmmaking process and have increasingly continued to document themselves. In 2008, my informants began creating their own video training insights series *Behind the Jump* (Parkour Generations [137]).

My initial intention had been to document the everyday practices, processes and lifestyles of parkour but as the research progressed I focused on the practice and act of parkour. From my work you do not gain great insights into the lives of the practitioners outside of their parkour world, although to a certain degree, their involvement with parkour informs their mindset and world view.

Much has been written on the ethics of documentary filmmaking and an awareness of the implications of the process of filmmaking and the final product on the lives of those who have been filmed. These considerations are extremely important but it is also important to be aware that the observer can also be vulnerable to positions of exploitation.

Nichols believes "filmmakers who choose to observe others but not to intervene overtly in their affairs run the risk of altering behavior and events and of having their own human responsiveness called into question" (Nichols 2001: 9). My response of choosing to stop collaborating with Ez and Asid was a subtle intervention and communication to the other members of the team, making them aware of the serious nature of my concerns for their well being and the levels of exploitation that were occuring. Whilst I offered no explanation to Ez and Asid, I discussed the matter with Stephane Vigroux, Dan Edwardes, Forrest, Andy Day and with Sticky and Blue.

The films produced and shared have had a positive impact and been of benefit to the participants as well as myself. The expository nature and parkour authority voiced by the experienced traceurs has been received well by the international parkour community who are geographically removed and not able to spend time with my informants.

The films' utility is to bring a visibility to a largely unrepresented aspect of parkour, to initiate change, to share and expand the cultural understanding of parkour as experienced by my informants beyond the established spectacle it is capable of producing. Whilst all of the films, documentaries and commercials featuring members of the original Yamakasi group have inspired and shown what is possible, there was initially, relatively little explanation of the processes and methods used to achieve such accomplishments safely and responsibly, especially to an English speaking audience. The parkour community is continuing to grow at a rapid rate, but the parkour that I have aimed to document (a mirror of the original practice) is currently experienced by a very small minority of traceurs due to a lack of explanation and understanding regarding the practice. As Rouch states, "Film is the only means I have to show someone else how I see him. For me, after the pleasure of the ciné-trance in shooting and editing, my first public is the other, those whom I've filmed" (Rouch, 43).

I continue to work and collaborate with Parkour Generations in our established feedback loop of encounters, questions, knowledge, observations, production and reflections, and I continue to do parkour.

January 2010, Group photo of the 'Off the Wall' open parkour jam at
Elephant and Castle, London. *Image courtesy of Brian Oppiah Obeng.*

Julie Angel

Chapter 3

Theorising the practice of Parkour

As previously stated in Chapter 2, through the anthropological processes of participant observation, feedback, and extended access, it has been possible to access, discover, describe and document the culture of parkour as experienced by a select group of traceurs. How and what this group does, mirrors the understandings of the individuals who were involved in parkour's creation. My anthropologically intended films represent my informants who are all male, therefore the gender politics of parkour have not been researched and represented within this project, as this requires a dedicated research project in itself.

By making documentary films, layers of knowledge were revealed that over time contributed to a more complete understanding of the practise of parkour as a whole. My understanding and initial impression of parkour changed and evolved due to the knowledge gained from the extended exposure and encounters I shared with my key informants and some of the pioneers of the discipline. This chapter aims to discuss and theorise parkour, situating it within Henning Eichberg's descriptions of body culture.

Eichberg states that the study of bodily discipline and the bodily production of activities such as games, outdoor activities, dance and sport, contribute to the history of human society and philosophy (Eichberg 2009a: 91) and is a field that whilst illustrative, has previously been too narrowly viewed as the social body, ignoring the dynamic body in motion (Eichberg 2007: 2). Eichberg promotes a wider view and praxis, suggesting the concept of 'body culture', practice in movement. He states there are three inter-connected dimensions to 'bodies in movement': 'bodily', 'emotional' and 'social movement' (Eichberg 2009a: 92). Whilst bodily movement can be seen as sports, play and games, he gives examples of fascination, anger, fear, pain and laughter as emotional movement. Social movement refers to how people interact and unite, and how this contributes to "the discovery of civil society and its inner contradictions" (Eichberg 2009a: 92). "Body culture shows the different levels of what we call 'culture' in human life. Body cultures range side-by-side with spiritual culture, which consists of the ideas, symbols and meanings of societal life and with 'material culture', which is the world of human-made things, instruments and technology" (Eichberg 2007: 2). The study of body culture is also political (Eichberg 2007: 5) by providing alternatives to sport and revealing internal contradictions within society as a whole.

The following theorisation of parkour is based on my observations and experiences, looking at the inter-related relations of the physical, psychological, spatial, political and social inherent in the parkour culture.

The physical experience & encounter of everyday actions

Historically parkour is part of a larger tradition of practical alterity or a culture of 'otherness'; expressions that could be interpreted as physical, spatial, emotional and social resistance in urban practices; subversions that make use of spaces and architecture in ways which they were not originally intended. Parkour continues the tradition of the body as a site of resistance.

Historical examples of such resistance include the visual re-appropriation of buildings that have been associated with protests, (Hartley, 6) for example, prison rooftop protests and activists climbing buildings and attaching themselves or banners (BBC News [21]). The act of 'buildering' (to climb a man-made structure designed for purposes other than climbing, (Arvin [15]) can be traced back to the 1920s at Cambridge University, when Geoffrey Winthrop Young, a Cambridge Graduate anonymously published, *The Roof Climbers Guide to Trinity* (Young, 1900). More recently, performance events such as the *Above the Below* project by David Blaine in Tower Bridge, 2003, or Anthony Gormley's *The One and Other*, have focussed on the situating of the body to create living artworks in a new inhabited space (Blaine [35]).

There are some participants who by 'disrupting' public spaces or events crave publicity, for example, Jimmy Jump invaded the pitch during the Euro 2004 Football Final, disrupting the flow of the game in the final five minutes of time, running across the pitch and throwing himself into the goal. On his website he writes,

"My treasure is my jump,

the fame is my liberty,

the power and the wind are my law,

My only patriot is Jimmy Jump"

Other stunts include risking his life running onto the track during a Formula One race (Jump, www.jimmyjump.com/ingles). The spatial practices acted out by Jimmy Jump and David Blane do not share the same motivation as that of traceurs who practice parkour.

Parkour enables people to re-encounter their everyday space. French cultural theorist Michel de Certeau was concerned with the ways in which people alter, adapt, appropriate and give new meanings to spaces both individually and collectively through the specific ways that they move through, and use, these spaces. He observed that, "The act of walking is to urban systems what the speech act is to language or to the statements uttered (de Certeau, 97-98). There is a process of appropriation by the walker in the physical space, akin to the way the speaker takes on a language. In the same way that de Certeau analysed the act of walking and stated that it could not be reduced to the simple representation of a graphic trail of where the walker went, (de Certeau, 99) the same could be said of parkour. It is not always of importance where the action took place, parkour can occur as easily in the natural environment as in the built, but it is the encounter; the physical and emotional experience of the act, the expressive nature, and the transformation of the space and person as a result, that is more worthy of attention and analysis.

Parkour is both a physical training methodology (with a specific approach to movement) and a potential route, both of which involve mobility and creative adaptation. Whether covering large or small areas, parkour rarely involves vast expanses of a city as erroneously stated by Sophie Fuggle who claims "parkour involves traversing wide areas of urban terrain" (Fuggle, 206). Parkour routes generally cover very small distances and include a limited number of obstacles. Parkour can be experienced in any environment (Angel, *An American Rendezvous: Day 1 Fast Forward* 2010, Angel, *Sarcelles* 2008) although, to-date, the narrow focus of any commentary and analysis has been purely on parkour within the built environment, (Archer 2010, Geyh 2009, Lamb 2008, Laughlin 2008, Mould 2009, Ortuzar 2009, Atkinson 2009, Bavinton 2007) which has, I believe, failed to address and recognise those who choose to train in the natural environment and the potential it offers. The uniformity and standardisation of straight lines, edges and level surfaces of the urban are less challenging for a traceur when faced with an equivalent movement in nature. Landing on an uneven rock face or tree branch requires a higher level of skill and accuracy than landing on a solid level surface of a wall. However, regardless of the chosen environment, the lived experience of parkour remains the same in terms of the spatial, physical, psychological and social.

Chris 'Blane' Rowat executes a precision jump from one rock to
another and Yann Hnautra vaults a rock at the American Rendezvous
event in Hocking Hills park, Columbus, Ohio 2010.

Despite the practice in essence being the same in the rural and
urban, parkour is more noticeable within the urban due to its
unorthodox style of movement compared to a less dynamic and
conformist majority. Other examples of body cultures in the urban
environment include; buildering, urban exploration, skateboarding,
inline skating and bmx.

There are variations and sub-groups within these activities:
within the skateboarding community some practitioners choose to
focus more on vert, street, pools or tricking, and some bmx riders
prefer digging trails to street riding, but they all share the experience
of adapting their perceptions of a given landscape to suit their own

needs and desires. Physically the desire could be to become faster and stronger, being able to execute more complex moves.

Psychologically it could be to feel joy or overcome fear, testing the limitations of the practitioner. Spatially it could be to be autonomous, appropriating sites in a manner and at a time of their own choosing, and socially it could be about spending time with friends, sharing experiences and creating new challenges. The politics of each of these activities differ due to the values, motivations and philosophies associated with each practice. Importantly, these participants choose when, where and how to move and involve a change in perception of the environment to satisfy their own needs. All of these combine and contribute to create a more embedded participatory expression of the self within the given environment.

Parkour is more open-ended than some of the aforementioned body cultures due to its body centric basis (there is no equipment) and ability to find opportunities in any terrain, in all weather conditions - rain, sleet and snow - as well as, training in the dry and warm. Whilst it is the obstacles or the urban furniture that is usually the primary focus, parkour as a training methodology can be practised in open spaces, choosing to exercise and condition the body in preparation for the movement over obstacles. Creating what Stephane Vigroux and many of the founders refer to as their 'body armour", (Angel, *Le Singe est de Retour,* 2006).

Parkour training in Gerlev, Denmark, Williams Belle does *quadrupedle* movements (see Appendix 1 for glossary of terms)

A group practising jumping, and group *quadrupedal* session.

Parkour represents an eradication of static obstacles which inhibit motion, like the inline skater, urban explorer, skateboarder, urban climber and bmx rider, traceurs seek out routes or a series of movements and actions that have not been pre-determined or defined. Objects become obstacles, they are re-perceived as forms and surfaces that provide opportunities for encounters; physically, psychologically, creatively and socially. Whether the object is a wall, rail, rock or fallen tree, there is a process of re-perception of such objects and an active engagement and appropriation by the traceur (although some objects, it has to be said, may be loaded with more symbolic meanings than others).

The interactions may be to pass over the obstacle, moving over, around or under it. Interactions might be playful, exploring routes and opportunities on the obstacle such as balancing, climbing and/or repeating conditioning drills, or it's focus may be one of an experience of overcoming fear relating to where you land or take off from on the obstacle. These actions initiate and explore the physical and emotional individual behaviour and limitations of the traceur.

Mathew Lamb describes the act of parkour as the "dialectical relationship between the built form and the body. This *'art of displacement'* functions as a way of understanding and locating the self within urban architectural space" (Lamb, 2008). Lamb's approach to look at the "corporeal connection with architecture" (Lamb, 2008) focuses on one half of the pursuit of parkour, the perceivable output. Yet, without the imagination or vision that parkour requires, parkour becomes just physical exercise performed against walls, that is, as a form of outdoor gymnastics. Parkour is not merely about jumping over walls, despite some common misconceptions, it is an imaginative reworking of the existing spatial configurations as well as a reworking of the corporeal and questioning of the self. It is the combination of these elements that creates and allows for parkour to happen.

Stephane Vigroux doing parkour at Latimer Road, London. Stephane jumps up to wall, precisions onto a rail, walks along the rail, precisions from the rail to the bench, precisions from bench to bench, walks along the bench to jump to the lamppost, from the lamppost steps onto the rail and catcrawls along the rail, precisions from the rail to the wall, crawls along the top of the wall, at the corner 180 catleap to the other wall, jumps the gap in the walls and crawls along the top of the wall back to the start.

A parkour route can involve several obstacles, for example, firstly jumping over a rail, completing a wall run, then a drop, then jumping over a rail. Although individual moves may not contain a high degree of difficulty, when they are combined and continuous, the levels of strength and agility necessary are increased. Traceurs train for efficiency in their routes, trying to eliminate any hesitation and unnecessary steps between obstacles.

Many locations that remain popular for parkour are ones that were originally (and somewhat ironically) designed for the movement or flow of people, such as, entrances or walkways; the liminal exteriors of society. "Places with concrete ramps, barriers and staircases that seem designed to direct and steer the human subject, as a mass rather than as an individual, which articulate human movement in terms of processing, delivery, outcome" (Grayson, 2008).

Dan Edwardes and Forrest use the walkways, rails, walls and stairs in ways they were not intended, instead choosing to kong over the rail, move on top of the rails, vault over the rails and wallrun up the wall.

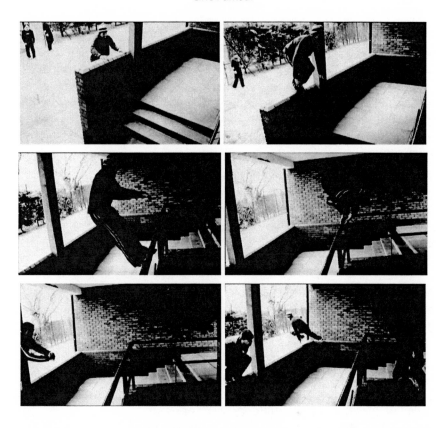

A route from left to right involving a wallrun, catleap to the railing, vault over the railings, vault another railing, run down the stairs then tictac or vault to clear the wall. This kind of route would be repeated many times as a circuit during training.

While many of these structures provide a route to guide pedestrians through conventional movements, they also provide new routes, created by - and for - the traceur. de Certeau said, "the ingenious ways in which the weak make use of the strong, thus lend a political dimension to everyday practices" (de Certeau, Xvii).

Parkour vision and environmental relations

The process of an imaginative re-perception and appropriation of the environment by the traceur results in new physical, spatial

133

and psychological connections to it. When the traceur re-conceptualises the space there is a dialogue; traceurs refer to this as 'parkour vision'. This occurs before the physical act of the parkour encounter. Traceurs experience a constant shift in the perceptual gestalt of the landscape around them. Their perception, openness, gaze and vision allows them to see and seek out opportunities for movement, an imaginative remapping of the familiar within their environments. Parkour makes every participant look at their environment differently. They see the potential for new encounters; to climb, crawl, vault, balance, jump, drop, roll or pull themselves up. They choose to initiate and execute challenges and achievements in their everyday surroundings beyond the specified norms.

The wall is no longer 'just' a wall, the tree no longer 'just' a tree, the surface 'just' a surface. Objects take on a new significance to the traceur. And all this matters and affects what potential there is for parkour.

Objects that were overlooked are now relevant and have something to say. The wall or ledge is transformed into a springboard, a take off pad or landing zone, it no longer maintains its initial function as a guide or divider, marking boundaries. The choice of movement made by the traceur brings attention, visibility and vitality to the spaces they move within through their appropriation. The city's transient spaces are visited and revitalised by hours of repetitive movement drills by the traceurs' presence. The empty potential of walls, rails, gaps, drops and edges is transformed and created into playgrounds of effort, activity and encounters through parkour.

One of the few remaining residents of the soon-to- be demolished
Aylesbury and Heygate estates in Elephant and Castle, London,
watching an evening training session.

Johnny 'Sticky' Budden describes the traceur's environmental
perception as having different visions and radars; "The more I
practice I'm seeing lots of opportunities and I'm seeing lots of
different visions. When you start out you see less visions than
people who have been doing it for a while. The more you practice
and the more you train and more experience you get the more
opportunities you may see and they come to you. There are some
things that I wouldn't see that Blue would see and there are some
things that Blue would see that Bam wouldn't see, and that's why it's
so good to train with everyone as they all have their different visions
and styles, and people with different style also have different
visions" (Angel, *Parkour Visions* 2006).

Paul 'Ez' Corkery, (now-retired from practicing parkour),
explained parkour vision as "becoming aware of your surroundings,
and becoming more in tune with your environment as opposed to
being a normal person where you are walking down the street and
oblivious to your surroundings and being herded in a certain way. It
just makes you see lines in architecture and understand surface
areas, you are looking for obstacles and in most cases these
obstacles are things that are put in place to guide you in a certain

way, i.e. railings or walls. They are built to herd you in a certain way" (Angel, *Parkour Visions* 2006).

Alongside the parkour vision, there is the accompanying interplay of dialogue and exchange that then follows. Williams Belle commented that every time he does *l'art du d'placement* it is like saying 'hello' to the environment and similarly when he watches someone else move, it is their dialogue that he witnesses. **The movements in parkour are expressions of the self, participating in, and with, the environment.** A wall, rail, bench or tree can now initiate a response, for example, "Can I vault over it? Can I balance on the top of it? Can I climb over it? Is it strong enough to hold me? Will I make it?" The imaginative exchange and dialogue that goes before the physical encounter is as much a part of parkour as the vault, the wall run, kong or tictac, the act of doing. The environment is the friend, the challenger and co-player in the parkour game, aiding the exploration of the limitations of body and mind.

The landscapes of creativity within parkour resonate with other creative practices. In my film *'The making of Traceurs, to trace to draw, to go fast'*, the artist Layla Curtis related to the creative practice of traceurs and how they see and interpret the environment. Curtis wanted to share the traceur's imagination and vision of the city's space and opportunities stating, "It's just so fantastic being with Stephane as he can see all these extra bits that I never even think of." "And I've never been able to speak to someone who can see those things that I can't see."

Stephane Vigroux demonstrates to Curtis the types of movement opportunities he sees with his parkour vision in the various locations stating "We can do everything, everywhere, with the number of people you want." And, he continued, "It's part of our sport to see and create movement all of the time with the environment around you." Stephane describes this as becoming like a natural reflex (Angel, *The making of Traceurs; to trace to draw, to go fast*, 2008).

The traceur's perception and vision is a product of their own understanding of what they believe they are capable of and therefore of being able to see the opportunities the environment presents to them.

Stephane Vigroux in mid-air in a kong to cat at the Imax subway walkway. The area had been a popular site for English traceurs for at least three years and has featured in numerous videos and TV reports due to its central location, public access and lack of security or policing. Stephane's considerable experience and physical abilities allowed him to execute this move but also, primarily, to have the vision to see it. To the best of my knowledge nobody had ever performed this move at this location before, focussing instead on the lower walls nearby.

Parkour requires a detailed understanding of the environment, whether it is the built form or in nature, as this helps determine the opportunities for parkour, and the safe execution of it. If a brick comes away from a landing then perhaps the landing has a smaller surface area and to land on, it is, therefore harder to achieve successfully. If anti-climb paint is applied, the surface will be slippery or sticky. If it is raining, more focus is required not to slip; the room for error increased. Spaces between, and the connecting points of the architectural edges, require more consideration than if someone is passively walking at ground level. Parkour involves a constant process of reading, responding and adapting to the materiality of the surroundings. Examples of points for consideration are: the distance between, the height above and below, the textures of the landing and the take-off points and the structural strong or weak points. An example of architectural and engineering knowledge understood by the traceurs, for example, is knowing that the point at which a railing has a welded intersection and pole underneath will support the weight of the body when landing a precision jump better than a long rail with no additional supporting welds or posts. "The materiality of parkour is fundamentally based upon the bodily relationship of the traceur with their built environment. The materials of the city have a direct impact upon the body of the traceur and the practice of parkour, enabling and disabling movements, suggesting and provoking actions, as well as, causing damage" (Laughlin 2008: 43).

From the film *Visions*, Sébastien Goudot and Kazuma contemplate a precision drop down to a small edge with a 30 foot drop on one side. Goudot climbs down and checks the landing area for texture and angle, then advises his friend on points to consider when landing. Kazuma jumps down and lands safely, then continues with his training.

Traceurs explore the multiplicity of their environment choosing a tactile and active relationship with the surfaces and textures that surround them. The tops of walls that are normally only visible from above are walked on and felt by hands grabbing them when landing a catleap, railings are balanced on, 'under barred' (see Appendix 1) through and landed on as opposed to merely walked around. The environment is felt and lived.

Stephane Vigroux executes a running precision on several tree trunks and then cleans and wipes the landing surface area to attempt the movement again.

In a training session at the Rendezvous 4 event in London, Williams Belle encouraged new participants to explore the obstacle with all of their whole body in order to take away the fear the body has of the obstacle, re-connecting the traceur to the environment physically as well as emotionally. The more physical contact the traceurs experience, the more their fear will subside (Angel, *Back to Basics* 2010).

Williams Belle at Rendezvous 4, demonstrating ways to train with greater body contact.

The physicality of the relationship with the environment and the confrontation of their emotions, enables the traceur to become more 'at one' and connected with the spaces where they practise parkour. They are not isolated from the spaces, but become an integral part of the landscape, a participant, a citizen, albeit momentarily.

Participatory active landscapes

Parkour does not aim to structurally alter the forms traceurs move within and on, taking the weight and pressure of the body landing on or passing over it, sometimes leaving only a surface residue of trainer marks on walls if any, a readable code or sign to other traceurs of their presence, unnoticed by some due to the unusual placement of the marks.

Images of actions and residues at District 13 in Paris. The image on the left shows the black lines of trainers gripping and sliding along the wall's surface at high levels in District 13 in Paris. The image on the right shows the kind of movement that created the marks.

Traceurs do not see their actions as destructive or threatening, they feel it is their right to move freely and they should not be limited to the existing routes and see their relationship with the environment as a positive one. Comparing the residual parkour marks to graffiti tags, Laughlin comments that "Traceurs might be described as hit and run choreographers; performing moves in unexpected locations, for the absent/unknown witness" (Laughlin 2004).

The marks left behind by the friction of the soles of trainers with the surface area of the walls, has even been brought into question by some traceurs, creating the 'Leave No Trace' initiative (Germaine, *Pilgrimage* 2008) painting over the marks left on walls from parkour. This has gathered momentum and is now a common theme among traceur gatherings where there is a clean up so that there are no water bottles or rubbish left after training. Parkour potentially improves areas, as well as, appropriating spaces. I have witnessed this many times in the Vauxhall Lane Estate area where traceurs on a regular basis will clear the area of rubbish left or thrown out by residents, enabling them to train more safely. As well as a general philosophy of parkour being non-destructive and not affecting the built form, it is their aim to form a harmonious relationship with the environment (Angel, *Asid, profile of a freerunner* 2006).

The traceur's desire is for an obstacle to remain unaltered. After being shouted at by a resident of a building that he had catleaped onto a garage roof, Johnny 'Sticky' Budden said "The thing I really hate is how people say 'get down from there before you break it or stop vandalising that! It's like, hang on a second, we need this. In fact in front of everybody over anyone I need this wall more than you because this is my baby, I need to practice on it, train on it, I don't want it worn away, I don't want the grip to go away, it needs to all be like this so I can train on it train on train on it. If a brick falls I'll be devastated" (Angel, *Canvas of the Street,* 2007).

With the heightened awareness of the environment for their own use, traceurs feel somewhat misunderstood by the public when their actions are deemed to be destructive. They believe it is only they (and some other body culture participants such as skateboarders and builderers) that pay such close attention and appreciate some of the less-celebrated examples of the built form in urban spaces (American Parkour [5], Angel, *Canvas of the Street*, 2007).

Traceurs encourage a participatory role where activity should be celebrated not discouraged within the existing framework of public space, bringing awareness and an openness to the potential of public spaces. Parkour has an international, cross-cultural appeal as a social phenomenon, risen out of a lack of both real and imagined sites of play (Angel, *Parkour World on You Tube Live,* 2008). By actively participating in and with the environment, sites of negative, little or no experience can become positive ones as something is achieved within them. The condition of 'no experience' as opposed to a negative experience, reflects a passive body; whereas parkour transforms the passive to active psychologically, physically and politically.

Parkour, while ignoring the originally intended functionality of a space, creates new sites of value and opportunity. For example, the railings outside the Shell Centre in London's South Bank became a precisions 'hotspot' for a while. The attachment was not to Shell, a large international corporation and the owners of the site, but to the physical elements that made up the railings and the space around it. The distance between the rails was challenging yet achievable and there were several rails in a row that allowed the traceur to gain momentum. They were not at great height so the focus was on the accuracy of, and sensitivity of the landings, without the risk of falling from a great height. The rails were well rooted and did not wobble. The connection to the architectural products such as the Shell railings created a new dialogue for the participant with that space, encouraging an increased engagement with the city. Railings then become a celebrated form: comparisons were made between different types, square flat tops or rounded edges: skinny or fat ones and attention paid to whether there was flat ground or stairs underneath to manage if you fall. The traceur's vision was to transform the guiding rails next to a set of stairs into a versatile training ground on which to practice precision jumps with a variety of take off and landing variations.

Forrest precision jumping between two rails at the Shell Centre.

Parkour plays out on the 'canvas of the street' (Angel, *Canvas of the Street* 2007) and the individual parkour visions and physical and emotional encounters are reminiscent of some of the ideas and elements of the Situationists movement. However, parkour's inquiring and expressive engagement with the landscape is not to be confused with some of the concepts linked to the Situationists, such as the dérive or a psychogeographical wander.

The psychogeography introduced by Guy DeBord and the Situationists International a group of avante garde artists and activists following on from the theoretical ideas of COBRA (Black, http://library.nothingness.org/articles/SI/en/display/242) - advocated the use of psychogeography as a political means. Furness states that it would allow people to creatively explore and see beyond the 'Society of the Spectacle'.

Furness states the 3 main ideas behind the dérive were:

1. A method by which to analyse and understand the city as it is.

2. To see the possibilities of the built environment.

3. To be used as a playful technique encouraging leisure (Furness, 303).

Furness's reading of the dérive sits comfortably within the framework of parkour and whilst the physical capabilities of traceurs would allow them to be effectual situationists, the political changes sought by Debord are not shared by traceurs. It is not their aim, as they do not view their actions as political in itself.

Traceurs and situationists both share the breaking of habituality of the normative route but the sensual relations and engagement with emotions, such as fear shaped by the objects around traceurs, are different. They are far more intentional and active. Parkour is not aimless, there is always focus, not least, because, without it there would be extensive injuries. The dérive is a passive drift whereas parkour is extremely active, intentional and involved. The two activities have different motivations. The physical nature of the movements of parkour and factors of risk do not allow for drifting. There are playful elements but the movements are always applied with intention, whether conscious or not. In contrast to the derive, it is about finding a route through, not allowing the route to unfold, although some could argue that this is the same thing.

Parkour shares and opposes some parallels with the Situationists in creating situations, but one of the main differences, however, is that parkour is only spontaneous at low level obstacles and beyond that it is only the extremely skilled and experienced traceurs who would be able to behave spontaneously without great risk of injury. As such, the opportunities for parkour and their 'parkour vision' is far more extended. Parkour involves educated risk and a constant adaptation of conditions relating to physical forms.

The Situationist's dérive is a drift, both conceptual and real. It never cites intentional highly focussed movements such as jumping or climbing for an exploration of the self. Theirs was a low level pedestrian pursuit. The dynamic multi -levelled abilities of a traceur could allow themselves theoretically to 'drift' in their parkour, whereas the lived reality is focused, intentional and an exploration of the imagination, self, body and materiality of the physical world.

In the dissemination of parkour, the traceurs I have worked with have presented parkour as having "no political agenda" (Edwardes [64]) yet simultaneously acknowledging what they call the 'bi-products' of practicing parkour: the fight against a 'cotton- wool', risk-averse society, rising obesity levels, lack of self discipline and respect not to mention, the reclaiming of public spaces as sites of play and expression. Politics is implicit in their actions if only, by the sheer nature of what they do in breaking away from the normative and pre-defined routes.

Socialisation, discipline and desires

As well as involving physical explorations in the environment, parkour encourages participants to enquire, experiment and explore the social controls exerted on the body in relation to how, when and where to move; how, when and where to play; what is social or anti-social and what should happen in private or public spaces. Parkour actively promotes a physical, psychological, spatial and social questioning of what is considered normal - and who has defined it as such - challenging the unspoken rules of social control and not always choosing to conform. By using things in ways they were not originally intended, traceurs actions of how and where to move, are not predictable and are political.

Traceurs' 'tactics' or intentions of movements (as with the other previously mentioned body cultures) are an example of what de Certeau describes as "antidiscipline" (de Certeau, xv) and a "procedure of everyday creativity" (de Certeau, xiv). Noam Chomsky describes the everyday process of organised life as the 'alienation and drudgery of labour', and like Henri Lefebvre, believes that people have their own satisfactions, which they use to break free from the work they do. Chomsky asserts that there is a universal human need for creative activities and free inquiry, and that the modern urban society stifles this need, and it is the social and political organisation of society that is to blame (Rabinow, 5). Lefebvre states there is "a fundamental desire of which play, sexuality, physical activities such as sport, creative activity, art and knowledge are particular expressions and *moments*, which can more-or-less overcome the fragmentary division of tasks" (Lefebvre 1996: 147).

Csikszentmihalyi states that "civilisation is built on the repression of individual desires" and that repression is necessary for maintaining social order and any complex division of labour. "Socialisation, or the transformation of a human organism into a person who functions successfully within a particular social system, cannot be avoided. The essence of socialisation is to make people dependent on social controls, to have them respond predictably to rewards and punishments." He states that this is most effectively achieved when individuals cannot imagine themselves breaking the rules of the social controls (Csikszentmihalyi, 17).

Foucault suggested that it was through a series of 'disciplines' that social controls and dominant relations of power were realised, resulting in 'docile' bodies. "The historical moment of the disciplines was the moment when an art of the human body was born, which was directed not only at the growth of its skills, nor at the intensification of its subjection, but at the formation of a relation that in the mechanism itself makes it more obedient as it becomes more useful, and conversely. What was then being formed was a policy of coercions that act upon the body, a calculated manipulation of its elements, its gestures, its behaviour. The human body was entering a machinery of power that explores it, breaks it down and rearranges it." Foucault continues; "Thus discipline produces subjected and practised bodies, 'docile' bodies" (Foucault 1991: 137-138).

Foucault describes disciplinary power as a force that, "compares, differentiates, hierarchizes, homogenizes, excludes. In short, it normalizes" (Foucault 1977: 183). He says, "The exercise of power consists in guiding the possibility of conduct and putting in order the possible outcome" (Foucault 1988: 789). This situates power as a device for determining responses, reactions, results and inventions.

Foucault suggested that one of the ways in which power actually operates in our society is by 'dividing practices' as a method of the 'objectification of the subject'. "The subject is either divided inside himself or divided from others" (Foucault 1982: 777-778). 'Dividing practices' are modes of manipulation combining the mediation of science and the practice of exclusion, usually in a spatial sense, and always in a social sense, e.g. the isolation of lepers in the Middle Ages; the mentally ill and the rise of modern psychiatric hospitals; prisons; confinement of the poor; medicalization, and stigmatisation, creating both dominated and dominating groups (Rabinow, 8).

Foucault argues that architecture and planning are spatial tactics and a political technology that contribute to the maintenance of power of one group over another, and this includes the control of movement and the surveillance of the body in space (Foucault 1982: 777-778). He stated that the organisation of individuals in space was achieved by interchangeable methods of enclosure, portioning, and of creating functional sites (Foucault 1991: 141-145).

Parkour serves to reverse Foucault's 'dividing practices' by being an activity that serves to include and connect participants to the 'political technology of architecture', creating an active body through a reorganisation of how individuals move in space. The modern spatial divisions; boundaries of walls and railings; public and private and the "No ball games" culture are ubiquitous in urban spaces and accepted forms of current dividing practices, separating subjects in a spatial sense but also a separation of the social, emotional and physical contact with the spaces and activities occurring within them. Parkour's approach is one of 'anti-discipline' to political and dominant spatial and disciplining practices.

The 'active' action of the parkour body and it's re-negotiation of space results in a reverse of Csikszentmihalyi's 'socialisation' and responds to Foucault's 'disciplines' of docility-utility, isolation and exclusion. The traceur body is not passive or 'docile'. The movement and route is defined by the traceur not the state; the autonomous actions of a traceur not having been pre-determined. The traceur is not confined by the fears embedded in a risk-averse society.

According to Eichberg there are the three spheres and logics of social life: state; market (including commercial logic) and civil society (Eichberg 2001: 10). State logic fits within the Foucauldian view that subjects the body to power, control, evaluation and the training of 'competences'. "This is the reification of bureaucratic control and 'management' " (Eichberg 2007: 6). In market logic the body is a means of production and subjected to instrumental use for consumption. "This is the reification of the commodity" (Eichberg 2007: 6). In civil logic, "the body is a medium to confirm or contest one's identity – inside and between self-organised and voluntary groups" (Eichberg 2009a: 89) whereby, the process is more important than the results. This third logic of a civil society is where parkour and other alternative body cultures become a tool for resisting, exploring and contesting perceptions of the self.

While Foucault discusses the histories of power, he also expresses a concern for freedom and the potential for explorations of the self, stating that while there are relations of power with domination and inequalities, there is also a free subject and therefore the possibility of resistance, reaction, responses and 'possible inventions' (Foucault 1982: 789). "Power is exercised only over free subjects, and only insofar as they are 'free'. By this we mean individual or collective subjects who are faced with a field of possibilities in which several ways of behaving, several reactions and diverse comportments, may be realised" (Foucault 1982: 790). He believes that, "to understand what power relations are about, perhaps we should investigate the forms of resistance and attempts made to dissociate these relations" (Foucault 1982: 780).

Foucault suggests there are three kinds of struggles relating to forms of power that are applied to everyday life; struggles against forms of domination (ethnic, social, and religious); against forms of exploitation which separate individuals from what they produce; or against that which ties individuals to himself and submits him to others in this way (Foucault 1982:781).

How a human being turns himself into a subject became the focus of Foucault's later works as opposed to 'power' (Foucault 1982: 778). He states that there are two meanings of the word 'subject'; "subject to someone else by control and dependence; and tied to his own identity by a conscience or self-knowledge" (Foucault 1982: 781).

Foucault comments, "Perhaps I've insisted too much on the technology of domination and power. I am more and more interested in the interaction between oneself and others and in the technologies of individual domination, the history of how an individual acts upon himself in the technology of self" (Foucault 1988: 19). Markula and Pringle suggest that this is not a transformation of power relations, but a way for "an investigation of the individual both as the object and the subject of power relations" (Markula & Pringle, 139).

Foucault proposes four major types of technologies:

1. "technologies of production, which permit us to produce, transform, or manipulate things";
2. "technologies of sign systems, which permit us to use signs, meanings, symbols, or signification;"
3. "technologies of power, which determine the conduct of individuals and submit them to certain ends or domination, an objectivizing of the subject:"
4. "technologies of the self are the various 'operations on their own bodies and souls, thoughts, conduct, and way of being' that people make either by themselves or with the help of others in order to transform themselves to reach a 'state of happiness, purity, wisdom, perfection, or immortality'" (Foucault 1988: 18).

Parkour represents a form of Foucault's 'care' or 'ethics of the self' (Fuggle, 219). The 'care of the self' consists of four aspects by which individuals subject themselves to a process of subjectivation: ethical substance, mode of subjection, ethical practice and telos

(Foucault in Markula and Pringle, 141). The four aspects allow for a transformation of the self in creating a new self, guided by one's own moral conduct defined by rules, codes, behaviour and choices. These choices are a result of self-reflection, problemitising and an awareness of a transformation into an 'ethical subject'.

The first aspect, 'ethical substance' is concerned with moral conduct and deals with issues, such as, desire and feelings (Markula & Pringle, 141). The second aspect, the 'mode of subjection', is dependent on choices made in deciding what is the topic of ethical substance and relies on oneself establishing and putting into practice sets of rules relating to the ethical substance. The third aspect, 'ethical practice', is the work that is then done according to the rules and conduct decided on in order to work towards transforming oneself into "the ethical subject of one's behaviour" (Foucault 1985: 27). The fourth aspect, 'the telos' is a kind of being that one works towards through the ethical practice, for example, to feel free, pure or immortal (Foucault 1983: 239).

In parkour the ethical substance for a traceur might be to want to move freely in any environment overcoming physical and emotional obstacles. The mode of subjection would be problemitising how to achieve this by asking what it is they need to work on to overcome that obstacle. For example, traceurs might ask of themselves, do I need to have less fear, or are my legs not yet physically strong enough to make that distance or withstand that drop? The ethical practice is then the subsequent training that addresses these issues. For example, engaging with fear by attempting similar moves and gradually increasing the levels of fear, or by working physically through repetitions of movements to increase the strength and ability to be physically capable of the move. The telos might be to become more 'at one' with the environment by achieving such movements and moving in a way, and at a place and time of one's own choosing, to feel free and empowered.

Traceurs are active subjects within dominant power relations who use parkour as a technology of the self; an active transformative tool, to create and understand themselves and move away from fixed notions of identity and behaviour. Through a process of critical thinking and self-awareness traceurs problemitise and set ethics by which they adhere to. Parkour becomes a 'practice of liberty', where traceurs practice freedom as a lifestyle, based on inventions and styles, that create ethics centered around creative environmental interactions and connections, to reclaim the body as an autonomous vehicle, away from the dominant notion of 'bio-power' and other dominant discourses.

The traceur is a continual work in progress recreating themselves through a constant process of creativity and invention. Parkour can be seen as a transformative lifestyle; set of ethics or an art. Foucault states, "Art has become something which is related only to objects and not to individuals, or to life. That art is something which is specialised or which is done by experts who are artists. But couldn't everyone's life become a work of art? Why should the lamp or the house be an art object, but not our life" (Foucault 1983: 236) Foucault referred to the creative potential for changing and re-invention of the self as the 'aesthetic self', and the chosen ethics were a stylisation, to give form to one's self, that allows for creative thinking to challenge one's identity (Markula & Pringle, 149).

In an interview with a representative from the website comunidadparkour.com, Stephane Vigroux expressed that for him, parkour was an art with the ability to create something from nothing; an encounter; expressions of the self and a creative re-perception of the environment. He also stated that he encouraged people "to think and reflect about their actions and training. Simply to have a better understanding about the reasons why they're practicing, training, jumping."

Stephane articulated parkour as having three potential strands:

"A method of training your body in an efficient way to overcome (physical) obstacles. Makes your body very strong and efficient through a natural way of training. A method of training your mind to overcome life's difficulties (non physical obstacles). There are many ways through practicing parkour that helps to be stronger and more balanced in your everyday life. And each individual will have his own way to do it and find answers. It is a personal work. One example is through the process of finding solutions and cultivating the habit of going over obstacles, your mind tends not be stopped by difficulties in your life and move forward. Another example is through cultivating your self confidence, by facing and overcoming your fears. A way to express yourself that connects you to the universe/life: An art form. Parkour cultivates your imagination and generates emotions. With nothing you create something."

More importantly perhaps, Stephane concluded, "For some people it is just about one of those points. For others it would be all three together. There is no right answer. Some even find other answers and definitions of it. What parkour is for you is what matters really"(Vigroux, [193]).

Traceurs are constantly being critically aware of their own 'practice' and ethics; their approach to how they train and move in feeling emancipated from society's dominant technologies to conform and subjectivate oneself. They reflect on their environmental awareness and how they recognise feelings of liberation in their new parkour visions of endless opportunities.

Dan Edwardes believes, "You can't hide in parkour, you can't fake it really, you can't hide from yourself when you are training. When you go out and train, every single time it's like looking at yourself in the mirror and immediately getting feedback on where you are that particular day; where you are physically, mentally; if you are injured, feeling sick; if you're not quite up for it. It really tests you every time you train. In many other disciplines or arts you can fake that, you can practise it but not really push yourself. In parkour, every session you are pushing yourself, every session gives you this feedback about who you are and what you are doing, and it's a journey of self-knowledge, in that way" (Edwardes, 2010).

All of this occurs within the framework of existing dominant power relations that are not a totalising force, but affords individuals the possibility for change and resistance. Markula and Pringle state, "The care for the self can assist today's individuals to play the games of power with a minimum of domination and replace the search for self-fulfilment with some other ethical substance" (Markula & Pringle, 147). The traceur's multiplicity, manipulation and diverse readings of the environment are a temporary deflection of the ruling social order and controls; a personal empowering strategy, merging the ordinary or everyday experience with one of play, fear, adventure, meaning, authenticity (as discussed in chapter 1), challenge and risk, creating their own forms of social and political organisation of active bodies. Jimena Ortuzar suggests that parkour, "is an act of flight. However, it is a chase with no pursuer, at least not one that is immediately evident or easily identified. Hence, the flight of parkour can be seen as an escape from the practices of power that govern our movement and regulate our behavior" (Ortuzar, 55).

Parkour's politics of space

The manner in which traceurs respond to the dominant politics of space could also be categorised as a form of 'pragmatic anarchism' as described by the anarchist architect Colin Ward, whose writings, such as *The Child in the City*, explore the relationships between people and their built environments; "Anarchism in all its guises is an assertion of human dignity and responsibility. It is not a programme for political change but an act of self-determination" (Ward, 143).

Stuart White describes Ward's form of anarchy as, "A form of social relationship characterized by self-defining individuals acting cooperatively as equals" (White, 20). This form of anarchism is not to be thought of as disruptive or violent, but more as having an experimental and experiential essence that contributes to more creative and individual experiences, whilst being socially anchored in an awareness for the environment as a whole, addressing social needs. Ward suggested; "Social changes, whether revolutionary or reformist, through which people enlarge their autonomy and reduce their subjection to external authority" (Ward, 143). Pragmatic anarchists proposed creating social changes by relations based on self-help and mutual aid, a form of 'social self-determination' a way of problem-solving as opposed to relations of subject and state, creating a 'revolutionary spirit' (White, 13-15).

Parkour embodies this spirit of revolution and the notion of 'direct action' for changing how people live, and importantly, how they perceive and experience themselves, their surroundings, and what sense of authenticity, citizenship and belonging they experience as a result.

In the film *ASID, profile of a freerunner*, Asid states that, "The discipline, it's a way of life, a way you can live your life in peace, a way you can live your life happy and free from all the boundaries around you, all the obstacles that define you into small spaces. You break out from all the small spaces and you see beyond all the obstacles around you and you don't feel trapped within the city that you live in, and it just sets you free, sets your whole life free" (Angel, *ASID, profile of a freerunner* 2005).

Identity, phenomenology and embedded perceptions of the self

The self-awareness that traceurs experience stems from becoming detached from external societal influences and allowing for a more autonomous and internal meeting of mind and body to experience the world, a reclaiming of the richness, depth and complexity of experience. By exploring the relationship between themselves and the natural world, traceurs understand themselves better. George Eric Brymer suggests that in extreme sports and high-risk scenarios, in addition to a quest of 'freedom to'; (for example, social controls), and 'freedom from, there is also a third dimension, a freedom of letting go and transcending existing ideas of limits and abilities (Brymer, 164).

The processes of learning, practicing, improving, and self-expression while doing parkour relies on a continuation of self-belief, of 'I can'; personal revelations of self-actualisation, self-realisation, self-determination and being. Confidence is gained from building upon physical and emotional competences, an evolving toolkit of skills and moments. The nature of the bodily acts and motility in parkour due to its challenging form, complexity and risk brings the impossible to the fore. During my research and documentation of parkour, I have observed traceurs breaking free from what Iris Young has referred to as "inhibited intentionality". Young states, "An uninhibited intentionality projects the aim to be accomplished and connect the body's motion toward that end in an unbroken directedness that organises and unifies the body's activity" (Welton, 265). Parkour's systematic training methodology is implemented to do this, aiding in the execution of a "bodily commitment". Welton believes that, "By projecting an aim toward which it moves, the body brings unity to and unites itself with its surroundings; through the vectors of its projected possibilities it sets things in relation to one another and to itself. The body's movement and orientation organizes the surrounding space as a continuous extension of its own being" (Welton, 226). These lived relations of space, positive ones of 'being' or being 'in tune', and the negative ones of frustration and fear that traceurs experience, are overcome through the unifying phenomena of parkour. Williams Belle says, "You must learn to discover yourself, how your body functions, you understand what you can or can't do. We all start with the body" (Belle W., 2010).

The nature of the movements in parkour and the infinite possibilities that environments present, mean that the open-ended nature or perceptual openness to the world is triggered through the new body-subject relationship created by doing parkour. In parkour the body-subject relationship is constantly challenged and changing as traceurs attempt to improve and progress, testing their tuning and exploration of the body, mind and self to different environments and conditions. As Stephane Vigroux stated in *Le Singe est de Retour*, the jumps he has to do now to experience the same kind of feelings he had when he started parkour need to be much larger, constantly challenging his fears and physicality in the act of parkour.

As Shirley Ardner discusses in *Ground Rules and Social Maps for Women: An Introduction* (Ardner, 2) "The environment imposes certain restraints on our mobility and, in turn, our perceptions of space are shaped by our own capacity to move about, whether by foot or by mechanical or other transport." Therefore, behaviour and space are mutually dependant. Traceurs experience the environment in a way that is normalised among fellow practitioners, yet their movements may appear anarchic and disruptive to a passing observer.

The restraints and patrolling of physical activity in developed Nations with increasingly unhealthy populations, such as signs declaring, "No Skateboarding, No Bicycles, No Ball Games", seems somewhat contradictory. Physical activities in unregulated public spaces - such as, running on the grass or a group of individuals practising martial arts, yoga or Tai Chi, BMX riders riding trails which they have dug out on a piece of waste land, or traceurs precision jumping between two walls - are viewed suspiciously, or as a curiosity, rather than a celebration and productive use of public space for healthier bodies and minds. All of the aforementioned activities choose to interact with the given environments in a far more direct way than how the passive general public does, whether it is a concrete ledge, a railing, or a disused piece of grassland.

In a similar parallel with skateboarding, parkour does not engage with architecture for its intended purpose of production and distribution of things, in this case it is concerned with the production of a new encounter, of the body and space. Borden described this in the skateboarder's context as "super architectural space" (Borden, 89) a space where architecture, body and skateboard are "erased and reborn in the encounter between skateboarder and skateboard architecture" (Borden, 2).

Stephane Vigroux in various stages as he executes a running precision
jump from a bench to a wall, creating the equivalent of a parkour 'super
architectural space'.

In the film *Feedback Loop*, (Angel, 2008) Thomas Couetdic discusses his experiences of parkour as stepping outside of the everyday process, a removal of the thinking mind with concerns on what happened yesterday or what to do tomorrow. It is in the act itself, a celebration, being in the present moment and taking in his surroundings. Now. He describes these sensations as providing a feeling of being 'natural' and experiencing an openness to what is around him. The French phenomenologist, Maurice Merleau-Ponty, promoted a similar idea of an imminent somatic perception remarking, "By thus remaking contact with the body and with the world, we shall rediscover ourself, since, perceiving as we do with our body, the body is a natural self and, as it were, the subject of perception" (Merleau-Ponty 1962: 239).

Brymer's doctoral thesis, *Extreme dude! A phenomenological perspective on the extreme sport experience*, states, "Phenomenology is, in its simplest form, a method for exploring the human experience and defining its nature from a view-point that requires the transcendence of cultural conditioning and its ensuing understanding of self and consciousness" (Brymer, 18). Phenomenology can provide a theoretical framework for the description and analysis of such experiences but according to Allen-Collinson, phenomenology's concern with subjectivity, first-person accounts, experience and meaning has sometimes meant it has been erroneously confused with qualitative research in general (Allen-Collinson, 279). There are many strands of phenomenology such as transcendental, hermeneutic and existential, but it is the existential phenomenology associated with Merleau Ponty that Allen-Collinson suggests is useful for studying the sporting body due to commencing from "a dialogic where world, body and consciousness are all fundamentally intertwined, inter-relating and mutually influencing" (Allen-Collinson, 282-283).

Writing with particular reference to the body's motility, Merleau-Ponty described a communing with the environment, the intertwining of the conscious, the body and the world. He reported, "It is clearly in action that the spatiality of our body is brought into being." The consideration of the body moving through space allows us to look at how the body ACTIVELY assumes both space and time (Merleau-Ponty 2004: 117). Merleau-Ponty's investigations into the spatial relations of the body concluded that it is through the body that we experience the world.

The sort of self-discovery and re-connection that Merleau-Ponty describes by this coming together and new body-subject is the same description often cited as a driving force for the continued practice of parkour by traceurs. All of the founders that I interviewed expressed they were 'looking for something' when they started the movements and training that were to evolve into the discipline, sport, lifestyle, body culture and art. I interpreted this as a search for identity, an exploration of the self, a way for them to find a way of being and to express themselves within their environment. It is my belief that it is this sense of 'being', felt when one moves through space; exploring one's own identity, that is the central attraction of parkour as a Foucauldian technology of the self, practise of freedom and can be described as the phenomenology of parkour.

Parkour is central to the lives of my key informants and doing parkour connects their lived bodily existence - their flesh and bones - the corporeal body moving in space and time, interacting with the environment, to their inner self, in search of a more authentic meaningful way of being, situating knowing and knowledge. The lived experience of parkour involves the transcendence of time, space, other and body as everyday experiences are re-evaluated and 'stylised' revealing the individual situated 'essences' of parkour as an expression of the corporeal for each participant. Parkour is then perhaps analogous to a 'phenomenological attitude', "an orientation to the world", a way of looking, "an attitude of attentiveness to the things of immediate experience" (Van den Berg 1972 in Allen-Collinson: 287).

Traceurs, like other body culture participants, feel their lives are enriched from their parkour experiences as they become more aware and capable in the personal, inter-personal and extra-personal spheres (Brymer, 200). As discussed in Chapter one, participants look for a more meaningful and authentic sense of self. Brymer suggests that by becoming more aware of one's inner being, one is more able perhaps to construct a social image (Brymer, 202).

All of the above experiences involved in parkour contribute to the formation of an enhanced sense of self and identity. As discussed in Chapter 2, parkour is an activity that allows participants to experience the 'flow' state, one that involves a letting-go of the sense of self, then experiencing a re-enforced sense of self, after an activity that involves entering the flow state, has occurred. This is tied up not just with the re-perception and subsequent alternative use of space, but the nature of the challenges experienced in parkour and developing the skills to exercise control in difficult situations.

Csikszentmihalyi believes that the momentary disregard for a sense of self becomes a very enjoyable experience; "When not preoccupied with our selves, we actually have a chance to expand the concept of who we are. **Loss of self-consciousness can lead to self-transcendance, to a feeling that the boundaries of our being have been pushed forward**" (Csikszentmihalyi, 64**).** "When the activity is over and self-consciousness has a chance to resume, the self that the person reflects upon is not the same self that existed before the flow experience; it is now enriched by new skills and fresh achievements" (Csikszentmihalyi, 66). Csikszentmihalyi describes the flow optimal experience as autotelic, one that is a self-contained activity, an end in itself and that it is not done "with the expectation of some future benefit, but simply because the doing itself is the reward" (Csikszentmihalyi, 67).

Whilst "flow" is obtainable in many diverse activities such as climbing, playing a musical instrument, sewing or reading, the heightened physicality and aim of controlling the body and its emotions - coupled with the creativity of producing new realities of movements - explains why many traceurs describe parkour as a transformative practice; people feel changed by their experience of parkour. It is not only their perceptions of space and the things they do in them, but it is the perception of themselves, their identity, the confidence and ease that they feel as a citizen, that is expanded and becomes more complex as a result of parkour. **Csikszentmihalyi states that "If one takes control of what the body can do, and learns to impose order on physical sensations, entropy yields to a sense of enjoyable harmony in consciousness**" (Csikszentmihalyi, 95).

This point was aptly exemplified by a traceur known as 'Cruise': "The best location for Parkour is that which lies just on or above your capabilities, which pushes you furthest while still being within reach" (Bavinton: 406).

The tuning to the environment, the coming together of the consciousness, the body and the environment when in action, is key to the traceur. The mind is focused equally on the environment as it is on the body's control and co-ordination of movements. Dan Edwardes explains "When I'm practicing parkour you feel the movements, the unlimited potential to move in the environment which normally you wouldn't move in very freely, that feeling is very good. You feel sort of connected to your environment, you feel connected to your body and you feel connected to the forces at play around you and within you, between you and your environment. You feel not in control of them but half in control and half controlled by them. You are one hundred percent there in your environment, you can't afford to be thinking of something else, you are just there, just you, your environment and physics. It's a very dynamic feeling, you feel very alive, very vibrant and full of power" (Edwardes, 2006).

Traceurs become very passionate about parkour; they give of themselves to it, heart and soul, blood sweat and tears, day after day, year after year. For some, this experience is so consuming that they start to take possession of it and feel a sense of ownership over parkour. It becomes 'theirs', they know it so well; it represents their experience, their ego, their identity. There is a tartalogical aspect to this; the parkour you do is 'yours' because parkour is you and you are your parkour, but this is where problems can arise: parkour has the potential for people to take it to a level of obsession. Traceurs can become their own prisoners, giving value only to the experiences and connections they have in their parkour experiences. It remains outside of the everyday in a form that is more than a tactic of an everyday act of creativity, but an all consuming behaviour. Williams Belle suggested that this can occur at the beginning of the practice as the thrill of discovering a tool for self-enquiry that is challenging while simultaneously presents a new reading of your everyday surroundings, can be extremely appealing and you can feel quite lost but you state, "I know myself better because I'm moving, I move my body over there, I know in a second if I can jump from here to there. But in reality you don't know yourself, you know your body but you ignore what's going on inside, you have no control over your mind, it means nothing" (Belle W.,

2010). This reflects the importance of the emotional aspect in parkour as well as the physical.

Fear and connection

The intentional actions and mind-body relationship in parkour is something that was of great concern to my research informants. Many body cultures have a level of mind-body focus and control, but what distinguishes parkour is the level of risk and fear involved in most actions, becoming potentially fatal at high levels. Parkour forces the participant to engage with, and counter, the fears and negative emotions that are revealed to oneself in their choice of actions. How the body and mind operate in relation to the environment and their experience of fear is paramount to the traceur.

The active emotional engagement and physical connection to spaces through parkour challenges conditioned patterns of behaviour and assists in the reversal of fear-reactivity (Edwardes [66]). As Stephen Saville describes: "Dynamic and mobile, it can be layered with other times and spaces, but also other emotions. Emotions like anger, excitement and joy can all be accompaniments to the fears encountered in parkour" (Saville, 903).

For traceurs to feel a connection to a place, Saville writes of the "emotional refiguring of spatial possibilities" (Saville, 892) experienced by traceurs and says that it is their engagement with fear that helps to create this connection. He argues that fear is not an entirely negative emotion in this context of "fear in place" and that there are different levels that can be experienced. All of this is possible, Saville suggests, once the traceur is open and vulnerable to the space, requiring a blurring of "bodily maturity and habit with play and spatial immaturity; neither maturity nor immaturity ever being complete" (Saville, 901). Parkour reconnects the openness of a child-like ability to enquire and move freely whilst having the maturity to achieve the physical strength necessary to achieve the necessary mobility.

In the short film, *The Outside In*, (Angel, 2007) when asked to sum up what parkour is to her, Karen Palmer answers, "Parkour is, honestly, just overcoming your fears, you just do it through your body that's all it is; just honing your body to overcome your fear, letting go of fear." Dan Edwardes explains "To practise parkour is to seek fear on a daily basis, to confront it head-on, to face it naked and alone" (Edwardes [66]).

Fear of the city itself (England & Simon, 202) can also be an issue relating to discourses of 'otherness' and difference in social contexts (Madge 1997, Pain 2001, Shirlow and Pain 2003, Valentine 1992 in England and Simon: 202). The actions and the spaces that people choose to move in are expressions of a perceived sense of safety where they experience a lack of fear and anxiety, by avoiding, for example, certain areas (England & Simon, 203). Stanko comments, "Generally speaking, researchers and policy-makers alike characterise the fear of the city as a destructive force, interfering with full participation in everyday life in a civilised society" (1990, 5 in England & Simon, 203). Fear is a repressive tool that reinforces dominant power positions of one party over another. Fear in a parkour context can be the fear of injury, pain, sporting failure, isolation, one's identity, (race, gender, sexuality) place, other and difference.

The fear of letting-go and facing the consequences of revealing one's identity by testing one's ability and of becoming aware of the fears embedded in how they control their behaviour, are all relevant to a traceur. The ability to 'let go' of and engage with fear by means of action and mobility within the practice of parkour is extremely relevant. By possessing the skills and ability to overcome the personal and/or unconscious fears that exist through socialisation the traceur creates a new position of power of the body and the individual over the materiality of the environment and the social controls within it.

Political scientist David Runciman comments that, "What the state can do is, over decades, over centuries, entrench peoples identities, organise their fears, organise their hopes" (Runciman, 2010). Fears that have accumulated over the period of a lifetime can shape people's everyday geographies and are "constructs that one uses to make daily decisions" (England & Simon, 202).

According to Corey Robin, fear is a political tool that can be divided into two types. Firstly, the apprehension of harm felt by people to their collective wellbeing, or the intimidation of people by governments and groups. Following on from the work of English philosopher Thomas Hobbes, according to Robin, fear is a tool of domination, that plays an essential role to the maintenance of political and social order, not the foundation for a just social and political order, as others might try and justify their use of political fear as a tool (Béland, 2005).

Fear is deeply personal and elusive: after more than twenty years of training that began at age nine, Williams Belle said that his continued motivation and reasons for training are to master his emotions. Whilst he has acquired an incredible mastery over the mechanics of his physicality that very few have currently achieved; (he can jump, balance, move over, under, around, etc.), it is still the emotional and psychological challenges that hold his interest. Williams says that, "At the outcome of the training you need to have learnt to control yourself, and it's not mastering the body, it's mastering yourself regarding your behaviour, your emotions, that's what's really important. Mastering your fear. Fear is a base that you must know, knowing what you can or can't do" (Belle W., 2010).

For the experienced, 'warrior class' of parkour (my final group of informants), they take their 'edgework' and journeys of self discovery to the extremity of their engagement with fear, needing what Thomas Couetdic describes as "a full 360 degree view" (Couetdic, 2010), that is, with no boundaries - imposed or imagined - including confronting one's own death. The fear, risk, danger, adventure and brutality sought in parkour, even at the extreme, are not negative experiences but ones that bring happiness and fulfilment, even if alarming when in the moment. Traceurs like Thomas are in a very small minority compared to the parkour mainstream for whom, like myself, it is a diversionary leisure activity; a challenging, joyful, interesting, active hobby that, while not consuming and life-threatening, is, nonetheless, a critically self-aware journey of discovery that challenges notions of fear, social controls and increases confidence, empowerment and inclusion by being active and open; of taking control of the body and of exploring and participating. Effort, fear, joy and satisfaction are relative.

Social landscapes, architecture, relations and encounters

The traceurs' desire to move, to reconnect with a child-like open enquiry and play in an adult context, is an attraction to 'difference,' to a changing of the self, and an acceptance of otherness. The 'other' is the form of movement; for example, encounters with built forms become exotic in comparison to the non-traceur; a cultural difference of mobility and spatial perceptions beyond the familiar and accepted social controls of predicted behaviour. The desire for freedom, movement and travel, (albeit travel on a local scale) embody the desire for new knowledge, to "engage with and know the world in its difference" (Fullagar, 57). Using Hegelian theory, Fullagar regards this kind of desire as a "social relation", a view into relations between self and other, and self and world. By embracing the alternative view of movement in the world around the participant they can open up to the idea of 'difference' elsewhere. Parkour encourages affinity with diversity in a world where, for example, the financial analyst trains alongside the unemployed seventeen year old, the young next to the old, the professional and amateur, the muslim and aetheist, male and female, sharing an experience, a utopian cross-cultural parkour 'differential space'.

Although parkour is currently dominated by men, the evolving culture promotes and perceives itself as having a participatory gender inclusive ideology. Belinda Wheaton suggests this is based on a responsibility of self and others (Wheaton, 2010). How issues of race and gender relate to inclusion, exclusion and difference, play out as a lived reality in parkour, has yet to be addressed and is a potential area for future research.

Sport is a key site of maintaining notions of hegemonic masculinity (Wheaton 2000: 434), identified by a combative competitiveness, aggression, toughness and courage (Wheaton 2000:435) whilst promoting homophobic and racist tendencies (Wheaton, 2010). However as with all culture, hegemonic masculinity is a contestable position and not fixed as there are gender politics within masculinity itself (Connell, 37). Whitson suggests that alternative 'new sports' and physical practices (of which parkour would be an example) can offer an alternative or transformative way of expressing masculine and feminine physicalities and identities that are not tied to domination or culture

(Whitson, 368). For example, Wheaton's ethnographic research into the gender politics of windsurfing culture in the UK provides some evidence of this, as she concludes that the recognised boundaries of masculinity are broadened within the culture she researched and participated (2000: 434).

Parkour values balance, agility, creativity and fluidity, skills that are more normally perceived as 'female' and associated with 'sports for girls' such as figure skating or gymnastics (Wheaton, 2010). Parkour also puts a value on aesthetics and has a lack of formal competition. Emotional engagement is not seen as a weakness but a valued commitment to the experience and demonstrates depth in the practice as well as striving for a position of 'harmony' with the environment. These characteristics occur simultaneously alongside a sense of adventure, fear and risk, traits more generally perceived as 'masculine'. Midol and Broyer suggest that within 'new sports' or body cultures, "Young men have been able to access something traditionally defined as feminine. The opposite is also true for young women. They have crossed over the well-marked dividing lines of the so-called sexual differences and challenged the views of the patriarchal society around them" (Midol and Broyer, 208).

Traceurs view parkour as a positive and healthy activity both physically and mentally. It gives them an increased, and more meaningful sense of self and the bond formed between practitioners when training creates strong friendships. The encounters created through parkour must also be considered in terms of the social, as well as, the physical, psychological and spatial.

Parkour culture organises itself around a system sociologist Barry Wellman refers to as 'networked individualism' whereby individuals are linked to one another, not tied or linked **TO** places, they become individuals **IN** places (Wellmann, Quan-Haase, Boase, Chen, Hampton, Isla de Diaz, Miyata 2003). Wellman et al suggest, "This shift facilitates *personal communities* that supply the essentials of community separately to each individual: support, sociability, information, social identities, and a sense of belonging. The person, rather than the household or group, is the primary sense of belonging" (Wellmann et al. 2003).

Wellman's research on how the internet is transforming or enhancing community, led him to suggest that networked individualism in networked societies involves a combination of becoming more individual through personalised and portable connectivity, while retaining a strong desire for community. Although becoming more independent there is still a desire for stronger relationships. Although there is more commercialisation, there is a longing for authenticity (Wellmann, et al, 2003).

Charles Taylor suggests that the search for an 'authentic self' is the result of western culture's modern identity suffering from three types of 'malaise': the lack of meaning, disenchantment (in that there can be no reasoned argument about values), and thirdly, the consequences for political life based on individualism leading to special interest politics as opposed to a greater common good (Taylor 1991: 4-9).

Taylor suggests "the loss of a heroic dimension to life" (Taylor 1991:4); the loss of resonance, depth, or "richness in our human surroundings" (Taylor 1991: 6); passion and the lack of a search for meaning and self-fullfilment leads to inauthentic lives.

Whilst Taylor acknowledges that the narcissistic 'dark side of individualism is "the centering on the self, which both flattens and narrows our lives, makes them poorer in meaning, and less concerned with others or society" (Taylor 1991: 4) is not the case with parkour. Parkour is a means of dialogue, a way of thinking, experiencing and being in connection to the external world and connection to a parkour tradition, lineage and culture of parkour peers and fellow practitioners, regardless of how young the discipline is. Taylor suggests that devaluing connections such as tradition, lineage and culture leads to alienation, disconnection, isolation and a sense that the self is insignificant (Weir, 544).

Like parkour, the web as a medium is unmediated and interactive; there is an openness and mobility, as well as, fluid temporary networks of routes of information and possibilities, allowing for encounters, communication and conflict. Personalisation through individual needs and desires are satisfied in online communications and interactions. The notion of the state is eroded on the web, of citizen verses state. The web challenges the real world ideals of identity and community as much as does the practice of parkour.

The temporary sense of connection, place, being and citizenship felt by the traceur when participating in parkour in the real world, is also experienced online in a form of what Wellman describes as 'e-citizenship'. Within the flux that is the parkour culture, identities, concepts of other and difference are made and remade. This is also mirrored online as parkour websites, teams and groups have come and gone, new ones born out of frustration toward the old.

Whilst parkour is highly individualistic, there is a culture and ideology of community among traceurs through their shared interest in the discipline. Hodkinson refers to this as "cultural substance" where regardless of any internal hierarchies and politics there is still a strong consciousness of group identity (Hodkinson, 136 in Wheaton 2007: 295). Negative representations of parkour identity are contested and discussed at great length, for example, the American Parkour website, chose to highlight the association of a cigarette company with parkour. The founder of APK (American Parkour) Mark Tarook, reacted that, "I really can't believe this. Words cannot express my frustration that someone in the parkour world would sink so low as to accept money from a cigarette company to do a parkour tour. You can rip my fucking lungs out before that day will happen with APK. I suggest we make every coordinated effort possible to show that this is exactly what we DO NOT represent. Money is a powerful thing, we need to fight it with creativity and outspoken outrage" (American Parkour [6]).

Blake Evitt, an American traceur researching the potential for parkour as a tool for social change, said of the Rendezvous 5 parkour event in London, "One of the most striking things about this weekend for me was the spirit of community that seemed to pervade all the events. While the atmosphere had subtle differences from the one that I encountered in France, (one might chalk that up to one being French and the other British), the spirit of cooperation, unity, and pursuit of the common goal of personal development and general fitness were the same. These events really seem to be the glue that binds a lot of these organizations together. The friendships and mutual respect that are forged by two days of blood and sweat seem to create a 'community' aspect to parkour that I think stems from the inclusive and progressive philosophy of the sport. An example of this is the accommodations set up for the event, with all of the "imported" instructors being hosted by Parkour Generations team members, and many of the foreign participants staying with friends that they had made at previous events. Maybe it is the stark contrast with the individualistic aspect of the sport that makes this sense of community so striking, but it gives me a lot of hope for the development of the sport, and the desire for it to outlast the labels of 'fad' or 'fashion' (Evitt [76]).

When there are internal politics and divisions within parkour, these are guided by what sociologist Sarah Thornton refers to as 'subcultural capital' (Thornton, 11) with subculturalists claims of authenticity relating to complex internal politics and hierarchies within the subculture that allocates positions of power and authority within it. Sports sociologist Belinda Wheaton suggests that research on windsurfing, skateboarding and climbing indicate that subcultural capital is based around characteristics such as "attitude, sporting prowess and commitment" (Wheaton 2007: 288). This is also true of parkour.

Public and private space of social encounters

Much of the everyday practice of parkour takes place in urban spaces that are increasingly sites of regulation by state and corporate bodies (Daskalaki, Starab & Imasa 2007), thereby, decreasing the availability of sites for non-commercial unregulated creative practices. Private corporations fear the risk of liability to their organisation over the risk to the parkour body if there is an injury to the participant or an accident to a member of the public caused by the traceur. As more public spaces are held by private corporations they become increasingly regulated and there are fewer opportunities for parkour to occur visibly and legally.

Parkour values educated risk and enquiry, encouraging activity beyond controlled or specified 'play' zones. The practice of parkour promotes the right of self-expression through freedom of movement, valuing play and aesthetics as part of a democratic society. Whilst parkour is in its nascent phase compared to other more established urban activities such as skateboarding or bmx, parkour is, by and large, impossible to regulate against, although attempts and warnings from councils indicate that there is a resistance to it, as well as, attempts to stop it (Murphy [129]).

Regardless of any imposed regulation, once embedded within the culture of parkour, traceurs experience liberation from the social control of their body, their movements and their perceptions of the environment. Mike Atkinson suggests that parkour "destabilizes and disrupts technocapitalist meanings of a city's physical and social landscape for its practitioners" (Atkinson, 169). Traceurs believe that parkour is realistically impossible to regulate against. Strategies such as the application of anti-climb paint have been applied to some areas where councils or residents feel at risk or are threatened by the kind of mobility and physicality that parkour presents.

In the film *Asid, profile of a freerunner,* Asid comments; "They can't stop parkour, even if they have signs up saying 'No don't do parkour, freerunning is prohibited', you cant stop it, how can you stop someone from moving, it's the art of movement, you cant stop someone, it's just silly, we'll always move. They aint going to put anticlimb paint on all the handrails on the street are they? Until they do that they are just out of their minds anyway" (Angel, *Asid, profile of a freerunner* 2006).

The resistance to traceurs in an area just moves the activity to another site with new opportunities for training and routes. With no shortage of environments to play in the traceurs adapt the type of parkour they do. *Quadrupedle* movements cannot be banned anymore than walking, whereas 'jumping activities' possibly could be. The parkour spaces created by traceurs are not fixed, but made and remade, used differently and adapted to suit their training.

A sign put up by the residents of the Latimer Road estate in London, the site of many regular parkour training sessions.

Spaces whether public or privately regulated where activities such as parkour take place are themselves not a neutral background but a contributing factor in shaping the social relations and identities that are produced and consumed within them (Soja, 1989). Spaces cannot be viewed separately from the cultural aspects of the landscape and there is a role in which identity, memory and historical moments all play a part (Dourish, 2006).

In contrast to Foucault's idea of people being controlled by the architectural elements surrounding them, architects reflecting upon the notion of "architectural determinism", take a different view suggesting much less-rigidly defined goals and a considerably less totalising influence. They explain: "We design to reflect, as well as to create, a pattern of behaviour" (Hillier, Bill & Burdett, Richard & Peponis, John & Penn, Alan, 233). Hillier, et al, questioned what the social implications are of a spatial patterning or determinism, and the social and psychological importance of encounters that are created or not. They seem to believe that architecture implies a much more relativised experience of space, one that is considerably more open to interpretation than Foucault's theory would imply.

Whilst recognising the role of architecture as less totalising than as presented by Foucault, Hillier, et al acknowledge that the spatial layout of urban areas can "create - or eliminate – 'life' in the sense that it determines a field of potential encounter and co-presence" (Hillier et al, 235) and that these elements are dictated by the product of architectural design. Their research concluded that the modern spatial transformations that have occurred in cities have produced and resulted in "the under-use, non-use and abuse of space – the 'urban desert effect' " (Hillier et al, 248). Whilst this differs from Foucault's dividing practise as a political tool of power, Hiller, et al's, research confirms some of the experiences I witnessed in my research. Traceurs have taken advantage of under-used urban spaces and their presence temporarily socially re-energises areas previously not used, particularly at night, serving to create new encounters both socially with residents, passersby, and fellow traceurs as well as architectural tactile encounters with walls, rails and other built forms.

Parkour is a direct response to this cultural emptiness, creating what Hillier, et al, refer to as a "virtual community", (Hillier, et al., 248) a "group awareness in a collectivity". Traceurs are members of a parkour community because of their shared spatial awareness and actions creating new landscapes of bodies. Like Hillier, et al's, 'virtual community' parkour as an urban culture or community constructs a "space of anti-structure rather than structure".

Traceurs during a warm down session after a parkour class taking place outside some garages near Latimer Road tube station, London.

The socio-economic factors of decreased availability for public areas for play and creative practices has played a role in the popularity and appeal of parkour in inner city areas in the UK, responding to a cultural emptiness.

Whilst the majority of parkour occurs in public spaces, there are conflicting perceptions of public space and the activities of who defines it: what is 'appropriate' or 'inappropriate' use, of 'citizen/non-citizen,' insider/outsider; the 'other' are often defined by those in positions of power who are able to make such claims, i.e. the dominant discourse of those who defined the initial intensions of the use of the space will state what are or are not normative practices.

Who can define public space faced with the competing values of different users, the pedestrian, the traceur, the cyclist, the skateboarder, and the consumer? Nathaniel Bavinton suggests that public spaces exclude many creative and spontaneous ways of engaging with the urban environment due to the material-spatially embedded power relations corresponding to the arrangement and order of fences, walls, stairs, ramps and railings. This is for the purpose of controlling flows of movement and to promote "conformity to ideological categories and concepts of public order and 'normal' behaviour" (Bavinton, 396).

England and Simon suggest that it is the fear and the supposed threatening nature of 'Other' that excludes difference from public space (England & Simon, 203). Fear discourses rely on dominant relations of power and can be used as a political tool for particular purposes. England and Simon believe this is to "define and maintain the shifting boundaries between deviance and belonging, order and disorder that are instrumental to the ways in which cities are lived and built" (England & Simon, 204).

Jeremy Nmeth writes that there is a legacy of public control "of groups deemed inappropriate, or 'out of place' in public space", (Nmeth, 2006) and that officials have their own view of public space which can be viewed as 'adult space' citing the example of the 2000 Municipal Code banning skateboarding in 'Love City' a world famous 'mecca of street skateboarding' adjacent to City Hall in Philadelphia. The Director of Planning at the time of its conception, Edmund Bacon, at the age of 95 supported the skateboarding community in fighting the Mayor's ban on skateboarding in the park, but Nmeth concluded that the skateboarders ban and exclusion from the area " is detrimental to processes of social learning and identity formation" (Nmeth, 2006).

Practices such as parkour, skateboarding and also more-collective group or shared experiences, such as the Critical Mass monthly bicycle rides, all "invert the function of a space while at the same time producing a new relationship to that space – even if the experience is temporary" (Furness, 304). The common themes are to break with the function and ideology of the environment. Furness suggests that through such experiences, people have the ability to realise that "materiality and culture are not static", and this effect can be largely influential in motivating people for political action, as well as a way in which to see beyond the confines of the 'Society of the Spectacle' (Furness, 305, Debord, 1983). Guy Debord described this as the 'capacity to revolutionise your own life' (Debord, 1957: 25). The motivation for Debord to encourage this kind of activity was political whereas the individual revolution for the traceurs is, firstly, one for their own well-being, mobility and identity; they are not always consciously aware of 'breaking free' of social constraints.

Traceurs, like the participants within the Critical Mass bicycle movement, as Furness explains, "call attention to the ideological norms that dictate both the prescribed function of the environment and the manner in which such environments are traversed" (Furness, 302).

The 'individual revolutions' and perceptional shifts experienced in parkour are constant. The impact has had positive effects for many who otherwise claim they would have followed a path of anti-social and destructive behaviour (Shelton [170]).

Productive play / ludic relations to space

Although there is the creation of an increased sense of self through parkour's 'liberational intent', traceurs do not necessarily see a difference or separation between their ordinary life spaces and the playful physical and creative spaces where parkour occurs, due to their open and creative perceptions of spaces and the possibilities they hold. If play is something that is supposed to happen outside of 'ordinary' life, (Huizinga, 1970) then what happens when play takes a more time-consuming role? De Souza and Sutko state that play is essentially part of all life, and belongs to the ' everyday spaces of ordinary life' rather than segregating compartments for 'ordinary' or 'play' (De Souza & Sutko, 448). When practising parkour, traceurs can engage with play at many occasions and bring play into acts of the everyday. The basic definition of parkour commonly given is 'to find a route from point A to point B', moving in a fast and efficient way. This can be a game and include elements of play, incorporated into the fabric of everyday life. Playfulness can be the result of social interactions formed through shared training experiences as well as the training itself.

In Pat Kane's book, *The Play Ethic*, he states that the crucial question relating to 'healthy play' - a term that parkour would easily suit - is "Where and when does it happen" (Kane, 44)? The benefits of ongoing play into adulthood has been noted by psychologists such as Csikszentmihalyi and Brian Sutton-Smith. Marano stated that "The opposite of play isn't work. It's depression" (Marano, 36-42). Kane defines play as "to engage oneself" (Kane, 4) and that it is the "richness and variety of our human games which make for a healthy and vibrant society" (Kane, 7) valuing play as a keyword equal to 'productivity', 'creativity', and 'labour'. It is this aspect of play and the ongoing processes of inquiry and experimentation that benefit the traceur.

The act of parkour involves the interaction with the environment, obstacles becoming the 'toy' or 'transitional object' as described by D.W. Winnicott, played with by the traceurs to aid the development and improvement of the relationship with the physical world. The wall, the railing, the ledge, the bench, are transitional toy objects of parkour. Kane describes the play moment as beginning "in a tension between experiment and safety- the need to fully test out all the possibilities of human beings" (Kane, 21). Traceurs operate within this play ethic, also conforming to Brian Sutton-Smith's Seven Rhetorics of Play.

The Modern Rhetorics:

- Play as progress (play in education, as healthy development).

- Play as imagination (play as art, as scientific hypothesis, as culture).

- Play as selfhood (play as freedom, voluntarism, personal happiness-the expression of individuality).

The Ancient Rhetorics:

- Play as power (the contest of players – in sport, markets, law, war, even philosophy).

- Play as identity (the play as the carnival, the binding rituals of community).

- Play as fate and chaos (the play of chance – gambling, risk, the cosmos at play).

The seventh rhetoric - "play as 'frivolity' (laughter, subversion, inversion and tomfoolery") is a mix of ancient and modern, a strategy of, "defence against all attempts at social authority and power" (Kane, 15).

Whilst traceurs know their actions to be at times playful, parkour is not always viewed as such. For example, a group of traceurs training together can be playful but maybe seen as alarmist or threatening to local residents, for example, if someone wants to pass by and there are people in the way vaulting railings. In so much as the traceurs 'read' their environment, they too are also 'read' by the public, being visible within the public domain. Their non-conformity is not always welcome, a desire for an on-going process of inquiry is not necessarily shared. The nature of their playful inquiry is not always obvious to an 'external' observer. One negative point-of-view presented in the press was that it is 'a method of training cat burglars of the future', and expressed how the mobility that parkour provides could be used for illicit activities. Anthony Minghella's 2006 film, Breaking and Entering featured a young traceur who was hired to break into architectural firms. Similar discussions have been used against the teaching and support of martial arts; are people being trained to fight or to defend themselves? Most practitioners of both parkour and martial arts will counter this argument with a view that it is a transformative practice and the increase they experience in gaining discipline, self- esteem and confidence would deter any will they had for any such negative actions.

Julie Angel

Stephane Vigroux and Sebastien Goudot precision jump the walls of a subway in Central London during the filming of the film City Gents, (Angel, 2007) as pedestrians walk by underneath, some noticing, some not. What may seem spontaneous, from the bystanders perspective, is not. To the general public, the traceurs actions can be viewed as part-play, performative, part-protest, part-celebration, but rarely, as the disciplined and highly-focussed past-time experienced by my research group.

Parkour's visibility in public spaces is ever increasing on an international level, yet its purpose function and value are yet to be established. The pressure brought to bear on many urban-based activities are related to the age of the participant, adults as well as young people are climbing, jumping, running, skateboarding, and cycling, but all outside to some degree of what is currently accepted as normal behaviour for anyone other than a child. For a child to explore or climb onto a wall is not questioned, accepting this as healthy curiosity and an extension and exploration of their physical capabilities, yet to view an adult or young person even who is not a 'child' explore and climb; play with their capacity for balance or strength especially in a city, is not valued or considered 'normal' practice. It is regarded as suspicious or inappropriate for an adult to be involved in child's play, especially when practiced in areas not specified for such activities. The lack of regulation situates parkour in a liminal space, entering the mainstream on sanctioned occasions, such as, an endorsed event, televised entertainment or display of performances, but when practiced of the traceurs freewill it is perceived differently sometimes.

A parkour performance in Trafalgar Square by Urban Freeflow in 2006 as part of celebrations commemorating Lord Nelson.

"If play is a preparation for maturity (Groos, 1901), then what are the mature doing when they play? Are they preparing for death? Perhaps they are not preparing for anything" (Sutton-Smith, 47 in Van Leeuwen & Westwood 2008).

Ivan Chtcheglov's essay, *Formulary for a New Urbanism* discusses the "banalization" and need for "constructing situations" and "the need to play with architecture, time and space...". Chtecheglov was a founding member of the Situationist International and the ideas of a move away from the banal to creating moments and encounters that resonate with many of the urban based body cultures (Chtcheglov [47]).

There are many different and conflicting views on the value and use of play; the Dutch historian and cultural theorist Johan Huizinga defined play in his seminal work '*Homo Ludens*' as "a voluntary activity or occupation executed within certain fixed limits of time and place, according to rules freely accepted but absolutely binding, having its aim in itself and accompanied by a feeling of tension, joy, and consciousness that is different from ordinary life" (Huizinga, 28).

French philosopher and writer, Roger Caillois, built on Huizinga's work in *Man, Play and Games* but had a more negative viewpoint stating that, "A characteristic of play, in fact, is that it creates no wealth or goods, thus differing from work or art [...] Nothing has been harvested or manufactured, no masterpiece has been created, no capital has accrued. Play is an occasion of pure waste: waste of time, energy, ingenuity, skill, and often of money..." (Caillois, 5 – 6).

Some may view the activity of parkour as a non-productive labour whereas the traceurs believe they work hard and receive nothing materially in return. As discussed in Chapter 1, the traceur's production is one of a meaningful authentic identity, a masterpiece of the self, of encounters and movements, a living labour operating within an architecture of freewill and mobility, creating new spaces and temporary spheres of liberation and new visions of imaginative opportunities. All of this improves the traceurs relationship with the physical world.

Parkour as a form of adult child's play invites ludic engagement with the environment and as a form of play, like other similar activities, it has been challenged by many as an activity lacking purpose for the well being of a community. "The connection of play to morally rejected idleness has given it, in the context of adulthood, a rather dubious reputation which sports and recreation sciences and industries try to reverse by pointing out the health and well-being benefits" (Van Leeuwen & Westwood 2008: 160).

Van Leeuwen and Westwood's call for more research into play give the example of the psychoanalytical approach of Winnicott (Van Leeuwen & Westwood, 154) in one that recognises play as a universal behaviour type, "having significance for health and wellbeing", whilst research into adult play has been left to the realms of mainly therapeutic contexts (Van Leeuwen & Westwood, 153).

Winnicott "describes play as taking place in a transitional space between the inner and outer reality which enables creative action". van Leeuwen and Westwood believe that this creates a transitional reality where attributes of the imagination meet attributes of objective reality where "one can experiment with different ways of relating to the external world" (Van Leeuwen & Westwood, 154).

Parkour exists within such a transitional space and blurs and extends the realms of physical possibilities whilst enabling new relationships with the external physical world. This is evident by the admission that some of the originators were inspired by the actions of animated 'superheroes' (Angel, What is parkour, 2008). Observers and commentators also see this 'articulated' fantasy; of "freeing the body from the bounds of the earth, of super-heroes, of Hermes, of flight" (Grayson, 2008).

Traceurs create their own transitional reality, temporarily becoming superheroes of their own realms, masters of movement, possessing greater strength and agility than other pedestrians through their physicality and their choices of locations for play and exploration, often choosing to move and seek out actions above the ordered movement below. They aim to improve on their previous abilities. They are on top of a wall not beside it; they balance on railings rather than going around them; they leave the walkway for more exhilarating routes setting themselves challenges and goals of repetitions and self-competition as their competence and confidence increases.

Climbing walls, gymnastics and athletic clubs provide similar activities but they do not allow for the activity to occur visibly in public space and maintains a restricted and regulated way in which it is acted out, detracting from the freedom felt to go of your own free will and time. De Souza e Silva and Sutko claim that "Play is essentially part of (all) life, that is, that playful activities belong to our everyday spaces of ordinary life." (De Souza e Silva & Sutko, 448).

Traceurs, like hybrid reality game play players "gain a different perspective" on urban spaces (De Souza e Silva & Sutko, 450). **The change in perception is an open-ended process.** "A change in the conceptualization of space, overlaying a game map on it, can change the perception and experience of that space" (De Souza e Silva & Sutko, 459).

The difference with parkour is that it is itself a 'game map' that provides new perceptions and experiences of the terrain. The parkour vision is the map, the gestalt landscape, whereas hybrid reality game players are given a map to overlay. Finding new visions of the environment and opportunities for movement is an ongoing game for traceurs then the play continues as the movement and effort of the physicality take over.

Play and games in relation to sport

In his writings on body culture Eichberg states, "In sport, play and games are considered educational entertainment for children and are used as warm-up, i.e. as marginal in relation to the central process of achievement. Play in relation to sport is experimentation, role play and a challenge to one's own identity, revolt, team-building, flirtation, contest and competitive engagement, the processing of fear and anxiety, background for a good laugh and so on. If play were to be taken seriously, a new approach would be required – play and games as experimentarium" (Eichberg 2009b: 307).

As stated, parkour can be a form of autotelic play, and as Allen Guttmann concludes in *Sports: The First Five Millennia,* out of organised play (games) comes competitive games (contests) that can result in physical contests (sports). He believes there are many different definitions of what constitutes an activity being a sport but concludes that "sports can be defined as *autotelic physical contests*" (Guttmann 2004: 2). He suggests that modern sport can be defined into seven interrelated formal-structural characteristics although there are always exceptions to these categories:

1. Secularism - premodern sports were sometimes connected to a religious event or site.

2. Equality – premodern sports often excluded people based on social status or ability.

3. Specialisation – modern team sports have specialised roles and playing positions, premodern did not.

4. Bureaucratisation – pre-modern sports did not have the administrative structures that modern ones do. They usually occurred under the order of local or religious authorities.

5. Rationalisation – premodern sports had very low levels of instrumental rationality compared to modern sports, for example, modern sports incorporate standardisation of objects (hurdles etc) in purpose built facilities.

6. Quantification – premodern sports had no systematic quantification of measurements or points.

7. Obsession with Records – premodern had none (Guttmann 2004: 4- 6).

Although parkour has the elements of equality and secularism it clearly lacks the rationalising, quantifying and bureaucratic nature of most 'modern sports'. According to Guttmann's categories, parkour is a 'pre-modern sport' born out of modern times that chooses the environment and self to be a co-player in the activity. Parkour occurs outside, with no acknowledgement of any designation of spaces that are set aside for sport or play.

Eichberg writes that, "Human movement can be seen as something which produces something. In modern sports, these are results and records. Go-for-it sports but also modern gymnastics and physical education are in a special way built around this It. By this reification, sport has differentiated itself from older games and play" (Eichberg 2009: 311).

In his writings on body culture and the change in where sporting activities occur, the historical shift from the middle ages onwards from the outside 'natural' environment to separate indoor locations, Eichberg comments that, "The physical culture of industrial society did not, therefore, only produce exercises of the body. It also necessitated the establishment of a separate environment in which to pursue them. Physical culture and building acted upon each other. This had not always been the case, nor was it by any means a matter of course that it happened" (Eichberg 1986: 100). As George Sage writes in the *Handbook of Sports Studies* "Prior to the Industrialised Revolution there was little in the way of organised sporting practices" (Sage, 262).

Vertinsky and McKay concur, that in a Foucauldian sense, the indoor gymnasium was, "structurally related to and arose simultaneously with the prison, the asylum and the school house in the context of a spatial disciplining and functionalisation of social life." (Vertinsky & McKay, 3). The gymnasium was a disciplining practice according to Foucault's discussion on biopolitical power and the concept of the body as a machine, "its disciplining, the optimisation of its capabilities, the extortion of its forces, the parallel increase of its usefulness and its docility, its integration into systems of efficient and economic controls, all this was ensured by the procedures of power that characterised the disciplines: an anatomo-politics of the human body" (Foucault 1978: 139).

Eichberg suggests that there are certain characteristics of achievement sports that reflect parts of the societies where they are dominant, for example, forms of competition and fighting he suggests lead to aggression that is often compared to the capitalist principle of competition. The production of results and "subordinating the joy of human movement in itself to this goal" (Eichberg 1998: 102) is compared to the focus on production growth in industrialist capitalist and state monopolist societies. The quantification of results and corresponding quantification of educational achievements, reduces the complexity of human achievement and human life. This sanctions and creates hierarchies, elitism and an artificial inequality instead of democratic solidarity. The spatial division of areas for sport and standardisation of sport contributes to a separation of sporting and non-sporting activities and separations based on gender, age and ability. The fragmentation of time and separation of times for work and leisure is compared with "advancing industrial exploitation and hindering human autonomy and the wholeness of life" (Eichberg 1998: 102). The discrimination against women and subjugation of women to dominant male patterns of sport parallels "the male patterns of industrial capitalist (and state monopolistic) production (Eichberg 1998: 102).

Eichberg argues that these patterns have been questioned by younger generations of Western metropoles, stating "Nations and peoples want to take their everyday life, including sport, into their own hands. They are experiencing the conflict between identity and alienation in body culture as well as in daily life." (1998: 103) He states there are a growing number of alternatives with a revival of indigenous folk games and sports, that are developed, "in the context of social and national criticism of international neo-colonial dominance in sports as tied up with the excesses of industrialist capitalism" (Eichberg 1998: 103). "The configurations of Western sports correspond to the patterns of Western industrialist capitalist societies (as well as those of the Eastern European state economic systems that prevailed until recently) (Eichberg 1998: 101).

Eichberg suggests that body culture has always changed throughout history and in the future there will be alternative areas of body cultures rooted in alternative concepts to everyday and bodily practices (Eichberg 1998: 101-105). He sites these alternatives as:

Cultural games - These will be reminiscent of the old carnival in the European Middle Ages, with "bodily demonstrations of the autonomy and self-liberation of the masses" (Eichberg 1998: 105).

The open-air movement - This indicates a political and social relation to nature in opposition to industrial annihilation (Eichberg 1998: 104).

Expressive activities - These types of activities focus on movement and on the body itself as opposed to the result produced. They also allow for more female participation. They promote creativity as opposed to a standardised norm (Eichberg 1998: 105).

Meditative exercises - These allow for a spirituality of sporting practice that connects body and soul, in contrast to a separation which Eichberg states is a very specific Western condition. Meditative exercises are not fixated with results and quantification. Eichberg states that this hinders the inner experience of the body (Eichberg 1998: 105).

Parkour, like many other spatial physical arts or body cultures, returns its participants to an older sense of the understandings of play and games. Whereas the modern sporting body is disciplined, measured, timed, ordered and adheres to performance, the parkour sporting body is playful, ambiguous, expressive and autonomous, yet promotes a discipline of strengthening mental resolve.

Parkour as practised by my research group is a high achievement activity; others (myself included) practise parkour in a way that could be more easily defined as an active leisure past time. For my informants and the founders, there is a brutality as well as disciplined artistry to the practice. When practised at their level it is a warrior-type culture as acknowledged by the founders themselves. They bleed, bruise, cry and set challenges of hardships for themselves to overcome physically and mentally, for example, the '300' challenge' and '1000 muscle-ups in 24 hours' (Parkour Generations [138]).

In *Quest for Excitement: Sport and Leisure in the Civilizing Process* by Norbert Elias and Eric Dunning, Elias, a German sociologist, claims that "modern sport" has a tendency to limit the dangers, aggression and brutality of the "sport". By making culture routine and rationalised, for example, bare-fist boxing introduced gloves, (Elias & Dunning, 21) these gloves then became padded, and boxers were put into ranks to facilitate a greater sense of fairness in their chances. This was part of a pattern of civilising social changes to changes of greater self-control (Elias & Dunning, 46).

Parkour is a return to a more brutal era of sporting practice, reflecting it's origins out of times of hardship (see Chapter 1). Traceurs choose to take their own abilities to an extreme level of challenge and experimentation, maintaining Couetdic's '360 degrees' of limitations. The aim is not to 'win' over the environment, the challenge, or another participant, but it is their own personal experience of enduring it, even if experienced collectively. The traceur experiences strength, weakness, pain and pleasure in the moment, an encounter and experience of the act of parkour in exploration of their limitations and identity.

Images from the day of training in Sarcelles by members of Parkour
Generations and Majestic Force demonstrate a range of emotions
experienced throughout the day; effort, exhaustion, focus, frustration,
joy and shared moments with friends.

If there are modern and pre-modern sports, defined by the
rationalising, specialising, and quantification of games and sports,
Guttmann acknowledges that there are also 'postmodern sports'
that involve more spontaneity and playfulness, and are less
rationalised. Ehrenburg referrs to these kinds of activities as 'les
sports californiens' (Guttmann 2000: 256) Wheaton suggests that
these types of activities are known by various terms such as,
"'extreme', 'alternative', 'lifestyle', 'whiz', 'action sports', 'panic sport',
'postmodern', and 'new sports'" (Wheaton 2004: 2). Parkour would
fit into the term defined by Wheaton as, 'lifestyle sport'. She uses
this to discuss activities such as surfing, windsurfing, skateboarding,

climbing, snowboarding and kitesurfing, based on the concept that there is a way of life associated with the practice and that the term, "reflects both the characteristics of these activities, and their wider socio-cultural significance" (Wheaton 2004: 4).

Conclusions

Parkour is a very specific spatial, creative, social, physical and psychological process and activity. There are certain elements that contribute to a healthy active autonomous parkour body. The socially-controlled body is challenged and changed by parkour to become autonomous. The autonomy is achieved through a re-perception of the landscape and a process of training and movement that involves a hyper-tactile engagement and dialogue with the environment. This re-connects the body and sense of self to the external physical world by engaging positively with fear and anxiety to achieve a greater sense of self and being. The activity occurs in public space and as such promotes inclusion, confidence and identity construction by revealing that culture and identity are not static; there are individual revolutions through an open ended process. As Dan Edwardes says, parkour is "a daily practise of self-knowledge" (Edwardes 2010). Williams Belle believes that, "As a person you have more confidence because you understand that it all comes from within you, you have a choice to see things in a certain way" (Belle W., 2010).

The disciplined approach of the accuracy and focussed intentions of the physicality of parkour keeps the traceur safe during the active engagement and confrontation with fear, engaging with informed levels of voluntary, self-imposed - rather than state set - levels of risk. The positive dialogue and confrontation of fear in parkour produces increased levels of confidence that then feedback into the experimentation of play and possibilities in parkour. Stephane Vigroux commented at Rendezvous 4 that parkour "is a method of training for me to get more confidence in my life, to face my fears and to understand more about myself basically" (Angel, *Parkour Generations: Rendezvous 4 Q&A part1* 2009).

In parkour, environments are redefined as open-ended landscapes of innumerable opportunities, providing feelings of strength and freedom, unbounded by the physicality of railings, walls, ledges, and structures that we are so familiar with and collectively adhere to through their inferred order and logic. In parkour, the motivation for negotiating and manipulating the environment from its functional intention, is to use it for the purpose and interest of traceurs in their development of themselves and their parkour, rather than operating within the systems of order, trajectories and discipline imposed by the state and corporate bodies which are, arguably, responsible for the ordering of architectural productions.

Parkour creates an active body and the spaces in which parkour occurs become a place for being, living and experiencing the environment. Parkour can create new 'social landscapes' (Low & Lawrence-Zúñiga, 216) diminishing levels of marginality, and promoting inclusion. Parkour provides connections that can lead to a more authentic and meaningful identity. Sites of parkour are where differences are shared and accepted; the space is turned into a place of parkour, a site of new meaning and new opportunities for sociality and identity, as well as the physical appropriation of the space. Thomas Couetdic comments that, "Originally I started parkour because I didn't have any self-confidence and I saw these guys training and I thought to do what they do they must have incredible confidence and complete control over themselves so I want to learn that. I didn't know if I could achieve that but at least I wanted to try my best and see if I could do something. (Angel, Parkour Generations: Rendezvous 4 Q&A part1, 2009)

The emotional attachments to sites created from parkour cultivate a sense of belonging and shared ownership. Traceur, Anne-Therese Marais explains, "Every time I choose a place to train, I make it mine for the time of my training. I choose my path, I choose my training. It is very personal" (Marais, 35). This feeling is emphasised more in urban spaces where new spatial and cultural identities are formed and there are more visible examples of dividing practices. Sites have been used (not just passed through), creating interactions with the physicality of the surroundings, no longer a separation of environment and body, there are social encounters and identity formation from traceurs interacting with one another.

The act of parkour becomes embedded in their daily lives and traceurs no longer feel excluded socially, or spatially, by re-gaining control over their mobility.

Parkour incorporates creative play, using 'toys' or transitional objects found in the surrounding landscapes of the participant, such as walls, rails, rocks and trees. This results in a re-perception of the self and the environment as ideas for movements and challenges are realised and experienced.

Parkour refuses to fit into rigid boundaries exact frameworks or categories, instead, it chooses to apply subtle or temporary resistance to any strategies or dominant forces not in alignment with the needs and desires of traceurs. Parkour's resistance is in gaining control and mobility over one's own behaviour, rather than behaving as a subject to the state. Traceurs' needs are of mobility, expression, play, and exploration. Parkour encourages autonomy, the individual and citizenship. This is achieved through open-ended engagements, contact and communication with the environment and others who share the practice, encouraging a more participatory sense of belonging. Traceur's self-determining actions and behaviour involve fluid, individual and transcient networks. When presented with un-mediated and non-deterministic choices, traceurs experience more-embedded participatory experiences and expressions of the self.

Currently, modern achievement sports do not allow for the heterogeneous forms of movement culture that exist. As an older form of play and physical contest, parkour has competitive elements but is not a competition sport. Instead there is an emphasis on experimentation and encounters that challenge one's own identity. Parkour rejects bureaucracy, standardisation and a rationalisation of the practice, instead it focusses on autonomy and expression, with mindful intentions. "Practices of sport in both their diversity and their historical change, thus, clarify inner contradictions inside social life more generally" (Eichberg, 2009b: 89).

Parkour is a transformative practice and 'lifestyle' that resists and minimises dominant modes of subjectivation and power relations through its liberational intent and code of individual ethics which lead to a more authentic sense of self. Traceurs constantly reflect and problemitise their own physical and emotional behaviour that they test, challenge and engage with every time they train. The effect of this is a move away from fixed notions of identity and culture, as well as a realisation of their own limitations and ability. This results in parkour acting as a 'practice of freedom' and art through which one conducts an authentic everyday life.

Julie Angel

Chapter 4

The Parkour Paradox, co-option for spectacle and institutionalisation.

As well as parkour being a physical, creative, social and spatial practice, it is also part of a system of contradictions. Parkour as a performance spectacle has been harnessed by corporatism through marketing and promotional campaigns (Nokia, Yota, Panasonic, Canon, KSwiss); used for entertainment purposes in feature films and video games (*Yamakasi, District 13, Casino Royale, Prince of Persia, Mirror's Edge, Brink*); and regulated and institutionalised as a sport (ParkourUK [148]). These have produced the parkour 'performer' and 'athlete'; the bi-products of parkour's move from an alternative practice to mainstream visibility.

However, as Wheaton says, the problem is that "The dominant and alternative culture has become indistinguishable" (Wheaton 2007: 289). Catherine Palmer reports that there has been an increased commodification of activities or sports labelled as 'extreme', 'alternative', 'lifestyle', or 'adventure sports'. This has involved the "shifting subjectivity of risk" and the "incorporation of an iconography of risk-taking behaviour into a whole range of popular cultural products." She acknowledges that activities within the above mentioned genres are now part of the mainstream landscape of popular culture (Palmer, 55).

Stephane Vigroux executes a running precision for the film *City Gents*, promoting Il Ponte bags.

Francois 'Forrest' Mahop teaching parkour at St. Augustine's school, London, as documented in the film *Jump Westminster*.

Sport and body cultures are never separate from society and parkour culture exists within the dominant economic and social relations of power in society. The cultural logic and ethical conduct (as discussed in Chapter 3) of parkour is produced by its own internal power relations and subcultural capital set by its internal hierarchies. The co-option of parkour for spectacle and sporting practices, exposes the tensions between internal parkour hierarchies, as well as, with and against external relations of power.

Although traceurs have been complicit in allowing parkour's co-option and appropriation for commercial spectacle or sportification, it is important to acknowledge that parkour has its own internal history of appropriation, originating from when David Belle chose to take his friend's (Hubert Kounde) advice and change the c to a k, appropriating the word 'parcours'. Whilst not co-opted in the same way as for commercial spectacle or sportification, this, none-the-less, demonstrates the autonomous and fluid nature of parkour and the willingness of traceurs to change and position it in a number of ways.

In 2003, on the set of the Channel 4 television documentary *Jump London*, Sébastien Foucan's then manager, Guillaume Pelletier, believed that parkour was a difficult term for an English audience so invented the term 'freerunning'. He presented it as a direct translation, using the terms 'parkour' and 'freerunning' interchangeably. After a few years Foucan fully appropriated this term to distinguish himself and his approach separately from David Belle's parkour (even though at times he also refers to parkour). A large proportion of the parkour mainstream has since appropriated the term and now regard 'freerunning' as a more-acrobatic and aesthetically-motivated version of parkour, enabling its use for more performative elements such as 'freerunning' competitions. Foucan however does not agree with this, it is not his understanding of freerunning and he is against competition; "It is not about being beautiful, it is about feeling and being connected" (Foucan, www.foucan.com). Wheaton describes the parkour verses freerunning debate as a "classic sub-cultural conundrum" (Wheaton, 2010) with various claims of authenticity on both sides, as different groups have different histories and therefore different values as to how they see their practice and the values they attach to it.

Parkour as a performance spectacle

The pioneering practitioners originally performed and demonstrated the sometimes incredible and impressive end results of their training, primarily, to communicate, share, inspire, and demonstrate to an audience beyond their local neighbourhoods of Lysse, Évry and Sarcelles, what they had created and what was possible. The physical achievements that have been accomplished to date in parkour have extended the perception of what is humanly possible for the body to achieve, and are worthy of celebration and visibility.

The spectacular actions contained within 'performed' parkour images, normally take place within the comfort zone of the traceur's skills when performed by experienced traceurs, even if this is perceived as 'extreme' or 'incredible' by a mainstream non-parkour audience. Rarely will experienced traceurs be motivated to take new or great risks to create a 'performance' aesthetic. In a similar parallel with climbing, the motivations for the activities do not come from a desire to create new aesthetics, but ones to improve self-esteem or a sense of self (Puchan, 172). As climber Joe Simpson explains, "If we did it for aesthetics, why on earth choose the hardest routes in the most difficult season? Why not just climb those routes that are well with in your ability rather than a struggle up horror stories that leave you unsure of the likely outcome from the very first step" (Puchan, 172)?

During a commercial shoot for Ecko clothing in District 13, Paris, Stephane Vigroux left the production group for 20 minutes at lunchtime upon the arrival of his good friend 'Kazuma'. He later showed me a jump that he did whilst the production crew including myself remained at lunch. It was exceptionally more difficult and spectacular than anything Stephane had agreed to do for the purposes of advertising clothing for the Ecko brand. For traceurs to achieve what they do, or break a new jump, it is important for them to 'feel' the movement and be able to enter the flow state. This might be in alignment with a commercial production's schedule, or it may not, depending on the conditions and pressures at the time.

Within and outside of the parkour community there are those who are eager to promote the parkour performance aesthetic. Their aim is for parkour's dominant meaning to be one of spectacular achievements, as opposed to a physical and mental approach to training the body. This is for the lure of material reward and 'celebrity'. To promote the parkour performance aesthetic, a video culture of showreels has been encouraged, and sponsored competition formats created; presenting parkour and/or freerunning as 'media friendly' (World Freerun Ents. [206], World Freerunning & Parkour Federation [208], Redbull Art of Motion [159], 3RUN SHOWREEL 2010 [2], Storm Freerun Volume1 [175]).

The competition events and showreels revel in a mediatised performance aesthetic, and are re-enforced by video recommendations and 'sponsorship' for participating practitioners (Urban Freeflow [186]) within parkour's own online 'subcultural media'. Thornton suggests that subcultural media is a vital network in defining and disseminating cultural knowledge that creates the symbols and meanings of subcultural capital to members of their communities (Thornton, 14).

Neil Blaine suggests some new sports or elements within them (as is the case with parkour), are content to become a 'mediatised' new sport, and from the start they will be viewed as a media sport (Blaine, 231). This occurs as interactions with the media have the ability to remake the substance of that culture (Blaine, 227). The growing mediatisation fits in with Blaine's suggestion of the post 1973 neoliberal economic model of:

"More culture, more of which is

Media culture, which helps to lead to

New growths of aesthetic awareness and activity and sensation-seeking, all of which lead to

More consumption" (Blaine, 230).

The media interactions with parkour have evolved around the spectacle of achievement and the excitement and awe created by images of the body suspended in space. The parkour performance spectacle relies on jumps and moves at height, situating the soft body freely in space against the solidity of an urban landscape. The substance of parkour becomes a single moment; once is all that is needed, in contrast to the 'once is never' philosophy of the approach to the training or the perfection of a combination of movements, (as discussed in Chapter 2) that leads to an enduring wellbeing and ability to continue to train for the participants, as exemplified by the founders discussed in Chapter 1. The substance of the mediatised parkour culture is about what happens in the air rather than the dialogue, relationship, and contact with the environment. The spectacle of a failed attempt or an injury occurring, can be just as spectacular as the commodifying of the body in space. There is little concern for the landing or safe execution of a move, the experience of the individual. Gymnastic backflips, spins, twists and even breakdancing moves are incorporated into 'the show' for competition, for example, Franck 'Cali' Nelle's performance in the Barclaycard World Freerun Championships 2008 (Nelle [128]).

Wheaton comments that there is a crossover that can occur at the elite level of 'lifestyle sports' where the lifestylers become part of the traditional sports landscape – such as of snowboarding in the Winter Olympics and the X Games - providing a competitive spectacle-based performance of many board sports such as skateboarding. However, as Palmer suggests, the increased commercialization of 'lifestyle sports', fails to acknowledge to those outside of the sports, that the motivations the 'true aficionados' have for such potentially fatal activities are not based in fun or relaxation, but, "because they provide a means of penetrating to realities not encountered in daily life." She continues, "It is these personally inflected motivations that are often overlooked in the increasing commercialization of risk taking" (Palmer, 67).

Within parkour culture it is only the elite or experienced traceurs who can safely 'perform' spectacle-based parkour. This was clearly demonstrated during the first *Barclaycard World Freerunning Championship* in 2008 where ill-prepared and inexperienced traceurs were willing to participate on offer of Barclaycard covering their travel expenses and accommodation in London. The (all) male young traceurs were excited to have the opportunity to meet and connect with other practitioners. However, many became injured during their 'performance' due to their inexperience of parkour in a context that differed from their normal training conditions. Another reason was their lack of physical fitness. This was evident in their performances as they could not maintain the pace and rhythm of their performances, becoming out-of-breath and visibly tired when required to do parkour constantly for two minutes without a break.

The event consisted of heavy, poorly executed landings, a head injury, knee and ankle injuries and many more. The parkour community reacted very negatively to this indoor event to the extent that comments were disabled from the YouTube channel showing the original highlights video and it has since been removed. The video was edited by the event's production company and as such there was little awareness of how the content would be read by the parkour community. Many traceurs believe the lack of understanding of the disciplined and exact approach to training, inexperience of the participants, and commercial association, presented parkour negatively as an activity where participants lacked control over their bodies, and as being overly-concerned in showmanship and entertainment, rather than presenting a skillful display of mind body co-ordination and creative expression.

Comments from the now deleted YouTube channel before comments were disabled stated,

"I cannot believe this, such faggotry EZ, enjoy your cash. Faggot."

"Its just shoddy, confused and shambolic gymnastics"

The comments demonstrate the hegemonic masculinity prevalent in sport as discussed in Chapter 3, displaying aggressive and homophobic attitudes. However, as Wheaton discusses, there is still a 'laddish' culture that young male traceurs operate within, even if at times they display a more progressive approach (Wheaton, 2010). Many of the negative comments were aimed directly at Ez (Paul Corkery), the gatekeeper for numerous young male practitioners. Himself a retired traceur, cum parkour 'entrepreneur', he joined forces with entertainment industry lawyers Jonathon Dembo and Dej Mahoney to explore how they could actively exploit the brand 'Urban Freeflow' and parkour, by creating "World Freerun Ents" (Dembo [61]). In response to claims that many within the parkour community were against the move into performance competition, his reply was simply "The people who are saying this are the ones who don't have any sponsorship". Adding, "They're also the ones who don't have any exposure" (Corkery [51]). However, this is incorrect as all the founders (who are infinitely more well known than Ez or any of 'his' sponsored athletes), expressed their opposition to such an event.

Whilst the movements of traceurs can indeed be spectacular, these spectacles are generally site-specific and are not always easily transferable to specific sites for performance or competitions. The spectacular 'image' produced by jumping from building to building may not be possible to recreate within the parameters of a given location. Parkour 'performances' typically involve scaffolding or a structure that allows for demonstrations of balance and jumping from one edge to another.

Public 'parkour' performances are usually centered around single acrobatic and gymnastic movements compared to the fluidity of combinations of movements and/or routes. The big cheers always come from the performance of a backflip, or a spinning, twisting; freely moving body in space. Very few specific parkour moves, such as 'catleaps' or 'precisions' warrant such celebration due to a lack of understanding of the skill needed to execute them.

The group 3Run were commissioned to perform at the world premiere of the feature film, *The Prince of Persia*, in London, 2010 which was broadcast internationally. 3Run are known for combining elements of parkour with gymnastics, acrobatics and tricking.

Practitioners who are more interested in the more performative aspects train in gymnastic centres with sprung floors to minimise the risk; focusing their training on new techniques and movements, without the harsh realities and fear of solid surfaces to land on. This differs greatly from the original parkour although it gives some their first step into parkour, for others, it is a way to access the commercial offerings available to performers (3run [1]).

Many newcomers regard parkour as a media spectacle and a route to becoming a commercial performer. The majority understand and know little of the disciplines' heritage or values. Stephane Vigroux commented, "For the moment the problem is that we have a misunderstanding of what it is really. It's not just about doing a backflip to impress your friends." "It's a school of life. It's an art where we practise everyday, not only physically but mentally also." He commented, "It's more about the attitude you should have during training rather than the exercise itself (3run [2]).

The extent to which parkour is performed, and for what reasons, remains a divisive issue amongst parkour communities. A common tagline on many parkour web forums (parkour.net, AmericanParkour.com) is 'Pro Parkour Against Competition', creating a language of contention within parkour communities.

Those who position themselves as "pro parkour" are expressing their interpretation of parkour as a critically-aware training philosophy of self improvement and parkour as a practice that has a self competitive nature: "Against competition" is not a stand against creative and expressive movements, but one that is against positioning parkour as a modern achievement sport with an emphasis on impressing and beating another practitioner. The tag sees 'competition' as a threat to the perceived core values of parkour, replacing the essence of it with an emphasis on performance spectacle. While many traceurs are 'pro parkour' they do not feel the need to offset parkour's identity by citing what it is against, that is, it is not a body culture that promotes formal competition with rules of engagement to adhere to. The phrase 'Against competition' also alludes to parkour becoming an elite activity rather than a 'sport for all'.

In a similar parallel with how baseball is perceived in Cuba and how it informs and is integral to the sense of Cuban identity, parkour provokes a 'politics of passion', defined by personal engagement from foundational issues that establish the nature of the parkour community (Carter, 4). The core values associated with an individual's interpretation of the concept of parkour embrace their sense of identity, self-worth, idealism and, at times, morals.

Traceurs are concerned with how the social relations, values and meanings they associate with parkour are possible to maintain if parkour is narrowly perceived as a media spectacle. However, some choose to participate in both the performance aesthetics and more sporting values, for example, Johnny 'Sticky' Budden', for example, currently signs his emails "Professional Freerunner & Parkour Coach", giving value to both the celebration and communication of the creative performance spectacle of 'freerunning' and the sportification of parkour. The terms are not in binary opposition, but complement each other and can co-exist within an individual's identity. Within parkour there appears to be an acceptance of parkour as a performance spectacle, but a rejection of the concept of formal competition.

In an interview with filmmaker Craig Pentak, Stephane Vigroux says, "I like the performance aspect of it, but the problem of competition, is parkour is a new discipline, it's a new sport, it's about to be established and recognised and I don't think doing a competition right now is the best thing to do for the sport. Parkour is really close to the media, to the show-off aspect; you know, do a backflip and perform in movies, stuff like that. All this stuff related to the ego is not really good. The competition thing is not really good" (Vigroux [191]).

Any criticisms from within the parkour community directed at parkour performers who participate in competitions, are met with the defence that their participation is driven by having fun and is about the camaraderie between competitors. On the 2010 *MTV Ultimate Parkour Challenge* series, contestant Daniel Arroyo said of the producers; "They really wanted to show the philosophical side of what we do, not just the skill. Some people out there have some major body awareness however they lack the passion and mindset. They carefully choose us based on personality, diversity in beliefs, and other moral/ethical decisions. All in all it was a very good move in showing what we do in a positive manner" (Arroyo [16]).

This somewhat naïve view did not reflect the fact that there were no variations in the views of the participants nor an awareness of the politics of representation. However, during the live television broadcast of *MTV's Ultimate Parkour Challenge* (Arroyo [16]) in the first edition of the series, the competitors behaved in a sullen and unenthusiastic manner. This they state was as a protest to how their 'art' was being represented. As Alec Furtado posted on the American Parkour forum "The hosts trying to incite some standard rivalry as they might expect in some other activity/sport and the guys just don't care. I think whats-his-name asked Tim what he has to say if his time got beat and he just says, Eh, I don't care, if he does, he does. At the end, Jenkin just acted completely careless when they announced that he won and you can tell they didn't know what to say(Arroyo [16]). "Yea dude, Oleg looked bored as hell. It made me feel bad lol and I loved how none of them cared about winning. It was hilarious how the judges were treating it like your normal competitive show, where people cry when they don't win, and they all just didn't care" (Arroyo [16]).

Dave S says, "This programme is clearly a terrible representation of Parkour, with a fundamentally wrong approach and a lot of nonsense being associated with Parkour. There were a few short clips of interviews that mentioned something that resembled Parkour, but that was as close as the show got to anything constructive" (Arroyo [16]).

In defence of the show but also demonstrating the participants' frustrations at the representations that MTV wanted to promote, Arroyo, the only participant to join the discussion online, diplomatically commented, "MTV is little by little allowing us to make our own changes to better satisfy our positions" (Arroyo [16]).

Wheaton suggests the participants in youth subcultures "are not simply victims of commercialism but mould and transform identities and meanings circulated in and by consumer culture" (Wheaton 2007: 288). Televised representations of parkour as seen in *MTV's Ultimate Parkour Challenge* and the *Barclaycard World Freerun Championships* expose none of the process or motivations for parkour. Parkour becomes a shiny product of achievement rather than an embodied sporting experience. Palmer states that; "Made-for-media versions of extreme sports are short-lived imitations of risk, rather than serious sporting initiations into activities in which physical fitness and technical nous are of paramount importance" (Palmer, 58).

Performance aesthetics and capital value

Whilst traceurs are content to perform parkour and have been actively involved in it's co-option for commercial purposes, they also express great frustration when their practice is reduced to a spectacle-based performance. When parkour is practiced outside, traceurs do not pay for the use of public space for their activity, they consume public space democratically. Yet at times they are willing to be paid to 'perform' parkour and be visible within those same public or private spaces at defined times for specific purposes. While normally resisting such practices in their everyday parkour (not seeking out public admiration and being content to train away from inquisitive eyes that may interrupt them), public 'performances' of parkour provide an aesthetic that contributes to what David Pinder describes as the state's production of space in the interests of capital (Pinder, 731).

Based on Pierre Bordieu's writings on fields of cultural production, David Ley's discussions on artists, aestheticisation and gentrification suggests it is possible for there to be changes in the volume and type of capital from cultural to economic, (Ley, 2530) through an artistic process; for there to be an act of transformation, "the movement of a product, and indeed a place, from junk to art and then on to commodity" (Ley, 2528-2530).

The gentrification of parkour from the streets of the everyday to a performance spectacle changes the dominance of economic and cultural capital within the 'field' of parkour. However, it is important to note that the value of various forms of capital - whether 'subcultural' economic or cultural - is dependant on how the different forms of capital are viewed from within a particular 'field'.

Within the 'field' of parkour economic capital is not as valued as cultural capital for the majority. The transformation from cultural to economic capital is unconsciously dismissed by the traceur performer. They view these actions as part of their road to a wider acceptance and an understanding of their art, thus, supporting their notion of cultural capital. They are happy to engage in brief associations whilst not commenting on the issue of their co-option, justifying the performance of "just moving" (Arroyo [16]).

David Harvey suggests that, "The continuous spectacles of commodity culture, including the commodification of the spectacle itself, play their part in fermenting political indifference. It is either stupefied nirvana or totally blasé attitude that is aimed at..." (Harvey, 168). Commodification of the parkour experience through performance and 'endorsed' training, as well as the commodification of the body, situates parkour as lacking in resistance and a part of a docile, mainstream public, where subjects operate within the dominant social and economic power relations.

However, the co-existence of parkour as a performance spectacle and one of a performance of the everyday, undermines the totality of a commodity culture and the constant political indifference. Traceurs choose to play in the grey areas of co-option to fulfil their desires, by being both complicit and subversive regarding the nature of their performance, for whom, when and where. Whilst many experienced traceurs, such as my research informants, are relatively fixed in their attitudes towards what they deem to be appropriate performances or not, the vast majority of parkour culture - the parkour mainstream - are more unstable and have a casual approach to cultural attachments, which is a characteristic of a consumer-based society.

As deCerteau explains, "Marginality is today no longer limited to minority groups, but is rather massive and persuasive; this cultural activity of the non-producers of culture, an activity that is unsigned, unreadable, and unsymbolised, remains the only one possible for all those who nevertheless buy and pay for the showy products through which a productivist economy articulates itself. Marginality is becoming universal. A marginal group has now become a silent majority" (de Certeau, XVII).

Parkour as an act of 'other', difference, excitement and spectacle, has aligned it with extreme sports and rendered it useful in promoting products and services aimed at a youth market alongside other 'extreme' activities such as surfing, bmx, snowboarding, and skateboarding (Relentess [160]). All of these practices share a mainstream of participants who do the activity simply for fun and as a leisure activity.

Whilst doing parkour requires no specialised equipment, it has not stopped parkour imagery being used to sell associated 'lifestyle' products. Puchan suggests that extreme sports are used to "promote ordinary products with the aim of lending an aura of the special, extraordinary or extreme" (Puchan, 173). The appeal of parkour for marketing campaigns and advertisers, has often stemmed around the concepts of 'alternatives', freedom, other, play, creativity, of looking at things differently and an extended mobility (Nokia, Yota, Canon).

However, behind every spectacle of performance there is the everyday act of training. Whilst the political indifference of traceurs is exemplified through their participation in a performed aesthetic, they simultaneously participate in a 'politics of difference' within their own parkour culture. Opportunities to perform are viewed as forms of temporary cultural attachments where the traceur is aligned with a product, service or institution for a moment in time. Wheaton regards the 'selling out debates' in parkour are the same as with other lifestyle sports and the way in which parkour is repackaged for mass consumption is a reason for concern (Wheaton, 2010).

Some traceurs will have their own ethics by which they choose which products to promote as they deem them to be in opposition or harmony to the values they associate with parkour. My key informants for example (Stephane Vigroux, Williams Belle, Thomas Couetdic, Dan Edwardes, Forrest) refused to promote an alcoholic drink and have made other exceptions when agreeing usage for commercial image rights, choosing to reject licensing agreements if they cannot negotiate their involvement on a case by case basis so they can decide if the product conforms to their 'ethical conduct'.

The motivations for some parkour performers are to gain positions of influence and recognition within the internal parkour hierarchies; to become 'parkour celebrities', whilst others, for example, Team Tempest, choose to position themselves as 'outside' the parkour community or culture, but nonetheless, use parkour to promote their performances and stunt work. Their website states: "Tempest set off to pursue the dream of making a mark in the freerunning world by adding style, creativity, and dedicated focus to the sport. The team's first event together was performing at the Taurus World Stunt Awards" (Team Tempest [180]). As with many practitioners Team Tempest also create their own media, broadcasting that Team Tempest, "loves to do nothing more than Film, Freerun, and have Fun. Join us for each webisode as we put our lives on blast for your viewing pleasure" (Team Tempest, www.tempestfreerunning.com/tempest-tv).

At times the cultural and economic capital of parkour is less-explicitly compromised than at others but the state's production of space for economic capital still dictates the levels to which cultural capital can occur. For example, the South Bank Centre in London plays host to the annual international Parkour Rendezvous event run by Parkour Generations, yet it is only on this one weekend of the year that traceurs are openly welcomed to train around the South Bank Centre, as long as risk assessments have been completed and waivers signed, leaving the centre devoid of accountability or 'risk' whilst maintaining a public position of 'support' for the practice of parkour, a practice that inevitably involves risk. The South Bank Centre has a history of endorsing occasional parkour performances and was featured in the performance documentary *Jump London*.

Images from the Rendezvous 5 event in London, August 2010 as traceurs gather at the start of the day, go about their training in small groups, and gather for an end-of-the-weekend group photo.

The spectacle of the event enforces the centre's position of one of visual culture and activities. The sight of over one hundred people training amongst the cafes and tourist attractions places parkour in the sphere of the mainstream consciousness where passersby stop to marvel and enquire about what it is they are doing. At this event there are performances of the everyday of training rather than a performance aesthetic. A passerby at Rendezvous 4 observing some ground level training remarked; "Fantastic, it's truly amazing!", (Angel, *Rendezvous 4 Day 1 of 2,* 2009).

Members of the public photographing some parkour training that took place within the South Bank Centre's grounds. Low level training at the Rendezvous 5 event, London, 2010.

Despite being aware of the contradiction in the South Bank's approach, members of Parkour Generations are happy to take advantage of the publicity and visibility. Parkour Generations see the event as a way to legitimise their activities as a training methodology rather than being viewed as reckless performance stunts carried out by adrenalin junkies

A security guard from the Southbank Centre stops Asid doing parkour during filming for the film *ASID profile of a freerunner. Image courtesy of Paul Holmes*

However, other spectacles have been more overtly contradictory in their endorsement of parkour as a performance spectacle. Institutions, such as, Shell have endorsed parkour as a performance spectacle by contracting Sébastien Foucan for a performance event hosted on their property, yet it bans traceurs from using it as a training ground.

The politics of the parkour spectacle

When parkour is performed as a spectacle within a regulated framework, it changes the politics of the traceur from an active body exerting subtle resistance and participating in pragmatic anarchism, to docility and passivity, participating in what Swyngedouw and Kaika refer to as, "The City of the Spectacle in which the body participates only as a passive consumer and not as a stage actor". Swyngedouw and Kaika state this has, "turned the city into a kaleidoscopic experience in which some call the shots, others lament the end of all certainties and most try to survive in the turmoil unleashed by an unfettered market dominance" (Swyngedouw & Kaika, 7).

This continues from Guy Debord's 1967 writings on the 'Society of the Spectacle'. Debord predicted; "In societies where modern conditions of production prevail, all of life presents itself as an immense accumulation of spectacles. Everything that was directly lived has moved away into representation (Debord 1967: 1).

The parkour performance spectacle simultaneously reflects and reproduces the dominant culture of spectacles. However, the extent to which parkour becomes a spectacle, that is, removed from the lived experience of an everyday parkour, is not fixed. There are distinct differences between parkour as a lived experience and the spectacle that Debord writes of, even if the parkour that is sometimes performed, becomes a spectacle in, and of, itself.

Whilst Debord's spectacle is mediated, the parkour experience involves direct action. Debord's spectacle separates and alienates (Debord 1967: 18, 20, 30, 32) whereas parkour reconnects and promotes an active dialogue, acting out the needs and desires of the traceurs. Debord's spectacle is rooted in relations of power (Debord 1967: 23) while the act of parkour is autonomous. Debord's spectacle is a mask, covering the means by which the everyday desires and passions of possibility are revealed (Debord 1967: 25). Whereas parkour communicates possibility. Debord's spectacle enforces separation (Debord 1967: 29) unlike parkour which is an act of spatial inclusion.

Swyngedouw and Kaika suggest that the staging of 'cultural spectacles' (of which the co-option of parkour for performance would be an example), try to "subvert, undermine, and marginalise the cultures of everyday life". Using London as an example of a 21st century urban experience, they suggest that, "In the millennial city, embedded in a neo-liberal utopian dream-cast, spectacle as the commodity-culture has become seemingly total" (Swyngedouw & Kaika, 10). They suggest that: "'alienation' and 'authenticity' need to be recaptured as potentially empowering and mobilising concepts and practices, not as remnants from the past that require reconstruction, but rather as possibilities that dwell in the future and are there for the making. Transcending alienation and making 'authenticity' should be seen as social and political projects, as promises that may and can be realized in the future; modernisation as a project of making authenticity, of reaching essence" (Swyngedouw & Kaika, 17).

Parkour as a sporting practice

Parkour, as a performance spectacle, has entertained audiences and ignited the imagination of consumers, so much so, that some of these consumers have been inspired to take to the streets, walls, rails, rocks and trees, exploring their own abilities and limitations. Images of spectacular parkour performances have encouraged an ever-increasing number of participants from the absolute beginner to the highly-skilled and competent. Parkour's popularity has resulted in greater demands for instruction on how to start and/or progress in parkour safely.

It has only been since the creation of the Parkour Generations and the Majestic Force collectives that experienced, 'elite-level', traceurs have sought to actively promote their particular methodology, by means other than spectacle, within the dominant mainstream culture. They have created coaching standards and a qualifications system, seeking recognition for their certification within already established sporting systems, such as, the AQA Unit Award Scheme in Parkour / Freerunning Unit 1 & Unit 2. This has involved institutionalising and rationalising some elements of the discipline. Currently various international communities are also following suit and developing their own parkour instructor qualification.

Many of the first and second generation of experienced traceurs believe that the explosion of interest in parkour, *l'art du déplacement* and freerunning, has necessitated a more-structured approach to communicating how participants can progress safely and responsibly. Whilst they feel a level of responsibility for passing on their knowledge, they also want to maintain the standard and quality of what they do. They do not want the discipline they created to disappear once they themselves choose to no longer train. Dan Edwardes, one of the directors of Parkour Generations believes, "It is absolutely essential to have a visible recognised teaching standard now in the world for the discipline, so that anyone who wants to learn, knows that this particular individual is endorsed by the founders and qualified to teach and that they are getting access to the discipline in the correct way and are not just imitating it from what they see on TV or on the internet" (Angel, *A.D.A.P.T. Parkour & L'art du Déplacement*, 2008).

In 2006 Stephane Vigroux explained "Somebody has to teach the way, because it's very particular, even me, I learnt from David and now I understand his way and I try and do it for me and when I meet people I try to give a little of what I know but I don't think nobody will find the way alone, on his own, I think because it is a very very particular way of thinking. When you know those guys you really understand why they are so good" (Angel, *Le Singe est de Retours*, 2006).

It had always been part of the founders' intentions that parkour be valued and integrated in some way into the mainstream sporting landscape, whether this was as an activity in its own right or as a way of training that could complement other activities, for example, for training athletes or firefighters.

As a result of the increased interest in the discipline, alongside the parkour that freely occurs in public spaces, there are now structured and scheduled parkour classes; as well as 'jams' or casual training sessions where friends meet.

The outdoor parkour classes run by Parkour Generations and Majestic Force involve small-scale group training sessions where the discipline is adapted and scaled to suit the participants' abilities and experience. The sessions occur in public spaces where they know their actions do not disrupt local communities (Angel, *First Step*, 2007).

From left to right, the group train 'balancing' by walking on a low rail and then holding a squat position on the rail; traversing along a wall and training wall runs; pistol squats on a static object and a moving object, helping to train balance and strengthen the legs.

As well as outdoor parkour classes that have arguably, made parkour more accessible, there are also more sanitised versions of the discipline available with indoor classes. Here students familiarise themselves with some of the techniques and prepare themselves physically, starting to create their own 'body armour'. This has furthered parkour's accessibility, adaptiveness and inclusivity. However, as Forrest discusses, in the short film *First*

Step, doing parkour indoors and outdoors are two different approaches. The real thing, he says, is when it is practiced outside where psychologically the activity is very different, than when the practitioner is faced with concrete. He accepts however, that training indoors is a good way to improve one's physical condition and an opportunity to work on some techniques. One student explained that they preferred training outdoors as, "Indoors, it's too safe. You don't get to understand all of the dynamics of 'the playground', so to speak. It's much more fun outside; you get to feel the harshness of it" (Angel, *First Step* 2007). However, during my research, I have seen far more injuries and accidents occur inside than outside. I attribute this to the perception of the indoors as 'safe' in contrast to the 'wild', frightening outdoors. The focus and concentration on the part of students appears to be higher when training outside than indoors.

By labelling or positioning some of these classes for "Beginners", parkour is presented as accessible to a cross-section of society that would perhaps feel uncomfortable about training outside. I have overheard students who are wary of participating in an outside class, as they fear they may be 'asked to jump across a building or climb up onto a roof'. These media-created myths are slowly being reversed as scaleable, progressive and adaptive training approaches to parkour are offered as a structured activity.

Indoor parkour classes utilise standard gymnastic equipment, such as, vaulting horses and crash mats, although they may be used differently than in a conventional gymnastics class. The gymnastics 'horse' was initially created to mimic the functions of a hedge to train the Renaissance acrobat equestrian performer to jump over it (Guttmann 2000: 253). Parkour constantly links back to the root of the invention, challenging students to clear the obstacle, thinking of it as a real hedge or a real wall. Likewise, the beam can prepare traceurs for the outdoor environment by encouraging them to experience it as a rail or narrow edge.

From left to right: students 'warm-up' with strength conditioning drills, such as, *quadrupedal* movements and pressups. Students practise various vaulting techniques, such as, the kong and slide monkey. Students work on their physical condition.

Parkour indoors is a self-reliant, physically-exerting workout but crucially, it lacks the fear, creativity, re-perception of the environment and self, and the interaction with public everyday spaces. These, for some, make up the essence of the practice and so, alongside any physical conditioning, students are always encouraged to train outside (Angel, *Indoor Academy* 2007). Some participants use the indoor parkour classes as physical conditioning to complement their own sporting practice, for example, to train for triathlons or as preparation for theatrical performances, and are not interested in the practice of parkour outdoors.

Parkour indoors becomes private and invisible to the public. The extent to which parkour type activities occur indoors is, at times, compromised due to the limitations of the venue, for example, participants may not be allowed to train wall runs or catleaps because of the risk of leaving trainer marks on the walls. Indoor classes must comply to a level of risk deemed appropriate by the hosting institution.

Parkour indoors is where parkour most explicitly connects its 'subcultural' roots to a dominant mainstream sporting model of 'regulated activities'. Parkour indoors is a hybrid of poorly-executed gymnastic movements accompanied with athletic flair and repetitions more akin to the discipline and mindful precision of martial arts.

The institutionalisation and 'sportification' of parkour and the creation of classes both indoors and outdoors (Parkour Generations [139]) has broadened parkour's reach in terms of age, gender and class of participants. Parkour in the UK is now on its way to being recognised as a 'sport' and in certain contexts has conformed to ideas of regulation, rationalisation and standards (Parkour UK [149]).

Although, at the moment, parkour is a predominantly male activity, I have observed a marked increase in female participation since the creation of more-accessible and regulated formal teaching structures. At least twenty percent of the participants at the adult parkour classes that I attend in London are now female. There is evidence of vibrant communities of female practitioners growing internationally where there are opportunities to learn from experienced traceurs in structured environments whether indoors or outside.

The creation of classes both indoors and out, has increased participation overall and enabled parkour to flourish as an unregulated creative outdoor practice. The institutionalising of parkour has, if anything, strengthened the parkour community as it has grown, even though there is a minority who question who is fit to 'qualify' someone to teach. Beginners socialise at classes and learn their first steps, then arrange to meet others to train outdoors at times and locations of their choosing.

Within the parkour culture there is a perceived need of governance with the creation of self-appointed national governing bodies. Traceurs acknowledge that what they do has been linked with an image of deviance and risk and there are safety concerns around the activity (Wheaton, 2010). Today, the UK has a National Governing Body for parkour, ParkourUK, created and led by the three directors of Parkour Generations – Stephane Vigroux, Francois 'Forrest' Mahop, Dan Edwardes and also Johann Vigroux.

Eugene Minogue (who instigated the first parkour classes within schools) is employed by Parkour UK. The Majestic Force collective, containing several members of the original Yamakasi group also support Parkour UK. The Parkour UK website states it aims to "support and develop parkour/freerunning in the UK, and to make the benefits of the sport accessible to any and all who want to learn. Parkour UK will always strive to maintain and improve the spirit of the discipline. We aim to provide guidance, support and assistance on all levels to all practitioners of the discipline, and to regulate and maintain the standards of coaching for the sport in the country. Parkour UK will oversee the development and management of the sport from grassroots teaching through to qualifying and insuring top-level instructors of this emerging discipline" (Parkour UK [147]).

The increased interest and broadened base of participants have also created opportunities for 'parkour camps' and holidays as a form of niche tourism, as well as, the large training events that occur internationally featuring experienced international guest instructors, for example, the Danish Streetmovement teams' bi-annual Streetcamp; Parkour Generations' week-long training experience/holiday in Morzine, Switzerland, the 'Jamming National Parkour Indonesia 2010' event, and the 'Brazilian Parkour Gathering'.

The opportunities for traceurs to become 'parkour professionals' (rather than, for example, entertainment industry professionals who profit from parkour's exploitation), such as members of Parkour Generations who offer a range of coaching, performance and design consultancy services, reflects the growth of the activity that has inspired and provided opportunities for many, myself included. The internal power struggles within parkour culture will continue to influence and mould the practice into new guises as a tradition of appropriation continues.

Parkour facilities

As well as the creation of structured sessions where people can learn and train parkour, there have also been specifically built structures to facilitate and support the growth and interest in parkour. The UK currently has two dedicated parkour facilities

(Edwardes [65]). In 2011, Westminster City Council built a 100 square metre outdoor, dedicated permanent parkour training facility designed by Stephane and Johann Vigroux and 'Kazuma'. Whilst for some this might seem contraversial and somewhat of an anti-parkour thing to do, it has always been the desire of the founders for the art to be recognised for its values and potential as a 'sport' as well as an art, even if it does not conform to achieving records or points. Parkour parks contextualise the parkour training. For traceurs a parkour park provides an efficient space for training different techniques and variations of routes and will become one of a number of training areas they frequent. The environment of the park still requires a level of creativity and adaptability even though it does not provide the opportunity for the active re-perception of the environment.

Whilst Westminster's park will not be open-access and will occur within the regulated and supervised private space of the Westminster Sports Academy, in Germany parkour parks have been created and situated within public parks. Other dedicated parkour parks exist in Poland and Denmark with plans for others within France and the USA.

A public parkour park in Dusselldorf, Germany. *Image courtesy of Eugene Minogue.*

The parkour park in Gerlev, Denmark.

The parkour park in Westminster, London, UK.

The development of parkour parks has been driven from the parkour community as many create fundraising events and engage with local councils to try and realise their ambitions (American Parkour [7]). Traceurs who are involved with the various projects are optimistic that the park will not help those who wish for parkour to be banned or not remain visible in public spaces. Instead, the existence of specific parkour parks will help to bring parkour into a more reasonable debate regarding its potential and benefit as a physical and creative transformative practice. Parkour parks consist of structures that are the bare bones of concern for traceurs, the surfaces, edges, and distances above and between 'obstacles'. They are reminiscent of abandoned building sites, not needing any frills or finishings to fulfill the traceurs' needs. They do not seek to mimic the aesthetic of the urban landscape, but aim to create an efficient environment for their training.

There are also several mobile parkour structures and parks already in existence, providing instant 'urban furniture' at venues or events that allow for parkour to take place within a specific area. These structures offer variations in how they can be set up, not wanting to conform to any set or over-rationalised presentation of the practice. Whilst experienced traceurs can host workshops or demonstrations in almost any environment, those who are still relatively new to the discipline require more obvious obstacles around which to create movements and opportunities (Parkour Generations [143]).

The social implications for parkour's institutionalisation

The social implications for parkour's institutionalisation are yet to be fully played out. Whilst the creation of a training standard and certificate has broadened the participant base in terms of age, class and gender, there is a concern that parkour's visibility in the public sphere as a training method may be limited if parkour is not better perceived as normative or valued to some degree from a mainstream perspective. If parkour is viewed narrowly as a performance for, and in public, (that should be trained in private), it would threaten the traceurs present ability to train freely as they do now, (although, as discussed in Chapter 3, it would be almost impossible to regulate against due to parkour's bodycentric adaptive nature). The majority of traceurs want to have good relations with the authorities as they are very protective of parkour's reputation and representation. The majority would welcome a more accepted normative stance to be taken. Dan Edwardes explains, "One of the biggest challenges was getting recognition of the fact that parkour is not a crazy anarchic sport that's about jumping off buildings, but is a very rigorous mental and physical discipline that's about self-improvement" (Edwardes [65]).

Without the formal creation of dedicated times and locations for learning parkour (whether indoors or outdoors), the discipline would remain predominantly within the same demographic. The sporting institutionalisation has come from within the parkour community rather than from commercial market forces or intermediary gatekeepers. As a result of classes and qualifications to have been created by some of the most informed and experienced traceurs, such as, the Yamakasi founding members; those in Parkour Generations and Majestic Force, the content and classes are deemed by others to be 'authentic', coming from parkour's grassroots, as opposed to 'unauthentic', that is coming from a mass-produced more commercial mainstream position. Markula Pirkko and Richard Pringle report that, "Within power relations of sport, it is determined what knowledge and what ethics counts as valuable and individuals at different levels of sport aim to influence these formations and thus, control others" (Markula & Pringle, 147-148).

Those against any form of institutionalisation of the practice and the resultant inclusivity that entails, are predominantly young males who yearn for an active label of 'other', that is, people who do something that is different from the mainstream. These participants believe a more open accessibility to parkour threatens to dilute the individuality they express by the label of "I am a traceur"; "I am a freerunner" or "I do parkour". However, the subcultural capital and influence the experienced traceurs of Parkour Generations and Majestic Force contain, have given a strong voice to support the discipline's institutionalisation.

Conclusions

Parkour is an autonomous artistic field, high in cultural capital when 'performed' as an everyday act, however its co-option for spectacle, shifts the volume of cultural to economic capital in its production and consumption of space. The synthesis of 'authentic' and commercially-produced parkour creates an aestheticised product, high in symbolic value, which could be described as 'parkour in the air', representing a body free and available to conform and be moulded by the dominant forces and logic in the production of space. The nature of the subtle resistance exerted in the act of doing parkour is appropriated and commodified for a consumer society in which the traceurs participate. There is little subtle resistance to the society of the spectacle as parkour is reduced to a mere representation of a more authentic and embodied experience to create cultural spectacles. However, in a similar parallel to performed skateboard tricks, Wilson suggests that such performances can be thought of as a "form of free expression" and a "temporary escape or sense of empowerment through movement" (Wilson, 386).

Although Wheaton suggests that, "Most lifestyle sports emphasise the creative, aesthetic, and performative expressions of their activities" (Wheaton 2004: 12) she argues that lifestyle sports participants, value the "intense experiences and the "inner" or "felt" body – not the commodified, astheticised, and disciplined body that many describe as symptomatic and expressive of contemporary consumer society" (Wheaton 2007: 298). Whilst Wheaton describes these actions as a commitment to pleasure, this is not always applicable to parkour as can be seen with my research informants for whom pleasure is found in the exploration of self and their limits. Their experiences are more closely affiliated with pain, fear and suffering as they challenge their emotional and physical limits, as opposed to more normative positive concepts such as pleasure and fun.

Traceurs are content to explore the co-option for spectacle to further their own needs and their desires for a wider acceptance of their everyday parkour practices, as well as, for individual material gains. The 'identity' of the 'parkour performer', through the act of co-option for spectacle, differs from the identity of the 'everyday' traceur. There are different values and cultural meanings aligned with the sometimes conflicting and multiple, fragmented, mobile 'parkour identities'. This reflects the individualisation and consumption of lifestyle choices through sport and leisure which are used to exchange and create social identity. This is in contrast to more traditional signifiers such as class, gender, ethnicity, religion or age.

Within parkour culture there is the identity of the 'traceur' and the 'freerunner' (taking freerunning as the appropriated form with an emphasis on visible creativity). Whilst there is obvious common ground between the experiences, parkour (as understood by my key informants and the founders), emphasises autonomy; effort; physical and mental endurance to overcome fear and physical pain; repetitive training drills; commitment and perfection over the fun, creativity and pleasure that is more associated with freerunning. The values that underpin parkour are more aligned with selfless, noble acts of heroic functionality and diminishing fear while the newly-coined term freerunning is less about valour and bravery, than visibility and leisure, a freedom of expression. These ideas are contested and refuted within the parkour community, as tastes, and styles while those who hold positions of influence, exert their control within the internal power relations and hierarchies of parkour culture. Parkour and - the related but, for some, distinct - freerunning reflect, produce and reproduce the histories and cultures that created them.

The differences in the problemitising and choices made in parkour as a 'technology of the self' dictate each of the 'parkour identities' and realisation of the 'ethical subject'. The goal or 'telos' of the traceur is, perhaps, recognition or material reward. The initial 'ethical substance' may be to ask of oneself, what part of my identity do I want to address or 'problemitise'? The 'mode of subjection' could be a different way of training or focus relative to the ethical substance. The ethical practice is the practices or tools with which the traceurs work towards their goal, for example the performer might concentrate on more original impressive techniques. Only after the original questioning and problemitsation can one engage in 'ethical conduct'. For example, the ethics of the performer may have a greater concern for aesthetics rather than exploring his or her relationship with their environment, yet he or she still choose to identify themselves with parkour.

The ethical conduct within parkour culture as a whole is fluid, fragmented, contradictory and provisional. While there is a certain amount of flux, Wheaton suggests that within most lifestyle sports cultures there is also "a high level of stability and distinctiveness in the culture's sense of collective identity and forms of status" (Wheaton 2007: 300). The subcultural capital, regarding tastes and status relating to the performance spectacle of parkour, is constantly shifting. The divisions within parkour culture (whilst sharing ideas of mobility and creative expression), are defined by the levels of 'cultural substance' given to aesthetics and style, as opposed to ,explorations of the self where more resistance is exerted. In his writings on *The Production of Space*, Lefebvre suggests "resistance is not a struggle with dominant hegemonic culture but is located at the levels of the everyday and the body" (Lefebvre 1991: 280).

The parkour performance spectacle is symbolic in its resistance, whereas the everyday act is an embodied act of resistance. The parkour performance aesthetic is a rebranding of urban stunts and acrobatics, continuing a tradition of cultural spectacles for entertainment. The parkour performance communicates little, if any, opposition to the dominant power relations within society.

The institutionalising of parkour has allowed parkour to reclaim its roots in sporting values of effort, discipline, adaptability, risk and the heroism of the empowered, individual body against the brutality of the environment and power relations rooted within, as opposed to, training towards a performed spectacle.

By creating indoor, domesticated versions, the practice has democratised itself by opening up to new environments in which parkour can be introduced and practiced. Whilst some might suggest this is a dilution of the values, the constant shifts and appropriations that occur within parkour culture may result in new future appropriations and terminology making clearer distinctions yet. Whilst there are obvious connections with parkour practiced indoors and outdoors, by the nature of the embodied experience in moving and using the body to overcome 'obstacles', outdoor parkour will always be a qualitatively different experience by offering practitioners a constant re-perception of their environment and questioning their relationship to and with it.

Parkour's mobile resistance is trained within the mainstream under the guise of health and wellbeing, and enjoyed and explored by a traceur's own desire. However, whilst some might suggest, as Wilson does, that types of escapist resistance involving pleasure-seeking and empowerment, that, in the end, "makes no difference" (Wilson, 401). I would disagree based on the observations and crime statistics provided for the *Jump Westminster* project.

Whilst the dominant majority may state what types of behaviour are deemed to be 'anti-social' (and this may include parkour type activities), more obvious actions, anti-social behaviours such as substance abuse, violence and theft were all seen to decrease substantially when young people engage in parkour. Therefore escapist resistance does make a difference to the lived experience of the individual and of those in networks around them, whether, family, work, social or, other forms of community.

There are various potentials and values within parkour culture that can be accessed by individuals who want to explore their own potential and move creatively and expressively. As Johann Vigroux stated when reflecting on the changing faces and representations of parkour over the past seven years, (particularly since the creation of the performance documentary *Jump London*), there is no right or wrong to what is or isn't parkour (Vigroux J., 2010). For those interested in learning the original way of parkour, it is now accessible through teaching and coaching offered by 'endorsed' groups who have been trained by some of the founders. For others, parkour will continue to evolve and grow.

Whether parkour is understood as a sport, performance, unregulated outdoor activity or hybrid, is dependant on the histories, motivations and the cultural values that individuals associate with their practice. How the mainstream public see and consider parkour will be determined by its mainstream representations and level of institutionalisation. The dominant performance spectacle images continue to travel through the online channels of dissemination via video sharing websites. These images inspire and celebrate the outcome of dedicated training encounters and experiences. The spectacles aid in the construction of a dominant representation of parkour as a performance and fuel the passionate debates over parkour's contested identity and values. The identity of practitioners does not have fixed boundaries as there are multiple ways in which traceurs come to embody their actions in parkour.

Parkour is still relatively young and, although some worry about the values associated with the performance spectacle of parkour lacking sporting values, there are those who believe the sportification of the practice may stifle the creative and innovative nature of parkour (Wheaton 2010). The contradictory elements within parkour are all reflective of the contradictions present in society and discourses on resistance, authenticity and consumer behaviour. In line with Swyngedouw and Kaika's ideas for the future, parkour is a 'modern project' involving an authentic realisation and 'essence', relating to individual needs and desires.

Conclusion

The aim in this thesis has been to document and explore the everyday practices of parkour as experienced by a select group of traceurs whose practice mirrors that of those who were influential in creating the art. My research aimed to reveal the subjective lived experiences of parkour, its essence, and what it means to those who practice the discipline. This has included discussions on the flow state, fear, autonomy, socialisation, parkour vision, and the relationship between self, body and the environment. I have endeavoured to understand these experiences from my informants' perspectives by becoming a participant observer immersed in parkour culture, learning to see the world through parkour eyes. In doing so I have provided a previously unrecorded culturally and historically situated understanding of the practice that contributes to the growing field of ethnographic work based around body cultures and 'lifestyle' sports.

My research offers an important contribution to knowledge by revealing and focussing on the performances of the everyday of parkour, as opposed to parkour performances for spectacle. This has bridged the gap and readdressed the balance of representations of parkour. My research has revealed parkour as a 'particular way of thinking' and demonstrates that parkour is not merely a physically, unregulated spectacular sport, but one that connects participants to a more autonomous, deeper inner self, revealing one's identity and potential through confrontations of fear, and challenging deterministic behaviour and socialisation. As Brymer states of transcendence through 'extreme sports', it alludes to "a deeper learning of what it means to be human" (Brymer, 318).

Whilst representations of parkour as a performance existed when I started my research, it was still a relatively new phenomenon and there had been no ethnographic research conducted at that time. Many of the founders and those with extensive knowledge and experience of parkour were initially not accessible. During my research I have had to work back through the generations of practitioners to access authentic voices from parkour's origins.

My fieldwork involved immersing myself in parkour culture and finding a role as a documentarian, as opposed to, simply training and doing parkour. This role gave me the connection and distance that was necessary to engage empathically, as well as, from a research perspective with the subject. Had I chosen to only train, my observations and conclusions would be similar to that of a typical practitioner with five years of experience, lacking in reflections beyond the physical behaviour and a concern for one's own progression. Stephane Vigroux concurs with this position stating that it is only with a combination of both deep involvement and distance that certain questions arise regarding the parkour experience. The wider view and understandings I have gained have been the result of contact with practitioners who have been practicing from eight to, more than, twenty years.

Whilst initially having some ambition to produce objective films, it soon became evident that I was a social activist within the parkour culture, especially after separating from my first group of informants, Urban Freeflow. The films I have produced are subjective, but this is not to say they offer a romanticised view: I am an artist/researcher who has had the pleasure of working alongside and researching other creative individuals who are critically self aware and reflective of their practices and actions. Parkour is not only a tool for self exploration, but also a tool for self expression, and I have endeavoured to find a balance between these two concepts through the films I have produced.

My aim has been to find a relationship between theory and practice in my parkour research. The practical video work, from my participant observation role, has been the tool for explorations into, and expressions of, parkour. The written thesis is a meeting ground of cultural and theoretical knowledge. As a participant observer, parkour documentarian I have tacked between the roles of insider/outsider, and between theorising, doing and documenting parkour. My understandings of parkour have been facilitated by creating a shared cinema that has helped to reveal the knowledge, understanding and focus I have to my informants. This has then fed into a feedback loop of film productions, discussion and theorising.

I have attempted to work within various theoretical frameworks relating to my filmmaking practice although these have evolved and changed over time as I have become more informed and also adapted to new avenues of research, having gained access to more experienced and informed traceurs. This has been a timely process as my research has occurred almost simultaneously with an emerging phenomenon. Each film opened up new topics for discussion, further film productions, and personal endorsements of my commitment to representing this artistic, sporting discipline.

Some of the films produced have been influential in promoting the sportification of parkour in the UK and internationally (*Jump Westminster* 2007) by concentrating on certain aspects of parkour such as its ability to engage with young people who do not participate in achievement sports. Other films have exposed previously unrepresented insights into the relationships of pain and pleasure, as experienced by the founding generation, as well as types of play and parkour vision experienced by traceurs in general.

The embodied and immediate experience of parkour is key to its cultural practise and it is this that I have attempted to document with sounds and images, as opposed to, relying solely on descriptive writing. However, using a phenomenological and optimal flow perspective has enabled me to discuss the emotional body subject and lived experience of the traceur's body mind relationship.

Feeling, sensing, and perceiving are key components to the parkour experience.

The main challenge of participant observation has been the process of selecting what was 'relevant' from such a cross disciplinary practice as parkour and what, therefore, has been in need of theorising. It has been a personal endeavour to find a selection of suitable theoretical frameworks through documentary filmmaking that has fulfilled the aim of finding the essence and substance of parkour beyond its mediatised representations. I have had to ignore much of my filmmaking experience, instead creating new modes of production based on the production feedback loop, forcing me to rethink my filmmaking practise whilst reflecting on what parkour is and is not; and, at the same time, contextualising the social relations of who says 'what', 'when' and 'why'.

Whilst the various films illustrated the complexities as well as contradictions, there is a challenge in formulating conclusions on such a varied practice, but that is the art's richness in that it reflects many of the contradictions present in the society where it is practised.

Whilst the filmmaking was organised around ethnographic intentions, the theoretical framework for the text has been based on Foucault's technologies of the self, situating parkour as a practice of freedom involving the confrontations of fear and explorations of the self through transitional spaces of play, in an experimental field of imaginative mobilities and new interpretations of the environment

I initially thought of parkour as an anarchic act of resistance, yet, over time, based on my experiences in the field and with reflection, I could no longer posit parkour within such a totalising view of power discourses. Foucault's later writings on the technology of the self provided the eventual theoretical framing that resonated with the self awareness and constant processes of problemitising, critical awareness, and finding methods of training, to work towards creating an 'ethical self' that was evident in those traceurs with the longest experience of parkour. This also provided a platform that explained the differences in the ethical conduct that created performances for spectacle, as opposed to, that of the everyday within parkour culture. Traceurs are not a homogenous group; their experiences of parkour are diverse; there are many embodied practices of parkour each with different ethics, motivations and outcomes. Using Foucault's later work helped me to highlight the liberational aspects traceurs experience which are key to their continued motivation. Parkour is an alternative practice of knowledge and experience as it involves the problemitising and reflections on how to improve one's self and can be a tool for identity construction and autonomy.

Wellmann's and Taylor's concepts of individualism offer key insights into the search for a meaningful authentic self and the complexities of a modern identity, reclaiming the right to experience life in all its variations of wonderment, magic and in the spirit of parkour. Eichberg's work on body cultures, alongside Guttmann's criteria of ancient and modern sports, helped to highlight parkour's contradictions and a way of connecting the past and the evolving present. As Marshall explains, "There can be no global evaluation or judgement of parkour, because it can be understood only in relation to its specific manifestations and contexts, including the medium in which they are represented, the historicity of a place, the life of an individual" (Marshall, 172).

Recognising that parkour is full of contradictions; I have suggested that a broader viewpoint and perspective is necessary, rather than the existing, somewhat-polarized views often held on the value of parkour as a sport, and/or performance. At the moment there is still a contested discourse within the parkour community on what is or is not appropriate with parkour as different voices compete for claims of authenticity and influence with claims of 'selling out' and debates on the 'dilution' of the art (Rowat, 2007).

During the period of my research, parkour has become an internationally practised past-time, which presented the challenge to stay up-to-date as well as to maintain access in an evolving activity of competing voices. It has only been during the past three years that it has been possible for me to have any direct dialogue with the founders.

In parallel with this, the arrival of Web 2.0, (Anderson, 2) meant traceurs were entering a new, more social and participatory phase, for facilitating the dissemination of parkour. The explosion in computer technologies and enabling of video sharing on the web, alongside the affordability and accessibility of video cameras and editing technologies, changed the media landscape for self documentation and expression, creating a niche parkour subcultural media. Whilst the web-based representations are participatory, they provide little explanation or any alternative perspectives on parkour. They are equally focused on the performative spectacle as are the more-mainstream media representations.

The complicity of traceurs, as well as my own involvement in the co-option and commodification of parkour for material reward when involved in commercial work and commissions, presented challenges as well as opportunities for a re-configuration of the representation of parkour as an activity with more depth than merely a twisting spinning body in space. My informants and I promoted the concept of combinations of movements and flow along with the active engagement and contact with the environment (whenever possible), especially when we had control and influence over the edit.

Parkour occurs both inside and outside of capitalist space as some traceurs choose to participate in the commercialisation of parkour as a means to an end to live a parkour lifestyle centred around training and critical awareness, if, and when, presented with such an opportunity. Parkour as a cultural form has a richness in self awareness and is constantly made and remade with new participants continuing to extend the realms of possibility and performance. As Andy Day commented, parkour, like skateboarding is caught up in it's own 'nexus of production' (Day 2010).

My research is not a complete ethnography of all aspects of parkour culture, a theme too broad to cover in one project, especially in a field that is still evolving. In addition to my own research, to date, parkour has been researched as a subversive practice offering resistance in cities (Mould 2009, Bavinton 2007) and there has been brief ethnographic work based on the embodiement of local cultures looking at small groups of people (Atkinson 2009, Saville 2008). As yet parkour has not been viewed on a transnational scale and is one area for potential future research.

I concur with Wheaton and Gilchrist who suggest other areas for future parkour research include: a comparative study of how parkour compares with other 'lifestyle sports' and body cultures in institutionalisation and commodification. How parkour relates to gender and race in terms of inclusion and exclusion. Does parkour offer alternative opportunities for expressing feminine and masculine identities? Further questions for future research on gender and parkour include: are male traceurs more reflective of their masculinity? What does the non-objectification and non-exploitation of women in parkour say about how women create their identities within a male dominated environment and how do they negotiate space? How do women counter the masculine public perception of risk-taking, danger and bravery? What are the barriers to participation? With regards to race, what are the multicultural aspects of parkour? Does participation reflect the demographic of local communities and how does exclusion, inclusion and difference play out as a lived reality of parkour? (Wheaton 2010, Gilchrist 2010) In addition to this, Wheaton and Gilchrist, recommend quantative research to determine the size of the parkour community, locally and globally (Wheaton 2010).

As a practice that is still evolving, it is also of interest to map the continued institutionalisation of parkour (Gilchrist 2010). How will training in parks or 'regulated' parkour spaces differ to training on the streets? What is the relationship between indoor and outdoor parkour, and how does coaching impact on this (Gilchrist 2010)?

By utilising a combination of both practice and theory, I believe that my adventures and experiences present a more complete view of parkour as an experience that would not have been possible without the combination of the two. I initially immersed myself in parkour by firstly creating a film about parkour, then progressing to create parkour-led films. This was then followed by a period of reflection, discussion and finally, theorisation.

The documentation, representation and interpretation of parkour solely as a text would have lacked the spatial and temporal nature so key to its actions. The films provide a shared language between myself and my informants, without which I could not so easily have expressed what I knew and understood about them, to them. The text allowed for previously, undocumented expressions and knowledge from 'films I never made', as knowledge and experiences gained when you do not have a camera are of equal value to times when you do. The text also allowed for a more critical perspective and a place to highlight parkour's contradictions and different manifestations. The continued inter-personal relations and quality of contact during the research have been key to the understandings gained from the research process.

Parkour culture constitutes an organic, evolving flux of individuals simultaneously exploring their autonomy through networks and communities of shared interest; choosing to train, discuss online, travel and share experiences and knowledge together. Parkour continues to attract attention from researchers, broadcast media, filmmakers, advertisers and the games industry. Parkour continues to be discovered and explored as traceurs find 'their way'. I now look forward to being able to do more parkour and to continue to explore the possibilities of exploring my own limits and behaviour on rails, walls, trees and benches as well as by creating films.

References

Primary Sources

Angel Julie, (2005) *Asid, profile of a freerunner*, Dir.

Angel Julie, (2006) MySpace, Dir.

Angel Julie, (2006) Parkour...Aint seen nothing like it...Damn!, Dir.

Angel Julie, (2006) Parkour Visions, Dir.

Angel Julie, (2006) Le Singe est de Retours, Dir.

Angel Julie, (2007) Canvas of the Street, Dir.

Angel Julie, (2007) City Gents, Dir.

Angel Julie, (2007) First Step, Dir.

Angel Julie, (2007) Indoor Academy, Dir.

Angel Julie, (2007) Jump Westminster, Dir.

Angel Julie, (2007) Parkour Sensei, Dir.

Angel Julie, (2007) Rendezvous 1, Dir.

Angel Julie (2007) Yamakasi Q&A Rendezvous II pt.1, Dir.

Angel Julie, (2007) The Outside In, Dir.

Angel Julie, (2007) Visions, Dir.

Angel Julie, (2008) A.D.A.P.T. Parkour & L'art du Déplacement, Dir.

Angel Julie, (2008) Feedback Loop, Dir.

Angel Julie, (2008) Parkour Generations: training with Kazuma, Ohio, Dir.

Angel Julie, (2008) *Parkour World on You Tube Live,* Dir.

Angel Julie, (2008) Rain, Dir.

Angel Julie, (2008) Sarcelles, Dir.

Angel Julie, (2008) The Making of Traceurs; to trace, to draw, to go fast, Dir.

Angel Julie, (2008) What is Parkour?, Dir.

Angel Julie (2009) Parkour Generations: Rendezvous 4 Q&A part1, Dir.

Angel Julie, (2009) Rendezvous 4 Day 1 of 2, Dir.

Angel Julie, (2010) An American Rendezvous: Day 1 Fast Forward, Dir.

Angel Julie, (2010) Back to Basics, Dir.

Angel Julie, www.youtube.com/slamcamspam

Bangs Andrew, (2009) emails 9.11.09

Belle David, (2009a) Audio interview

Belle David, (2009b) 10.12.09 Msm

Belle Katty, (2007) Video interview

Belle Katty, (2009) Audio interview

Belle Williams, (2010) Video Interview

Christie Mike, (2005a) Video Interview

Couetdic Thomas, (2010) emails

Edwardes Dan, (2006) Video interview

Edwardes Dan & Mahop Francois 'Forrest', (2008) Video interview

Edwardes Dan, (2010) Video interview

Day Andy, (2010) Parkour Symposium, University of Brighton

Foucan Sébastien, (2010) Video interview 19.1.10

Hnautra Yann, (2008) Video interview

Hnautra Yann, (29.11.09) Video interview

Vigroux Johann, (2010) Video interview

Vigroux Stephane, (Nov. 09) Audio interview

Wheaton Belinda, (2010) Parkour Symposium, University of Brighton

Wiseman Frederick, (12.4.10) Q & A, Curzon Cinema, London

Secondary Sources

1. 3 Run, *3Run*, retrieved 18.10.10
    http://www.youtube.com/user/3runtube?blend=2&ob=4

2. 3 Run, *3RUN SHOWREEL 2010*, retrieved 26.11.10
    http://www.youtube.com/watch?v=XFErnYDHFF0

3. Adler Patricia A., Adler Peter, (1989) *The Gloried Self: The Aggrandizement and the Constriction of Self,* Social Psychology Quarterly, Vol. 52, No. 4, 299-310 American Sociological Association

4. Allen-Collinson, Jacquelyn, (2009) *Sporting embodiment: sports studies and the (continuing) promise of phenomenology,* Qualitative Research in Sport and Exercise, 1: 3, 279-296

5. American Parkour, *Current Affairs Program Slams Parkour*, retrieved, 20.2.09
http://www.americanparkour.com/smf/index.php?action=printpage;topic=13915.0

6. American Parkour, *Parkour Event Sponsored by Cigarette Company*. retrieved 14.8.10
http://www.americanparkour.com/smf/index.php?topic=29014.0

7. American Parkour, Parkour Parks (fundraising), retrieved 18.10.10 http://www.americanparkour.com/content/view/5411/1/

8. American Parkour, *Project Pilgrimage*, retrieved, 30.6.09
http://www.americanparkour.com/content/view/2042/318/

9. Anderson, Paul, (2007) *What is Web2.0? Ideas, technologies and implications for education.* JISC Technology and Standards Watch, retrieved 1.12.10
http://www.jisc.ac.uk/media/documents/techwatch/tsw0701b.pdf

10. Angel Julie, retrieved 29.3.10
http://www.parkourgenerations.com/biography.php?p=julie

11. Angel Julie, *Parkour Documentary*, retrieved 10.05.06
http://www.youtube.com/watch?v=WkHPQPozDRs

12. Angel Julie, *Parkour Generations: Visions*, retrieved 3.12.10
http://www.youtube.com/comment_servlet?all_comments=1&v=O

13. Archer, Neil, (2010) *Virtual Poaching and Altered Space: Reading Parkour in French Visual Culture,* Modern & Contemporary France, 18: 1, 93-107

14. Ardner Shirley, (1997) *Ground Rules and Social Maps for Women:An Introduction* Oxford

15. Arvin Ard, retrieved 18.2.09 http://www.buildering.net/

16. Arroyo Daniel, retrieved 18.10.10

http://www.americanparkour.com/smf/index.php/topic,26474.300.html

http://www.americanparkour.com/smf/index.php/topic,26474.0.html

http://www.americanparkour.com/smf/index.php/topic,26474.20.html

http://www.americanparkour.com/smf/index.php/topic,26474.40.html

http://www.americanparkour.com/smf/index.php/topic,26474.300.html

17. Atkins, Barry, & Krzywinska, Tanya, (2007) *Videogame, player, text.* Manchester: Manchester University Press

18. Atkinson, Mike (2009) *Parkour, anarcho-environmentalism, and poiesis,* Journal of Sport and Social Issues, 33 (2), 169-194

19. Barbash Ilisa, & Taylor Lucien, (1997) *Cross-Cultural Filmmaking,* Berkeley: University of California Press

20. Bavinton Nathaniel, (2007) *From obstacle to opportunity: Parkour, leisure, and the reinterpretation of constraints*, Annals of leisure research, vol 10 no 3&4, 391-412

21. BBC News Online, Asylum Seekers end Sydney rooftop protest, retrieved 6.11.10
http://www.bbc.co.uk/news/world-asia-pacific-11379285

22. *Corey Robin. Béland Daniel, (2005)* Fear: The History of a Political Idea, *Canadian Journal of Sociology Online January-February, retrieved 29.11.10*
http://www.cjsonline.ca/pdf/fearpolitical.pdf

23. Belle David, *David Belle Interview*, retrieved 6.1.10
http://www.americanparkour.com/content/view/4895/378/

24. Belle David, *Parkour*, retrieved 23.1.10
http://www.newyorker.com/online/video/festival/2007/Parkour

25. Belle David, *SpeedAirMan*, retrieved 1.5.08
http://www.youtube.com/watch?v=kWJHSyjVMY8

26. Belle David, (2009c) *Parkour Texte et entretiens de Sabine Gros La Faige,* Intervista

27. Belle Jean Francois, *1997 Portes ouvertes de la Brigade de Sapeurs Pompiers de paris. Le Sport utilitaire devient sport spectacle*, retrieved 11.11.09
http://www.wmaker.net/parkour/1997-Portes-ouvertes-de-la-Brigade-de-Sapeurs-Pompiers-de-paris_a26.html

28. Belle Jean-Francois, *L'initiateur Raymond Belle*, retrieved 23.1.10
http://www.wmaker.net/parkour/Raymond-Belle_r4.html

29. Belle Williams, *Rendezvous 4 Q & A, part1,* retrieved *28.8.09*
http://www.youtube.com/watch?v=owXGhQclhTc

30. Belle Williams, *RDV4 Day 1 of 2*, retrieved 20.12.09
http://www.youtube.com/watch?v=Ljrmkr014qE

31. Belle-Dinh Châu, *Yamakasi, 10 ans après*, retrieved 9.11.09
http://www.dailymotion.com/video/x7s0au_vsd-a-30-ans-yamakasi-10-ans-apres_creation

32. Belle-Dinh Châu, *Yamakasi Q&A Rendezvous II pt.1,* retrieved 22.1.10
http://www.youtube.com/watch?v=cfm_xUV2xkl

33. Bennett Andy, (1999) *Subcultures or Neo-tribes? Rethinking the relationship between youth, style and musical taste.* Sociology, Vol. 33 No. 3, 599–617

34. Black Bob, (2000) *The Realization and Supression of Situationism*, retrieved 15.6.09
http://library.nothingness.org/articles/SI/en/display/242

35. Blaine David, (2003) *Above the Below*, retrieved 6.11.10
http://davidblaine.com/video/2003-above-the-below-brief/

36. Blain Neil, *(2003) Beyond 'Media Culture': Sport as Dispersed Symbolic Activity,* in Blain Neil & Bernstein Alina (eds.), *Sport Media Culture: Global and Local Dimensions,* London: Routledge

37. Borden Iain, (2001) *Skateboarding, Space and the City,* Oxford: Berg

38.   Brymer George E., (2005) *Extreme dude! A phenomenological perspective on the extreme sport experience,* doctoral thesis, University of Wollongong

39. Budden Johnny 'Sticky', *Strength*, retrieved 12.4.10 http://stickyparkour.com/BlogNew/?p=299

40. Burghardt, Gordon M., (2004) *The Genesis of Animal Play*, Cambridge, MA: MIT Press

41. Caillois Roger, (2001) *Man, Play and Games*, trans. M. Barash, Urbana & Chicago: University of Illinois Press

42. Carter Thomas F., (2008) *The Quality of Home Runs, The Passion, Politics, and Language of Cuban Baseball, London:* Duke University Press

43. Cert Vince, *The Virtual Revolution*, Ep 2, *'Enemy of the State?'* BBC2, retrieved on BBC iplayer, 16.2.10

44. Christie Mike, Jump, issue 1, 48 retrieved 22.2.10
http://www.urbanfreeflow.com/jumpmagazine/

45. Christie Mike, (2003) *Jump London*, Channel 4 Television, Dir.

46. Christie Mike, (2005b) *Jump Britain*, Channel 4 Television/ Carbon Media, Dir.

47. Chtcheglov Ivan, *Formulary for a New Urbanism*, retrieved 18.3.09 http://library.nothingness.org/articles/SI/en/display/1

48. Clifford James, (1988) *The Predicament of Culture, Twentieth-Century Ethnography, Literature, and Art*, Cambridge, Massachusetts: Harvard University Press

49. Coakley Jay & Dunning Eric, (2000) *Handbook of Sports Studies*, (eds.) London: Sage publications Limited

50. Connell Raewyn W. & Messerschmidt James W., (2005) *Hegemonic Masculinity: Rethinking the Concept,* Gender and Society, Vol. 19, No. 6, 829-859

51. Corkery Paul 'Ez', retrieved 18.10.10
http://www.independent.co.uk/news/uk/this-britain/jumpedup-plan-to-stage-world-competition-sees-free-runners-falling-out-445746.html

52. Csikszentmihalyi Mihaly, (1990) *Flow : the psychology of optimal experience,* New York: HarperCollins

53. Curtis Polly, *New rules to protect school playing fields,* retrieved 31.3.10
http://www.guardian.co.uk/education/2004/aug/27/schools.uk1

54. Daskalaki Maria, Starab Alexandra & Imasa Miguel, (2008) *The 'Parkour Organisation': inhabitation of corporate spaces,* Culture and Organization Vol. 14, No. 1, 49–64

55. Day Andy, retrieved 2.10.07, www.kiell.com

56. Debord Guy, (1957) *Report on the construction of situations and on the international situationist tendency's conditions of organization and action,* in: K. Knabb (Ed.), Situationist International Anthology, Berkeley, CA: Bureau of Public Secrets, 17–25

57. Debord Guy, (1967) *Society of the Spectacle,* retrieved 20.10.10
http://www.marxists.org/reference/archive/debord/society.htm

58. Debord Guy, (1983) *The Society of the Spectacle,* Detroit, MI: Red and Black

59. de Certeau Michel, (1988) *The Practice of Everyday Life,* London: University of California Press

60. Deleuze, Gilles & Félix Guattari, (1987) *A Thousand Plateaus: Capitalism and Schizophrenia* Trans. Brian Massumi, Minneapolis: University of Minnesota Press

61. Dembo Jonathon, retrieved 18.10.10
http://www.allourbusiness.com/about.php

62. De Souza e Silva, Adriana & Sutko Daiel M. (2008) *Playing Life and Living Play: How Hybrid Reality Games Reframe Space, Play, and the Ordinary,* Critical Studies in Media Communication, 25:5, 447-465

63. Dourish Paul, (2006) *Re-Space-ing Place: Place and Space Ten Years On,* Proc. ACM Conf. Computer-Supported Cooperative Work CSCW, Banff, Alberta, 299-308.

64. Edwardes Dan, *Connections: Coaching Parkour,* retrieved 1.6.09
http://www.parkourgenerations.com/blog/2009/06/58-connections-coaching-parkour.php

65. Edwardes Dan, *Running Free*, in Leisure Management, issue 4, 2010, retrieved 29.9.10,
http://www.leisuremanagement.co.uk/digital/index1.cfm?CFID=321 5592&CFTOKEN=99366781

66. Edwardes Dan, *Moving Through Fear*, retrieved 10.11.07,
http://www.parkourgenerations.com/articles.php?id_cat=2idart=10

67. Eichberg Henning, (1986) *The Enclosure of the Body - On the Historical Relativity of 'Health', 'Nature' and the Environment of Sport,* Journal of Contemporary History, Vol. 21, No. 1, 99-121

68. Eichberg Henning, (1998) *Olympic Sport: neo-Colonialism and alternatives*, in Bale John & Philo Chris (eds.), *Body Cultures: essays on sport, space, and identity*, Routledge

69. Eichberg Henning, (2007) *How to study body culture – Observing human practice*, retrieved 27.10.10, http://www.idrottsforum.org/articles/eichberg/eichberg070606.html

70. Eichberg Henning, (2009a) *Body Culture,* Physical Culture and Sport. Studies and Research, Vol. 46, 79-98

71. Eichberg Henning, (2009b) *Pull and Tug: Towards A Philosophy of The Playing 'You',* Sport, Ethics and Philosophy, volume 3, number 3, 305-324, Routledge

72. Eichberg Henning, *Thinking Contradictions; Towards a Methodology of Configurational Analysis or: How to Reconstruct the Societal Signification of Movement Culture and Sport,* International Seminar, How Societies create Movement Culture and Sport, Institute of Exercise and Sport Sciences University of Copenhagen, retrieved 26.10.10 http://www.ifi.ku.dk/formidling/udgivelser/rapporter/engelske/kd_how_societies_2001.pdf/

73. Elias Norbert & Dunning Eric, (1986) *Quest for Excitement: Sport and Leisure in the Civilizing Process,* Oxford: Blackwell

74. England Marcia R., & Simon Stephanie (2010) *Scary cities: urban geographies of fear, difference and belonging*, Social & Cultural Geography, 11: 3, 201-207

75. Estroff Marano Hara, (1999) *The Power of Play*, Psychology Today, July/August, 36-42

76. Evitt Blake, retrieved 25.9.10,
http://making-the-jump.blogspot.com/

77. Foucan Sébastien, retrieved 18.10.10,
http://www.foucan.com

78. Foucan Sébastien, Biography, retrieved 19.1.10,
http://www.foucan.com/?page_id=15

79. Foucault Michel, (1972) *The Archaeology of Knowledge,*
New York: Pantheon

80. Foucault Michel, (1978) *The History of Sexuality*, translation
by Hurley R., New York: Vintage Books

81. Foucault Michel, (1982) *The Subject and Power,* Critical
Inquiry, Vol. 8, No. 4, 777-795

82. Foucault Michel, (1983) *On the Genealogy of Ethics: An
Overview of Work in Progress*, H.L. Dreyfus & P. Rabinow
(eds.) Michel Foucault: Beyond Structuralism and
Hermeneutics, 2nd edn, Chicago: University of Chicago Press

83. Foucault Michel, (1985) *The History of Sexuality Volume 2:
The Use of Pleasure,* London: Penguin Books

84. Foucault Michel, (1988) *Technologies of the self. A seminar with Michel Foucault,* in Martin Luther H., Gutman Huck and Hutton Patrick H. (eds.) London: Tavistock Publications

85. Foucault Michel, (1991) *Discipline and Punish The Birth of the Prison,* London: Penguin

86. Foucault Michel, *Michel Foucault. Of Other Spaces (1967), Heterotopias.* Retrieved 20.2.09
http://www.foucault.info/documents/heteroTopia/foucault.heteroTopia.en.html

87. Freestyle Festival, retrieved 19.1.10
http://www.freestyle-festival.co.uk/freerunning.php

88. Fuggle Sophie, (2008) *Discourses of Subversion: The Ethics and Aesthetics of Capoeira and Parkour,* Dance Research, Volume 26, 204-222

89. Furness Zack, (2007) *Critical Mass, Urban Space and Vélomobility,* Mobilities, 2:2, 299-319

90. Fullagar Simone, (2002) *Narratives of travel: desire and the movement of feminine subjectivity, Leisure Studies,* Volume 21, Issue 1, 57 - 74

91. Geyh Paula, *Urban Free Flow: A Poetics of Parkour,* retrieved 17.2.09 http://journal.media-culture.org.au/0607/06-geyh.php

92. Gormley Anthony, (2009) *The One and Other*, retrieved 6.11.10 http://www.antonygormley.com/#/shows/past/solo

93. Grayson Richard, (2008) *Traceurs: to trace, to draw, to go fast*, Chelsea Space

94. Guttmann Allen, (2000) *The Development of Modern Sports*, in Coakley Jay & Dunning Eric (eds.), Handbook of Sports Studies, London: Sage

95. Guttmann Allen, (2004) *Sports: The First Five Millennia*, Amherst: University of Massachusetts Press

96. Hartley Alex, (2003) *LA Climbs, Alternative Uses For Architecture*, London: Black Dog

97. Harvey David, (2000) *Spaces of Hope,* Edinburgh: Edinburgh University Press

98. Henley Paul, (2009) *The Adventure of the Real : Jean Rouch and the Craft of Ethnographic Cinema,* London: The University of Chicago Press

99. Hillier Bill, & Burdett Richard, & Peponis John, & Penn Alan, (1987) *Creating Life: Or, Does Architecture Determine Anything?* Architecture & Comportement/ Architecture & Behaviour, 3 (3) 233-250

100. Hodkinson Paul, (2004) *The Goth scene and (sub) culture substance* in Wheaton Belinda (2007) After Sport Culture: Rethinking Sport and Post-Subcultural Theory, Journal of Sport and Social Issues, volume 31, no.3, 282-307

101. Huizinga Johann, (1950) *Homo Ludens*, New York: Roy Publishers

102. Johns David P. & Johns Jennifer S., (2000) *SURVEILLANCE, SUBJECTIVISM AND TECHNOLOGIES OF POWER : An Analysis of the Discursive Practice of High-Performance Sport*, International Review for the Sociology of Sport, 35, 219-235

103. Jump Jimmy, retrieved 20.9.04 http://www.jimmyjump.com/

104. Kane Pat, (2005) *The Play Ethic*, London: Pan Books

105. Knowles Richard T. (1997) *Fantasy and Imagination* in McLean George F. Civil Society and Social Reconstruction, The Council for Research Values and Philosophy

106. Lamb Mathew, (2008) *We Gotta Get Out of this Space: The Art of Parkour in Rethinking Architectural Space and the Body*, Paper presented at the annual meeting of the NCA 94th Annual Convention, TBA, San Diego, CA, retrieved 2.2.09 http://www.allacademic.com/meta/p259185_index.html

107. Laughlin Zoe, (2004) *Sewing The City: Parkour and the Traceurs of Narrative Threads,* retrieved 21.2.09
http://www.asifitwerereal.org/zoe/archive/Parkour/parkour.htm

108. Laughlin Zoe, (2008) *The Materiality of Parkour Actions: What you can do with the city,* Canadian Centre for Architecture

109. LeCorre Erwan, retrieved 30.6.09
http://movnat.com/archives/423

110. Lefebvre Henri, (1991) *Production of Space,* Oxford: Blackwell Publishers

111. Lefebrvre Henri, (1996) *Writings on Cities,* Oxford: Blackwell Publishers

112. Ley David, (2003) *Artists, Aestheticisation and the Field of Gentrification,* Urban Studies, Vol. 40, November, No.12, 2527–2544

113. Low Setha M., & Lawrence-Zúñiga Denise, (2003) *The Anthropology of Space and Place: Locating Culture*, Malden, MA: Wiley-Blackwell

114. Lyng Stephen, (1990) *Edgework: A Social Psychological Analysis of Voluntary Risk Taking*, American Journal of Sociology, 95: 4, 851-886

115. Lyng Stephen, (2005) *Edgework The Sociology of Risk-Taking*, (ed.) New York: Routledge

116. MacDougall David, (1998) *Transcultural Cinema*, Princeton, New Jersey: Princeton University Press

117. Mahop Francois '*Forrest, RETOUR VERS LE FUTUR (BACK TO THE FUTURE),* retrieved 26.1.10
http://www.parkourgenerations.com/blog/2009/06/59-retour-vers-le-futur-back-to-future.php

118. Mahop Francois 'Forrest', *RETOUR VERS LE FUTUR 3: "DE L'ATHLETISME AU PARKOUR",* retrieved 26.1.10
http://www.parkourgenerations.com/blog/2009/08/57-retour-vers-le-futur-3-de.php

119. Marais Anne-Therese, (2010) *Role Model*, Spiked, Issue 6, 32-35

120. Marano Hara Estroff, (1999) *The Power of Play*, Psychology Today, July/Aug, 36-42

121. Markula Pirkko, & Pringle Richard, (2006) *Foucault, Sport and Exercise,* London: Routledge

122. Marshall Bill, (2010) *Running across the Rooves of Empire: Parkour and the Postcolonial City,* Modern & Contemporary France, 18: 2, 157-173

123. Massey Doreen, (2004) *Geographies of Responsibility*, Geografiska Annaler.Series B, Human Geography, Vol. 86, No. 1, Special Issue: *The Political Challenge of Relational Space*, 5-18 Blackwell Publishing on behalf of the Swedish Society for Anthropology and Geography

124. Merleau-Ponty Maurice, (1962) *Phenomenology of Perception*, New York: Routledge & Kegan Paul

125. Merleau-Ponty Maurice, (2004) *The World of Perception*, New York: Routledge

126. Midol Nancy, & Broyer Gérard, (1995) *Toward an Anthropological Analysis of New Sport Cultures: The Cse of Whiz Sports in France*, Sociology of Sport Journal, 12, 204-212

127. Mould Oli, (2009) *Parkour, the city, the event*. Environment and Planning D: Society and Space, volume 27, 738-750

128. Nelle Franck 'Cali', Barclaycard World Freerun Championships 2008, retrieved 18.10.10 http://www.youtube.com/watch?v=FkUiRngtaE0&feature=related

129. Murphy Liam, *Freerunning banned by Wirral Council*, retrieved 24.9.09 http://www.liverpooldailypost.co.uk/liverpool-news/regional-news/2009/07/28/freerunning-banned-by-wirral-council-92534-24252436/

130. Nichols Bill, (1991) *Representing Reality*, Bloomington, Indianapolis: Indiana University Press

131. Nichols Bill, (2001) *Introduction to Documentary,* Bloomington, Indianapolis: Indiana University Press

132. Nmeth Jeremy, (2006) *Conflict, Exclusion, Relocation: Skateboarding and Public Space,* Journal of Urban Design, Volume 11, Issue 3, October, 297 - 318

133. Orlando Valérie, (2003) *From Rap to Raï in the Mixing Bowl: Beur Hip-Hop Culture and Banlieue Cinema in Urban France.* The Journal of Popular Culture, 36: 395–415

134. Ortuzar Jimena, (2009) Parkour or l'art du déplacement A Kinetic Urban Utopia, The Drama Review 53:3, 54-66

135. Palmer Catherine, Death, danger and the selling of risk in adventure sports, in Wheaton Belinda (ed.), Understanding Lifestyle Sports. Consumption, identity and difference, (2004) London: Routledge

136. Parkour Generations, Behind the Jump, retrieved 20.6.08
http://www.youtube.com/watch?v=NUMuxmp3lb4

137. Parkour Generations, Behind The Jump: Vol 8 - Train Small, See Large, retrieved 10.4.10
http://www.parkourgenerations.com/videos.php?details&id=57

138. Parkour Generations, Naoki Ishiyama 1000 Muscle-Up Challenge, retrieved 30.11.10
http://www.parkourgenerations.com/naoki.php

139. Parkour Generations, Parkour Academy, retrieved 18.10.10
http://www.parkourgenerations.com/classes.php

140. Parkour Generations, Parkour for Schools Programme, retrieved 20.4.10
http://www.parkourgenerations.com/classes.php?p=schools

141. Parkour Generations, Parkour Parks, retrieved 18.10.10
http://www.leisuremanagement.co.uk/digital/index1.cfm?CFID=321 5592&CFTOKEN=99366781

142. Parkour Generations, Parkour Research Ongoing, retrieved 19.1.10
http://www.parkourgenerations.com/news.php?my=december2009#953

143. Parkour Generations, Park Structures, retrieved 25.9.10
http://www.parkourgenerations.com/business.php

144. Parkour Generations: Rendezvous 4 Q&A part 3, retrieved 26.1.10 http://www.youtube.com/watch?v=jKTl2tw0Ni4

145. Parkour Generations, Rightmove TV Commercial Featuring Agota, 29.9.10 http://www.youtube.com/watch?v=WBxbp6l0bXs

146. Parkour.net, retrieved 15.6.08 http://parkour.net/

147. ParkourUK, retrieved 18.10.10
http://www.parkouruk.org/download/afPE_Statement.pdf
http://www.parkouruk.org/#About

148. Parkour UK, A.D.A.P.T., retrieved20.4.10
http://parkouruk.org/#Adapt_intro

149. Parkour UK, Parkour - Updated afPE position statement
(Jan 2010), retrieved 24.1.10
http://www.parkouruk.org/download/afPE_Statement.pdf

150. Perks Robert, & Thomson Alistair, (1997) The Oral History
Reader, London: Routledge

151. Pinder David, (2008) Urban Interventions: Art, Politics and
Pedagogy, International Journal of Urban and Regional
Research, 32: 730–736.

152. Pink Sarah, (2007) Doing Visual Ethnography, second
edition London: Sage Publications Ltd.

153. Plunkett John & Deans Jason, BBC to tackle weighty issue,
(10/7/04)
http://media.guardian.co.uk/site/story/0,14173,1270164,00.html

154. Portelli Alessandro, (1997) The Battle of Valle Giulia: Oral
History and the Art of Dialogue, Madison: The University of
Wisconsin Press

155. Pringle Richard, (2009) Defamiliarizing Heavy-Contact Sports: A Critical Examination of Rugby, Discipline, and Pleasure, Sociology of Sport Journal, 26, 211-234

156. Puchan Heike, (2004) Living 'extreme': Adventure sports, media and commercialization, Journal of Communication Management, Vol 9, 2, 171-178

157. Rabinow Paul, (1991) The Foucault Reader, an introduction to Foucault's thought, London: Penguin Books

158. Rannikko, Ulla J., (2010) Going beyond the mainstream? Online participatory journalism as a mode of civic engagement. PhD thesis, London School of Economics and Political Science.

159. Redbull Art of Motion, retrieved 18.10.10 http://www.redbull.com/cs/Satellite/en_INT/Event/Red-Bull-Art-of-Motion-021242758003880

160. Relentless, Relentess Advert, retrieved 18.10.10 http://www.youtube.com/watch?v=oqkFqpjqCec

161. Rouch Jean, (2003) Ciné-ethnography, London: University of Minnesota Press

162. Rowat Chris 'Blane', Dilution, retrieved 1.12.10 http://blane-parkour.blogspot.com/

163. Ruby Jay, (2000) Picturing Culture: explorations of film and anthropology, London: University of Chicago

164. Runciman David, (2010) Enemy of the State?, retrieved 16.2.10The Virtual Revolution, Ep 2,' BBC2, accessed on BBC iplayer,

165. Sage George, (2000) Political Economy and Sport, in Coakley Jay & Dunning Eric (eds.), Handbook of Sports Studies, London: Sage

166. Sandbag, Sandbag's One Giant Leap 2009, retrieved 23.1.10 http://www.youtube.com/user/sandbagcampaign#p/u/18/WC0qo2crPtU

167. Sands Robert, (2002) Sport Ethnography, Leeds: Human Kinetics

168. Saville Stephen John, (2008) Playing with fear: parkour and the mobility of emotion, Social & Cultural Geography, Vol. 9, No. 8, 891-914

169. Shahani Shawn, Parkour The Evolution of the Disparate Tradition, retrieved 9.2.09 http://shawnshahani.files.wordpress.com/2008/07/parkour-the-evolution-of-the-disparate-european-tradition.pdf

170. Shelton Alli, PKMAX Video Podcast - Episódio 01 – Curitiba, retrieved 30.6.09 http://www.youtube.com/user/rachacuca666#play/uploads/11/577wSjhLEos

171. Shogan Debra & Ford Maureen, (2000) A NEW SPORT ETHICS : Taking König Seriously, International Review for the Sociology of Sport 35: 49-58

172. Shopes Linda, (2002) Making Sense of Oral History, History Matters: The U.S. Survey Course on the Web, retrieved 20.11.10 http://historymatters.gmu.edu/mse/oral/

173. Soja Edward, (1989) Postmodern Geographies: The Reassertion of Space in Critical Social Theory, London: Verso

174. Stoller Paul, (1992) The Cinematic Griot, Chicago & London: University of Chicago

175. Storm Freerun, Storm Freerun - Volume 1, retrieved 26.11.10 http://www.youtube.com/watch?v=dHy9W9LpvlQ

176. Swyngedouw, Erik & Kaïka, Maria, (2003) The making of 'glocal' urban modernities, City, 7: 1, 5-21

177. Tarook Mark, Art of Motion, Why It's not News, retrieved 25.9.10 http://www.americanparkour.com/content/view/5754/1/

178. Taylor Charles, (1989) Sources of the Self, Cambridge: Cambridge University Press

179. Taylor Charles, (1991) The Ethics of Authenticity, Cambridge, Massachusetts: Harvard University Press

180. Team Tempest, retrieved 18.10.10
http://www.tempestfreerunning.com/about/past
www.tempestfreerunning.com/tempest-tv

181. ten Brink Joram, (2007) Building Bridges The Cinema of Jean Rouch, London: Wallflower Press

182. Thornton Sarah, (1995) Club Cultures: Music, Media and Subcultural Capital, Cambridge: Polity

183. Thorpe, Holly A., (2007) Boarders, Babes and Bad-Asses: Theories of a female physical youth culture, PhD Thesis, University of Waikato

184. Tuan Yi-Fu, (1971) Phenomenology, and the Study of Human Nature, Canadian Geographer, xv, 3

185. Tuan Yi-Fu, (1990), Realism and Fantasy in Art, History, and Geography, Annals of the Association of American Geographers, Vol. 80, No. 3 (Sept.), 435-446, Taylor & Francis, Ltd. on behalf of the Association of American Geographers Stable

186. Urban Freeflow, retrieved 18.10.10
http://www.urbanfreeflow.com/2010/03/27/uf-international-all-stars/

187. UrbanFreeflow, Urbanfreeflow's U$FTV Vol.1, retrieved 7.4.10 http://www.dailymotion.com/video/x6deu8_urbanfreeflows-uftv-vol1_sport

188. Van den Berg J.H., (1972) A Different Existence, Pittsburgh: Duquesne University Press.

189. van Leeuwen Lieselotte & Westwood Diane, (2008) Adult play, psychology and design, Digital Creativity, Vol.19, No. 3, 153-161

190. Vertinsky Patricia, & McKay Sherry, (2004) Disciplining bodies in the gymnasium: memory, monument, modernism, London: Routledge

191. Vigroux Stephane, An Interview with Stephane Vigroux, retrieved 10.9.10 http://www.youtube.com/watch?v=_d1AxUPPcF8

192. Vigroux Stephane, Discussion between Stephane Vigroux and Trevor Kjeldal, retrieved 25.9.10 http://parkourpedia.com/about/interviews-and-articles-of-interest/discussion-between-stephane-vigroux-and-trevor-kjeldal

193. Vigroux Stephane, Interview (Original language), retrieved 1.11.10 http://www.comunidadparkour.com/stephane_vigroux_francia.html

194. Ward Colin, (1973) Anarchy in Action, London: George Allen & Unwin Ltd.

195. Weir Allison, (2009) Who are we? : Modern identities between Taylor and Foucault, Philosophy Social Criticism 35: 533

196. Wellmann Barry, Quan-Haase Anabel, Boase Jeffrey, Chen Wenhong, Hampton Keith, Isla de Diaz Isabel, Miyata Kakuko, (2003) The Social Affordances of the Internet for Networked Individualism, Journal of Computer Mediated Communication 8, 3

197. Welton Donn, (1998) Body & Flesh, A philosophical Reader, (ed.) Oxford: Blackwell Publishers Ltd.

198. Wesch Michael, An anthropological introduction to YouTube, retrieved 20.10.10 http://www.youtube.com/watch?v=TPAO-IZ4_hU&feature=channel

199. Wheaton Belinda, (2000) "New Lads"? : Masculinities and the "New Sport" Participants, Men and Masculinities 2: 434-456

200. Wheaton Belinda, (2004) Understanding Lifestyle Sports. Consumption, identity and difference, (ed.) London: Routledge

201. Wheaton Belinda, (2007) After Sport Culture: Rethinking Sport and Post-Subcultural Theory, Journal of Sport and Social Issues volume 31 no.3, 282-307

202. White Stuart, (2007) Making anarchism respectable? The social philosophy of Colin Ward Journal of Political Ideologies, 12: 1, 11-28

203. Whitson David, (1994) The embodiment of gender: Discipline, domination and empowerment, in Birrel S. & Cole C. (eds.) Women, sport and Culture, 353-371, Champaign, Il: Human Kinetics

204. Wiebe Sarah, Opinion. Re-Thinking Citizenship: (Un)Healthy Bodies and the Canadian Border, retrieved 30.6.09 http://www.surveillance-and-society.org/articles5(3)/opinion.pdf

205. Wilson Brian, (2002) *The Canadian Race Scene and five theses on youth resistance,* Canadian Journal of Sociology, 27 (3), 373-412

206. World Freerun Ents., retrieved 11.10.10 http://www.worldfreerun.com/

207. World Freerun Ents. *Venue,* retrieved 18.10.10 http://www.worldfreerun.com/venue

208. World Freerunning & Parkour Federation, retrieved 18.10.10 http://wfpf.com/

209. Young Iris, (1990) *Throwing Like A Girl,* Bloomington: Indiana University Press,

210. Young Geoffrey w., (2009) *The Roof Climbers Guide to Trinity,* Cambridge: Oleander Press

Appendix 1

Parkour Glossary of Terms

Monkey work (*Quadrupedal*)

Conditioning movements using all four limbs to strengthen and work the joints without any impact. All of the movements are practiced going forward and backwards.

Chris 'Blane' Rowat

Cat Balance

The opposite arm and leg are moved forward one after the other whilst balancing. Practiced forward and backwards.

Tracey Tiltman

Kong Vault (*saut de chat*)

A through vault, both hands are placed on the obstacle and the legs dive through. Variations are a double kong where the hands are placed twice, tapping each time and the diving kong where the take-off is extended and the arms are extended and the vault is akin to 'diving' into the vault. A kong is often used in a combination with other movements, for example a kong to precision or a kong to cat (catleap).

Chris 'Blane' Rowat

Slide monkey Vault

A lateral vault where the outer leg goes over the obstacle first, the trailing leg then tucks under the lead leg to closely go over the obstacle.

Tracey Tiltman

Speed Vault

A single footed take-off, only the hand makes contact with the obstacle as the body follows over as quickly as possible, landing on the same foot as the take-off.

Dominic Willoughby

Step Vault

Very similar to the speed vault but the outer leg foot makes contact with the obstacle and then the takeoff foot steps through.

Shirley Darlington

Catleap (*saut de bras*)

An arm jump, you leap towards the wall or obstacle and land with both hands, arms bent, grabbing the top of the wall/obstacle, then climb up.

Annty Marais

Tictac

You approach the obstacle, one footed take off then kick off one wall to then land on another.

Thomas Couetdic

Precision Jump – standing or running

A one or two footed take off jump, landing on a specific point. The take off can be from either standing or running.

Thomas Couetdic

Wallrun (*passe muraille*)

A one footed take off then kicking upwards against the wall, grab the top of the wall and climbing up.

Dan Edwardes

Palm Spin

The body rotates 360 degrees around the hand rested on an obstacle, either the top of a surface or against the flat side of a wall.

Bobby Gordon-smith

Underbar

The body moves through the obstacle feet first.

Chris 'Blane' Rowat

Drop Jumps (*saut de fond*)

The body drops or jumps down, landing softy on the balls of the feet or using a roll to absorb the impact.

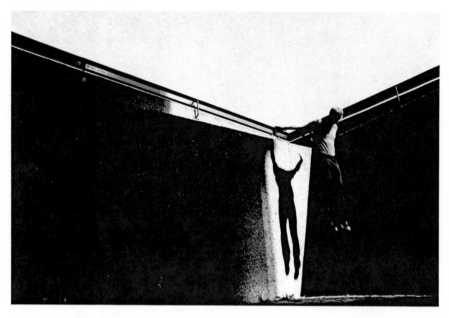

Chris 'Blane' Rowat

Swinging and Hanging movements (*laché*)

Hanging with both hands from any horizontal obstacle you swing and let go, reaching towards another edge. In the urban setting this is frequently practiced on scaffolding.

Chris 'Blane' Rowat

The Roll

Landing feet first you then transfer your body weight to your hands and make contact with the shoulder and then the hip to avoid the head and spine making contact with the surface.

Kristian McPhee

Traceurs

Unlike other physical disciplines that take the name of the activity as the basis for the name of the practitioner, for example, people who climb are climbers, people who practice parkour are not parkourers. The name that is now commonly used for someone who does parkour is a traceur. The word traceur has been appropriated from the name of a team, 'Tracers', that consisted of David Belle, Sebastien Foucan, Stephane Vigroux, Johann Vigroux, Sebastien Goudot, Steve 'Kazuma' Rognoni, Michael Ramdani, Jerome Ben Aoues, Romain Moutault and Rudy Duong (Vigroux [191]). Some choose to refer to female parkour practitioners as traceuses or use the term traceur for both.

Ciné Parkour

Julie Angel

Appendix 2

Terminology Timeline

1986/7   **Parcours**

(a course or a route) Raymond Belle discusses his training with his

son David

1997   **L'art du déplacement**

Sébastien Foucan gives the name to the practice for the French

television *Stade 2* feature.

1997   **Parkour**

Herbert Kounde suggests to David Belle that he creates a word so

he can feel an ownership over the training that he was doing.

2003   **Freerunning**

English translation proposed by Guillame Pelletier during the
production of the British channel Four documentary *Jump London.*

Groups:

Yamakasi

Name of the group that appeared in the Stad 2 TV piece and Fire fighter performance. The name of the group was also a sort of 'concept' for some of the group so for them there were more than the 9 in the group, including many people who were present in the early years of the training.

Tracers

David Belle, Sebastien Foucan, Steve 'Kazuma' Rognoni,

Stephane Vigroux, Johann Vigroux, Jerome Ben Aoues, Michael

Ramdani, Sebastien Goudot, Rudy Duong, Romain Moutault

Individuals:

Traceur/traceuse (male/female)

Someone who practices parkour, appropriated from the group name 'Tracers'.

Freerunner

Someone who practices freerunning or parkour

Appendix 3   Parcours Timeline: Some of the Key Events

Year					
1986/7	Phung Belle, Châu Belle Dinh, Williams Belle	David Belle	Yann Hnautra, Frederick Hnautra	David Malgogne	Started moving, playing, and seeing opportunities for training outdoors
				Laurent Piemontesi	Joined their friends in their games and training
1987/8	Sébastien Foucan, David Foucan	Guylain N'Guba-Boyeke	Malik Diouf	Charles Perriere	Laurent Piemontesi

1988-97 The friends from Sarcelles, Lisses and Évry all give of themselves and support each other in developing the essence of their practice: a training methodology, set of values, ethics and spirit

1997

Jean Francois Belle — Jean Francois asks his brother David Belle if he and his friends would like to perform for the Paris Firefighter event. Jean Francois begins filming the group of friends

The friends receive their first media coverage - a magazine article published in Lisses

First TV appearance on Stade 2, a positive portrayal

Paris Firefighter Performance

Yamakasi name and group created

Châu Belle Dinh, Williams Belle, David Belle, Yann Hnautra, Sébastien Foucan, Guylain N'Guba-Boyeke, Malik Diouf, Charles Perriere, Laurent Piemontesi

Invitation to perform at *Notre Dame de Paris* musical. David Belle and Sébastien Foucan leave the group; the remaining 7 take part

1998

Luc Besson — Luc Besson invites Yamakasi to be involved in a feature film after their *Notre Dame de Paris* performance

David Belle — David begins using the term 'parkour' (rather than 'parcours' or 'l'art du déplacement')

David pursues an acting career, creating *SpeedAirMan*, a showreel video

SpeedAirMan is made available to download on the internet through www.style2ouf.fr

Sébastien Foucan — Sébastien concentrates on his own creative projects and artwork

Stephane Vigroux — Stephane sees *SpeedAirMan* and begins training with David Belle

Tracers group created — David Belle, Kazuma, Romain Moutault, Jerome Ben Aoues, Rudy Duong, Stephane Vigroux, Michael Ramdani, Sébastien Goudot, Johann Vigroux, train together

Sébastien Foucan — Sébastien joins the Tracers group

1998 - 2000 Various media coverage and commercial events featuring 'parkour' and 'l'art du déplacement' by different groups and individuals

2000

Sébastien Foucan — Sébastien focuses more on his own goals

Yamakasi — 6 months are spent shooting *Yamakasi, Les Samouraï des Temps Modernes*

Yamakasi perform as ninjas in the film *Taxi 2*

2001 Theatrical release of *Yamakasi, Les Samouraï des Temps Modernes* in France

296

2001 cont'd

Thomas Couetdic — Thomas Couetdic begins training with Johann Vigroux, Sébastien Goudot and Michael Ramdani in Lisses and Tours

Yamakasi — Châu Belle Dinh and other members of the Yamakasi begin teaching small groups

Domain name parkour.net is registered

2002

Stephane & Johann Vigroux — Stephane and Johann begin training with Sébastien Foucan instead of David Belle

Sébastien Foucan — Sébastien features in the Nike commercial *Angry Chicken*

Yamakasi — Yamakasi feature in the American TV show *Ripley's Believe It or Not*

David Belle — David appears in BBC ident *Rush Hour*, Kazuma is stunt double.
Cyril Raffaelli is stunt coordinator

Parkour.net becomes active with general information and forum

2003

Yamakasi — Yamakasi film *Les Fils du Vent*, shooting in France and Thailand

UK based website and forum urbanfreeflow.com created

Sébastien Foucan, Johann Vigroux, Jerome Ben Aoues, Stephane Vigroux — Group invited to feature in the Channel 4 documentary *Jump London*

2004

David Belle, Cyrill Raffaelli, Kazuma,   Group begin filming *Banlieue 13* in France
Stephane Vigroux, Romain Moutault & others

Sébastien Foucan   Sébastien asked to create a team for *Jump Britain*

Yamakasi   Yamakasi train young people from Évry to take part in *Cirque du Soleil*

Stephane Vigroux   Stephane moves to Thailand

Ph.D parkour research begins

Theatrical release of *Banlieue 13* in France

298

Julie Angel

ABOUT THE AUTHOR

Dr. Julie Angel is a London based independent filmmaker, artist, writer and academic. She regularly trains parkour and continues to follow and document the evolving culture of parkour.

www.julieangel.com

Julie Angel

Julie Angel

Julie.Angel©

CPSIA information can be obtained at www.ICGtesting.com
Printed in the USA
LVOW061530271211

261231LV00001B/270/P